a **classroom guide** for stud

Designing
with Pro/**DESKTOP**®

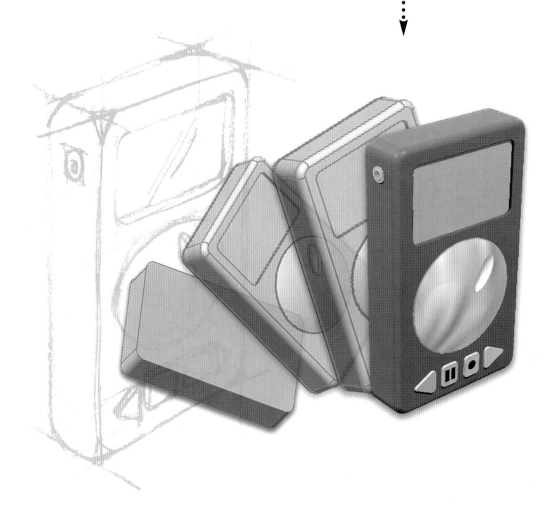

a d e s i g n e d w o r l d l e a r n i n g p u b l i c a t i o n

Designing
with Pro/**DESKTOP**®

Published by
Designed World Learning, LLC
1933 Highway 35
Suite 105-124
Wall, NJ 07719
www.designedworldlearning.com

©2005 by Designed World Learning, LLC

All rights reserved. No part of this book may be reproduced in any form or by any means without written permission from the publisher. This book may not be stored in a retrieval system or be transmitted by any means including, but not limited to, electronic, mechanical, photocopying, or recording, without written permission from the publisher.

No patent liability is assumed with respect to the use of the information contained herein. While every precaution has been taken in the preparation of this book, the author, publisher or seller assumes no responsibility for errors or omissions. Nor is any liability assumed for damages resulting from the use of information contained herein.

International Standard Book Number: ISBN 0-9763351-0-7

Copy Editor: Adrienne Russell
Layout and Design: Lori Lozinski
Illustration: Pat Hutchinson

Trademark Acknowledgements:

All product illustrations, product names and logos are trademarks of their respective manufacturers. All terms in this book that are known or suspected to be trademarks or services have been properly capitalized. Designed World Learning, LLC cannot attest to the accuracy of this information. Use of an illustration, term or logo in this book should not be regarded as affecting the validity of any trademark or service mark.

Pro/DESKTOP® is a trademark or registered trademark of PTC, Inc. Designed World Learning, LLC is not associated with any product or vendor mentioned in this book.

Printed in Canada

about the author

John Hutchinson is a professor of Technological Studies at The College of New Jersey. He holds a Ph.D. from the Pennsylvania State University. He has authored numerous articles on technology education curriculum and philosophy, as well as technical articles on microelectronics. He is the co-author of the textbook, *Design and Problem Solving in Technology*, published by Glencoe McGraw-Hill.

Designing with Pro/DESKTOP®

table of contents

Preface		vi
00	A Short History of Design & Technology	1
01	Getting to Know Pro/DESKTOP®	11
02	Extrude Profile Feature & Round Edges Command	39
03	Modeling Challenge Using Extrude Feature and Constraints	81
04	Sketches	127
05	Project Profile Feature	193
06	Revolve Profile Feature	217
07	Assemblies	239
08	Sweep Profile Feature	271
09	Animation	297
10	Design Evolution, Animation & Style Projects	329
11	Pro/DESKTOP® and Engineering Drawing	391
Keyboard Shortcuts		427
File Types and Extensions		428
Vocabulary & Glossary of Terms		429
Index		430

preface

Designing With Pro/DESKTOP® focuses on the use of Pro/DESKTOP 3D modeling software to design, develop and present new products. An introductory text for middle or high school students, it will introduce and develop basic and intermediate skills in the use of the software in a context of product design and engineering. Within these pages, students will learn the skills necessary to do design work with powerful 3D parametric solid modeling software program, Pro/DESKTOP from PTC.

This book is not intended as a comprehensive text on computer-aided drafting or design, but rather presents a logical and interesting guide to the basic skills and knowledge needed for design work. We believe this text to be an ideal supplement to other resources in courses where Pro/DESKTOP will be used as part of an introductory or intermediate level course in technology, or any course where Pro/DESKTOP will be used as a design tool.

The goal of the author was to develop a book that is an approachable, affordable and useful school text. For this reason, not every option available has been covered. A text covering all the features of Pro/DESKTOP would be impractical. Students who develop advanced expertise with Pro/DESKTOP will undoubtedly discover and learn features of the software not covered here.

Every effort has been made to blend technical skill building with application to real design problems. Wherever possible, exercises and projects have been chosen that have relevance to students' lives. These activities introduce, develop and reinforce the basic operation and use of Pro/DESKTOP and help students learn about design.

00

a short history of design and technology

Introduction

People have been designing for a long time. Early humans created tools from materials they found in nature, including wood, bone and stone. In fact, whole epochs of history have been named after the most common materials used to make tools: the Stone Age, the Bronze Age and the Iron Age. The creation of tools made survival possible. They were used to hunt, make shelter and clothing, and sometimes small ornaments or jewelry. To make a tool, someone had to imagine something that did not yet exist. In other words – **design**.

Early tools were designed and used by the same person. Gradually, it became apparent that certain individuals were more skilled than others at creating tools. These people began to specialize in tool design and tool making. While these tools may have been used by many members of the tribe, only a few people were skilled enough to make them well.

As tools evolved, humans were capable of doing more things – and doing them better. For example, hunting became more efficient and safer when the bow and arrow were developed. Using a spear required being closer to wild game and their teeth and claws. But, the bow and arrow allowed hunters to remain at a safe distance from their prey.

For many thousands of years, life changed slowly, and tool making was a skill highly valued among all people. Small tribes would follow the herds of buffalo or other large animals. These hunter-gatherers would also move with the availability of certain wild plants critical to their diet. When seasons changed or when they ate all of the plants in a particular area, the tribe would move to a place where the animals and plants were more abundant. These were nomadic people who traveled where food was to be found. They did not own much because they did not stay in one place very long. Their shelter was temporary and they had little need of much beyond clothing and basic tools, because that was all they could carry. It is said that it took about 25 square miles to support one person in a hunter-gatherer tribe. A tribe of 20 people would reuire an area roughly 500 square miles, or an area 25 miles wide by 20 miles long.

The Agricultural Revolution

At some point in time, roughly ten thousand years ago, the practice of agriculture began. It did not happen all at once. Instead, it probably occurred in only a few places and took hold slowly. Some anthropologists believe that agriculture grew out of the knowledge women held about plants. Men typically did the hunting, but women gathered the plants and knew a great deal about how and where they grew.

Agriculture changed almost everything. When you plant seeds, you need to take care of the growing plants and stay around for the harvest. Unlike the small nomadic tribes, farming could support larger communities. Early agriculture decreased the land area needed to support a person from 25 square miles for the hunter-gatherer tribes, to about 3 square miles. Because of this, more people could live together and communities developed.

When you stay in one place instead of constantly moving, you can create better shelter. Agriculture created the environment

4 industrial revolution

for architecture. To store food, containers were needed, so pottery developed. To identify who owns the food in the pot, writing developed. Agriculture stimulated the creation of tools, the plow and the wheel, buildings, writing, government, laws, taxes and many other things we take for granted in our lives. These advances in technology took thousands of years to develop and spread.

The Industrial Revolution

In the mid 1700's, before the American and French Revolutions, a new source of power was developed: steam. Before this time, wind, water and animal muscle power were used to mill grain and pump water. Towns grew up around rivers because they provided a source of power. Wind power, while widely used, was only available when strong winds blew, so it could not be counted on to run machinery. The new steam engines, however, could be constructed almost anywhere.

The steam engine helped drive the creation of mechanical devices and the development of techniques for creating products in large quantities. Factories grew up around the steam engine and with larger quantities of an item produced, the price of each product went down. More people could afford to have more things.

The textile industries were the first to be affected by industrialization. In fact, there is a story of a disgruntled textile worker named Ned Lud who lost his job to the new automated equipment. Ned Lud led a band of thugs to destroy the new textile machinery. Today, people who are against new technology, or are sometimes just ingnorant of it, are called Luddites, after him.

The appearance of products was driven by the technology. At first, little attention was given to how a manufactured product looked. The main concern was to produce the item cheaply and make a profit. Design was still largely a concern for craftsmen and women, affecting one-of-a-kind items for the wealthy, like architecture and art.

It took time for the Industrial Revolution to reach North America and to have an effect on the lives of people here. During that time, steamships and railroads were created, both driven by the new steam engine.

The 1800's: The Industrial Age in America

President Thomas Jefferson made a deal with Emperor Napoleon Bonaparte of France to buy a large tract of land west of the Mississippi River in 1803. When Lewis and Clark took off to explore the new Louisiana Purchase in 1804, transportation and communication had changed little since the Romans of two thousand years before. Lewis and Clark literally walked and paddled across America and it took them two years.

At this time, a trip between Boston and New York took three days. It took almost two days to travel between New York and Philadelphia. The time it took to communicate between these cities was, in most cases, the same as the time it took for the mail to travel, since both used the same route. Traveling

1800's industrial age

usually involved fording rivers, since few bridges existed, especially as you traveled farther west, away from the Atlantic coast.

By 1850 or so, all this would change. The telegraph would make communication almost instantaneous, from days and weeks to seconds. At the same time, the railroads emerged. It wasn't until May 1869, that the transcontinental railroad was completed across the United States. Though, local regional railroads were already being used over the country well before that time. If you could stand the soot and smoke from the wood burning steam engines, the railroad got you to your destination in almost unbelievable speed, considering your alternative was to walk or ride a stagecoach.

The last several decades of the 1800's saw the invention of the electric motor, the car, the telephone, and a huge chemical industry. There are many historians that believe that the ninteenth century (1800's) was the time of the most significant technological change in human history, even when compared to the twentieth century. This is because the changes were so radical. Steady improvements were made to these technologies through the twentieth century, but the impact of their first appearance in the 1800's is almost beyond measure.

The Industrial Age lasted well into the twentieth century. The Wright brothers flew the first airplane in 1903, and Henry Ford figured out a way to make automobiles by "mass production," which lowered the cost so many more people could afford to buy one. The first radio was developed and Morse code was used to communicate with ships at sea and between continents. The first commercial television broadcast took place in 1936.

The Great Exhibition of 1851:
The Rise of Industrial Design

In the Crystal Palace in London, a great exhibition of arts and industry was held in 1851. This exhibition was intended to attract manufacturers from all over the world to show off their products. At the time, Queen Victoria was the ruler of Britain, but it was her husband, Albert, who promoted the exhibition and led the Royal Commission to plan it.

The products displayed at the exhibition were decorated with exotic designs. At the time, design was considered something you applied to the surface of an object to suggest that a craftsman had given it some attention. It was not something done during the development of the product. The fancy decorations became known as Victorian design, after the name of the Queen.

Arts and Crafts Movement

About 10 years after the Great Exhibition, William Morris started a company that produced carefully designed, quality products to compete with the factory made products of the time. They produced furniture, jewelry, metalwork, and textiles. Morris wanted to return to the craft tradition of hand-made products. He, and others, believed that the factories alienated

Arts and Crafts

art nouveau/ art deco

Art Nouveau

Art Deco

workers and the machines created less skilled workers who took no pride in what they were producing.

Art Nouveau

The Arts and Crafts movement did not last. Because it looked backwards toward a simpler time of hand craftsmanship, its products could not compete in price with the factory made products. But, the design style evolved.

Art Nouveau, French for "new art," was a design style that took ideas from the Arts and Crafts movement. Art Nouveau used curving lines and intertwining patterns based on flowers, trees and vines, and long, flowing hair.

Art Deco

In Paris, France in 1925, an exhibition was held called the "Exposition Internationale Des Arts Decoratifs et Industriels Modernes." Even if your French is a bit rusty, you can probably translate this into roughly, "International Exposition for Decorative Arts and Modern Industry." It was at this exposition that a number of well-known designers unveiled their latest works. Even though each designer had his/her own style, the influence of the new materials and industrial techniques of the time was clear. Almost forty years later, this movement was named the Art Deco style and the name has stuck.

The Art Deco style is characterized by straight lines and curves, and geometric shapes. The streamlined shapes were applied to everything from aircraft, trains, cars and ocean liners, to radios, clocks and furniture. The expression, "form follows function" was introduced at this time and describes how the shape and form of an object should follow its function, or how it is used. Of course, vehicles that travel fast should be streamlined, but this style was also applied to things that stood still.

The Technological Age

Thousands of inventions and improvements to existing technologies took place in the twentieth century. One of the most important was the computer, first developed in the 1940's by the military to calculate the path of artillery shells. Early computers filled large rooms and required huge cooling systems to carry away the heat from thousands of vacuum tubes. Like all technologies, computers evolved and became more efficient. The invention of the transistor allowed computers to eventually fit on a desk. Today, there are "one-chip" computers the size of a postage stamp.

Also important are the health benefits brought about by technology and science in the twentieth century. Penicillin, the first antibiotic, was discovered by Alexander Fleming in 1928. In a few years, factories were producing antibiotics in large quantities and the modern pharmaceutical industry was born. Because of these improvements to health, people lived longer and the life expectancy increased 30% in North America during the years 1900 to 2000.

Because we live in the middle of this technological revolution, it is difficult to understand what the world was like before people had the tools and products that we have today.

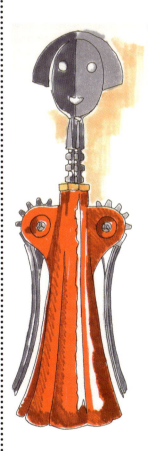

10 technological age

00. A Short History of Design and Technology

Contemporary Design

Technology changes how we live our lives, but it also changes how we think about ourselves and our world.

This brief history of design and technology does not do justice to the subject. Each tool and device has its own history, as it evolved and improved. However, each tool and each product was designed. Some were designed by an individual and some were designed by teams of people who carefully applied their knowledge, skill, creativity and ingenuity to solving a problem. When you design, you share some of the same obstacles and satisfaction of these early technologists.

01

getting
to know
Pro/DESKTOP®

01. Getting to Know Pro/DESKTOP®

Introduction

Computer-aided design (CAD) is the name given to the process of designing products on the computer. CAD is used by architects, interior designers, engineers, industrial designers, fashion designers, ship designers, aircraft designers, shoe designers and almost every other kind of designer you can think of. There is a wide range of CAD programs, some aimed at specialized design fields, such as landscape architecture or textile design. This book is about a particular kind of CAD software used for product and component development. It has unique features that allow the designer to smoothly move from the initial, "hazy" ideas of a project (sometimes called the "fuzzy front end" of design), through the refinement of these ideas, to the final stages of modeling and production of an actual product. Pro/DESKTOP is a CAD program intended for use by industrial designers or engineers in what might be called "general purpose product design."

Figure 1.0

In this first chapter you'll learn about Pro/DESKTOP®, a 3D product design solution created by PTC® (Parametric Technology Corporation). PTC launched the 3D CAD (computer-aided design) industry in 1987 with its flagship CAD software, Pro/ENGINEER®. Today, PTC is a leader providing Product Lifecycle Management (PLM) solutions to more than 35,000 companies worldwide.

Used by millions of designers, engineers and students, Pro/ENGINEER began as a 'high-end' CAD program—highly complex, with a long learning curve. Today's Pro/ENGINEER, totally redesigned in 2001, is now among the fastest, easiest solutions available. In every area of product development—from industrial design to sheet metal to manufacturing— engineers use

Pro/ENGINEER® to create products of all sizes and complexity, from simple cell phones to jumbo jetliners and Indy 500 racecars.

As part of their commitment to help schools prepare students for the real world of product development, PTC® has made Pro/DESKTOP available to teachers and students through the company's Design & Technology in Schools Program.

Figure 1.1
Scaled Composites Space Ship One.

Pro/DESKTOP is ideal for students learning 3D software because it is both powerful and easy to learn and use. It features many of the same capabilities of high-end CAD tools, in a smaller, simpler package. Many companies use Pro/DESKTOP to develop early design concepts before moving them to more complex CAD programs, while other companies use it as their primary design tool. One such company is StarChaser Industries.

StarChaser Industries is using Pro/DESKTOP to develop a series of unmanned and manned rockets, including the Thunderbird pictured in Figure 1.0. A cutaway view shows the life-support capsule on top the Thunderbird rocket. StarChaser has been competing with other private companies in an effort to make access to space affordable for commercial purposes, such as launching satellites and future tourist travel. StarChaser competed in the "X-Prize" competition for the $10 Million prize.

The "X-Prize" was awarded to the first private company that launched three people 100 kilometers (62.5 miles) high and landed them safely back to earth; then, launched them again in the same rocket within two weeks. The X-Prize was won by Scaled Composites in October of

01. Getting to Know Pro/DESKTOP®

2004 with their "Space Ship One." **Figure 1.1** shows Space Ship One hanging underneath the "White Knight," the aircraft that transports the craft to an altitude of 70,000 feet. The rocket is then dropped and travels straight up to the edge of space.

The design of aircraft and rockets, as well as most of the things you use everyday, is now done on computers. Computer-aided design reduces the time it takes for a company to bring a product to the marketplace, which saves the company money. A company that saves money developing a product can sell that product at ***lower*** cost. CAD also helps companies make changes and improvements in the design of products more quickly and less expensively.

The design of a new product is what makes it a success or a failure. Well-designed products do what they are intended to do, they do it well, and they do it for a long time. Another way of saying this is: "a well-designed product gives the customer value." CAD offers companies a way to allow designers, engineers, marketing people and others to participate in the development of products throughout the product development process. Products created in this way tend to be better designed and more successful.

Why CAD?

Designers use many strategies and techniques to investigate design ideas and communicate them to others. These techniques include free-hand sketching, finished drawings, renderings, and three-dimensional models. Critical to the role of a designer is the ability to draw well enough to express and develop ideas visually. Because the language of drawing, like the ability to design, has been under appreciated in school, few children or adults feel comfortable with this skill. In the last few years, however, the designer has gained a new set of tools in computer-aided design software.

CAD software can permit the designer to create designs more rapidly, as well as designs that are more accurate and more rapidly rendered. Design files created in CAD software can be shared among various stakeholders in the design, allowing rapid refinement of design ideas. Many CAD software packages even permit files to be exported that lead directly to the production of a prototype through computer-controlled machines.

Pro/DESKTOP allows the designer to create satisfying images in a friendly and intuitive way, circumventing the need for good drawing skills. Many students even report that the program's ability to create forms, manipulate lighting and simulate surfaces helps them understand and learn the ideas behind the drawing skills.

Design
There are many definitions of design. Nearly all of the definitions, however, have in common the understanding that design involves the making of choices among a number of (often conflicting) factors that will influence the final outcome. In industry, the design of a product may involve such choices as materials, ergonomics, production processes, aesthetics, environmental impact, distribution and marketing of the product. Within each of these factors there are often many more choices that must be made. For example, within the realm of environmental impact, the materials, processes, finishes, packaging, and disposal of the product when its useful life is over, should be considered. When students study design and technology, they take on the role of designer. When students design, they are weighing these and other factors and are gaining a deeper understanding of the technological world.

Throughout this book we will show you how to use the Pro/DESKTOP program and provide you with challenges that will help you learn

01. Getting to Know Pro/DESKTOP®

about design. The challenges will begin with step-by-step instructions, but as you become more familiar with the software, the challenges will be less specific. This will give you the opportunity to apply what you have learned about Pro/DESKTOP and to make more of the design decisions yourself.

Design is Different from Drafting
Design is a kind of thinking we use to make things. Design thinking happens when we get an idea about something that we want, then figure out how to make it. Human beings are born with the ability to design, but learning more about design makes the ability more powerful. We use this kind of thinking every day to plan what we wear, to arrange our room, to draw a map, and to cook a meal. In its more complex forms, professionals use design to create all of the technological products around us—from skyscrapers to space vehicles, and from clothing to software.

Computer modeling is used by designers, architects and engineers all over the world. It wasn't too many years ago when there were no computers (or the computers were not powerful enough) so all design work was done on paper. Times have changed and now almost everyone has access to a computer, and design software has become both powerful and affordable.

When we design we make drawings and models so that we can evaluate what we have imagined. Design is a process that involves thinking, analyzing, thinking again, analyzing again, and so on. While design involves many other things, getting an idea out of your head and to a place where you can look at it, evaluate it, and change it is of primary importance. Writers jot down notes, make rough drafts of their thoughts, refine the wording, and rewrite again. A designer does the same thing with her ideas about products.

Drafting is making drawings of the final solution so that it can then be manufactured, constructed and produced. In other words, design is figuring out how to do something and drafting is showing others how to do it. A designer and an engineer will design a car, then call in a draftsperson to make drawings of the designs so that others can manufacture it. The drawings created by the draftsperson are used to figure out the size to cut material, locate where holes must be drilled and figure out where all the parts go in the assembly of the product.

Drafting began with paper and pencil drawings and moved to computer-aided drafting programs as computers were developed. But, new, more powerful computer software has changed the way products are designed and produced. Three-dimensional design software, like Pro/DESKTOP, not only lets the designer model and test the design before it's built, it also produces final drawings, eliminating the need for a draftsperson.

The Pro/DESKTOP Program

Pro/DESKTOP is a 3D design solid-modeling program that allows the user to create realistic 3D images of parts and products. The term *solid-modeling* means that each object you create, no matter how complicated, is still a geometric solid. If you have taken a course in geometry, you will appreciate how complex it would be to describe in mathematics even simple solid objects you see around you. Even a pencil is quite a complex solid. What makes Pro/DESKTOP so powerful is that the program also creates all the mathematical information needed to actually make the part automatically. The information is in the form of geometric data that special programs can read and translate into code. This code is then used by computer-guided machines to produce the shape of the part.

the pro/DESKTOP program

01. Getting to Know Pro/DESKTOP®

In the highly technological society of today, most products and parts are made by machines. People manage the machines, that is, they set them up, adjust them, clean them, and get them ready for the raw materials that will be used to make the parts. People also troubleshoot and fix problems with the machines. In many cases machines can make products more quickly and more accurately than people can.

However, it would not make sense to have everything made by machine – for machines to have all the jobs. People must work to earn money so they can afford to buy the things machines make. It makes sense to use machines to do the things that people cannot do: work in dangerous environments, make highly accurate parts and make the production of products more efficient. But, one of the most important issues facing society today is the question of the limits of that efficiency. In other words, "How will we know when too many jobs have been replaced by machines?" The answer to this question is not simple. You may get one answer from the board of directors of a company, and a different answer from the board of directors of the labor union representing the people who work at the company.

Humans vs. the Machine

When we create new technologies we create dilemmas. A dilemma is a situation in which you find there are no clear right or wrong choices. The invention of the industrial robot is such a dilemma.

Robots can do difficult, hazardous, and very precise work, often doing things that people cannot do. However, robots can sometimes do work that people do and perform it better and longer. A robot can work in the dark, work 24 hours a day for weeks on end without stopping (no coffee breaks or sick days) and never complain that the factory is too noisy or cold. But, the people who used to do the work are now not taking home a paycheck.

The issues are complex. Perhaps the displaced worker can find another job that pays the same or more. Perhaps not. Here are a few of the arguments both for and against replacing people with machines. Of course there are many more. Can you think of any arguments that have not been included here?

Pro
- Robots do not require health insurance or other benefits;
- Robots can work in factories that have minimum light and heat so the company saves on utility bills;
- Robots can do highly dangerous jobs.

Con
- Older workers who lose their job have a poor chance of getting another job at equivalent pay;
- Unemployed people cannot afford to purchase the products made by the company that replaced its workers with robots;
- There is evidence that communities that have large numbers of worker layoffs, divorce rates rise, stores go out of business, and crime rates go up.

design link: machines replacing workers

01. Getting to Know Pro/DESKTOP®

Figure 1.2 Industrial CNC machine

Figure 1.3 Rapid-prototype machine and rendered 3D parts

The process of making parts and products automatically is called Computer-Aided Manufacturing or CAM. The machines are often called Computer Numerical Control or CNC machines. Figure 1.2 shows a CNC machine that can be found in school technology labs. Figure 1.3 shows a rapid-prototyping machine that creates models in 3D using plaster.

The Pro/DESKTOP software program can create:

- 3D solid models of parts and assemblies of parts
- realistic images of a part or product – like the images you might see in a catalog;
- drawings that can be used by someone to hand-make the part or product;
- output files that can be used by machines to make the individual parts.
- output files for virtual reality viewing, like VRML on the web.

There are three environments in Pro/DESKTOP and they are called the interfaces: ***Design Interface***, ***Drawing Interface***, and ***Album***

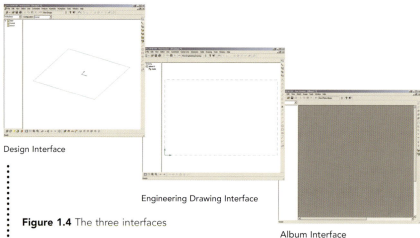

Design Interface

Engineering Drawing Interface

Album Interface

Figure 1.4 The three interfaces

Interface. Design is 3D (3 Dimensional), Drawing is 2D (2-Dimensional) and is sometimes called drafting, and Album is for creating realistic renderings that are very much like photographs. Most parts are created in the **Design Interface**. The images on page 20 are screen shots of the three interfaces. It is easy to tell which interface you are in by the look of the screen.

The creation of an object is usually done in the **Design** interface. The object is rendered in the **Album** interface. Rendering is the application of color and textures and might include placing the object on a background, such as the clouds in Figure 1.5. Pro/DESKTOP also allows you to change lighting effects to create interesting shadows and highlights on surfaces.

Figure 1.5 MP3 Player rendered in Pro/DESKTOP

Rendered objects are only pictures of the model you have designed. They do not have the geometry to actually make the part. Rendered images are often used by designers to show to clients and other people working on the product design. A carefully rendered image can be so realistic that it can be used in a catalog even before the real product is made.

The **Drawing** interface creates what are called orthographic drawings (Figure 1.6). In the past, this style of drawing was used primarily by the people who made the parts and products. It was common for machinists and skilled craftsman to have orthographic drawings spread out on a shop table and refer to them often as they cut, shaped, drilled, welded, and glued parts together to make products. Today, much of this work is done by machines, so the necessity for orthographic drawings is reduced. Chapter 11 has been devoted to the **Drawing** interface.

01. *Getting to Know Pro/DESKTOP®*

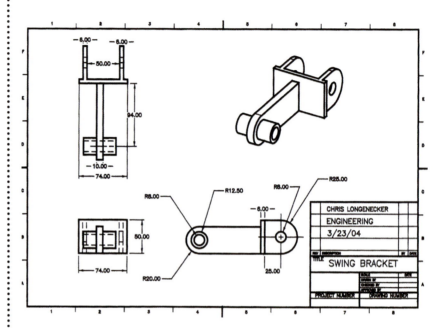

Figure 1.6 Orthographic Drawing
Drawing courtesy of Chris Longenecker, Lenape High School.

Context Sensitive Help Icon

There are a number of commands and design operations that will not be covered in this book. If you come across something that interests you, there are several choices to help you find out more about it. The **Context Sensitive Help** command is located on the Standard Toolbar at the top of the screen. Click once on the icon and then click on any other icon or tool on the Pro/DESKTOP screen and a new small window with a detailed explanation will open. Also, the **Help** pull-down menu at the top of the screen is useful to look up how to use tools, create features and other important information.

The Pro/DESKTOP Design Screen

The Pro/DESKTOP Design screen is divided into five areas: the *Design Window*, the *Browser Window*, the *Design Toolbar*, the *Top Toolbar Area* and the *Bottom Toolbar Area*, as shown in Figure 1.7. You will also see the vertical Design Toolbar on the right side of the screen that contains the most commonly used tools. These windows and the vertical toolbar are labeled in the figure.

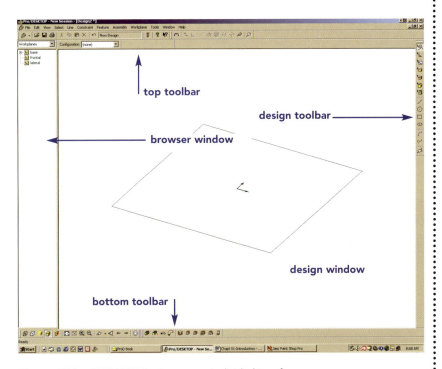

Figure 1.7 Pro/DESKTOP Design screen is divided into five areas.

24 the pro/DESKTOP design screen

01. Getting to Know Pro/DESKTOP®

Working in the **Design interface**, you will draw lines and shapes on something called a **Sketch** that sits on a flat **Workplane** (see below). Pro/DESKTOP then allows you to turn these 2D shapes into 3D objects.

In Pro/DESKTOP, the term **sketch** is used to describe the place where you draw 2D shapes, something like a piece of paper. But the term sketch is also used to describe the actual lines you put on that "piece of paper." It is easy to get confused about whether someone is talking about the actual lines or a sketch on a workplane.

Pro/DESKTOP has a number of different operations it calls Features that turn 2D shapes (on sketches) into 3D objects, including: Extrude, Project, Revolve, Sweep, and Loft. In addition, you can also round corners, distort the shape of flat surfaces, and create other 3D effects.

Here are a few examples of the Features in Pro/DESKTOP:

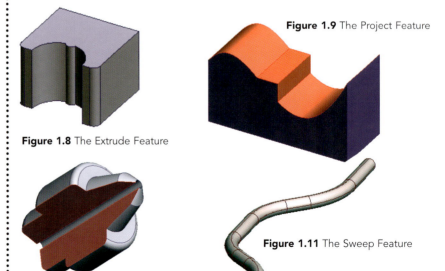

Figure 1.8 The Extrude Feature

Figure 1.9 The Project Feature

Figure 1.10 The Revolve Feature

Figure 1.11 The Sweep Feature

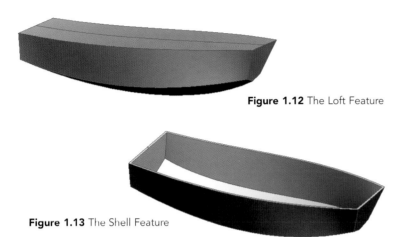

Figure 1.12 The Loft Feature

Figure 1.13 The Shell Feature

Each project requires a combination of some or all of these features. In this book, each project has been selected so that it only requires specific features. This will allow you to learn how to use each feature and not have to learn them all at once. Advanced projects in this book will assume you have learned the basic features.

More on the Pro/DESKTOP Design Screen

Browser Window

On the left side of the screen is the ***Browser Window***. The Browser Window keeps track of the Workplanes, Sketches and Features you use while you are designing. It will not keep track of every change you make to a sketch, such as changing the length of a line or each time you change the location of a circle. However, in the Browser Window you will be able to make changes to Features you have used and add new Sketches and Workplanes. More about the Browser Window will be explained later.

26 the pro/DESKTOP design screen

01. Getting to Know Pro/DESKTOP®

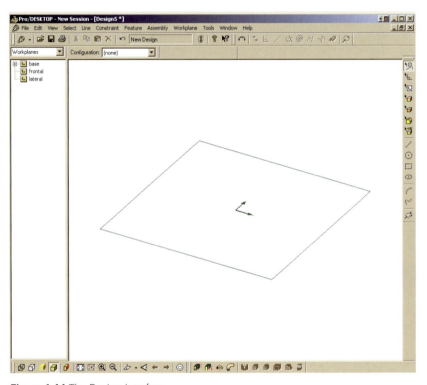

Figure 1.14 The Design Interface

Design Toolbar

The vertical toolbar on the right side of the screen (**Figure 1.15**) contains the tools you will use most often. These tools fall into three categories: ***Selection Tools***, ***Drawing Tools***, and a ***Delete Line Segment Tool***. You will use this toolbar constantly, so the sooner you become familiar with each tool and what it does, the easier it will be for you to use Pro/DESKTOP.

Figure 1.15 Toolbar

Selection Tools

There are seven *Selection Tools*. From the top they are:

Line Select Tool – used to select a sketch line. When this tool is selected all sketch lines on your design are visible.

Constraint Select Tool – used to select a dimension (or other constraint) when you want to change or delete it. When this tool is selected all the constraints on your design are visible.

Workplane Select Tool – used to select a workplane. When this tool is selected *all* workplanes are visible. Sketch lines are *not* visible in this mode.

Edge Select Tool – used to select an edge of a 3D solid when you want to round it or chamfer it (not used for sketch lines). Sketch lines are *not* visible in this mode.

Face Select Tool – used to select a face (surface) of a 3D solid; used often to place a new workplane and sketch on a face. Sketch lines are *not* visible in this mode.

Feature Select Tool – used to select a Feature, such as an extrusion; you can sometimes redefine a Feature (change the length of the extrusion, for example) by double-clicking on the Feature with this tool. Sketch lines are *not* visible in this mode.

Part Select Tool – used to select a part during an assembly or used to select a part in a design. Sketch lines are *not* visible in this mode.

Drawing Tools

Line Tool – used to draw straight lines

Circle Tool – used to draw circles.

Rectangle Tool – used to draw rectangles; hold down the shift key while drawing with this tool to draw a square.

Ellipse Tool – used to draw ellipses.

Arc or Fillet Tool – used to draw parts of a circle.

Spline Tool – used to draw squiggly lines.

Delete Line Segment Tool – used to cut out a line or line segment. Lines with curves usually have two or more segments and each piece is deleted separately.

Constraints Toolbar

Located near the top of the screen is another tool you will need. It is located in the Constraints toolbar. Although there are a number of tools on this toolbar, you will only need to know one right now.

The Sketch Dimension Tool is used to specify a dimension for a line, circle, arc or angle. Once you have constrained a line (or a circle, etc.) you can only change its size by changing the constraint using the Constraint Selection tool.

Don't worry if you do not remember all the tools. When you start using them, each tool will start to make sense and after a little time you will use them without really thinking about it. The reason for showing them to you here is so you can refer back to this page when you begin to use the Pro/DESKTOP program.

The Pro/DESKTOP Environment

Workplanes and Sketches
When you begin a *New Design*, Pro/DESKTOP automatically gives you three workplanes and one *sketch*. The three workplanes are the *Base Workplane* – it lies flat (horizontal); *Frontal Workplane* – a vertical workplane; *Lateral Workplane* – another vertical workplane that is 90 degrees to the Frontal Workplane.

There is a sketch called *Initial* on the *Base Workplane*. This is usually a good place to begin a design, although there are times when it is better to start on one of the vertical workplanes. This will be discussed later in the book.

Pro/DESKTOP allows you to create other workplanes almost any place you wish. You can create as many sketches as you want on each workplane. Chapter 4 shows you how to create new workplanes and sketches.

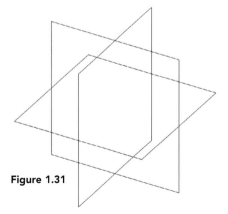

Figure 1.31

In Figure 1.31 you see the three workplanes. The flat Base Workplane, the vertical Frontal Workplane, and the other vertical Lateral Workplane. All three workplanes intersect at their centers. The Workplanes are all visible when you click on the Select Workplanes tool in the Design Toolbar. You cannot see sketches in the Select Workplanes mode, although you can see solids. Pro/DESKTOP is designed so that you only see things appropriate to the mode you are in. Otherwise, the screen would become very cluttered in a short time.

The workplanes in **Figure 1.32** are more visible because the command ***Show workplanes as glass*** was checked in the ***Options*** menu. This may help you visualize the workplanes while you are first learning Pro/DESKTOP, but it will probably become annoying when you become more proficient with the program. To turn on this command, go to the ***Tools*** pull-down menu and select ***Options*** at the bottom of the list, then select the ***Performance*** tab. Click in the box next to "Show workplanes as glass." To turn off this function, just click in the box again.

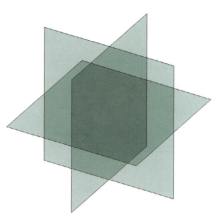

Figure 1.32

The Browser Window

Figure 1.33 shows a portion of the Browser window on the left side of the screen. The Browser is a running history of the evolution of your design. The yellow box with the arrows represents a workplane and the pencil represents a sketch.

Figure 1.33

The Browser window also contains other useful information. If you click on the down arrow next to the word ***Workplanes*** at the top of the Browser window, you will see there are actually three different

01. Getting to Know Pro/DESKTOP®

the pro/DESKTOP environment

Browser windows that you can choose: **Components**, **Features** and **Workplanes** (Figure 1.34). You will learn more about the other two Browser windows as you become more skilled in using Pro/DESKTOP.

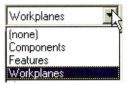

Figure 1.34

The Browser window is handy for creating new sketches on existing Workplanes. Another useful thing you can do with the Browser Window is find out which Workplane and Sketch particular lines in your design belong to. As designs become more complicated, the ability to identify a sketch or Workplane can save you a lot of time.

Tip: You can add sketches to any workplane by positioning the cursor over the workplane icon or name in the Browser window, then right mouse-click, and select New Sketch from the floating window. **Figure 1.35** shows a new sketch being added to the lateral workplane.

Navigation

When you are designing with Pro/DESKTOP you will want to change views and move the object around the screen so you can see the top, bottom and sides, as well as zoom in and out. Here are a few commands and tools so you can get a better look at what you are designing.

Arrow Keys – Use the arrow keys on the keyboard to rotate the object (Figure 1.36).

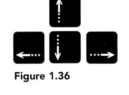

Figure 1.36

Shift+W – This is a very handy keyboard command. It will change the view of the design window so that you are looking straight down on the active workplane and sketch. Often, you will use this command immediately after creating a New Sketch (Figure 1.37).

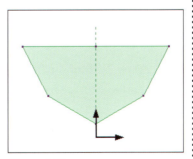

Figure 1.37
Shift+W Command

Figure 1.35

01. Getting to Know Pro/DESKTOP®

Figure 1.38
Shift+T Command

Shift+T – This command changes the view to Trimetric, which is a 3D view that is good for viewing sketches while you are applying Features. (**Figure 1.38**)

 Center mouse button or wheel – Clicking and holding the center mouse button allows you to manipulate the object by moving the mouse.

 Hold down the Shift key while clicking the center mouse button – This combination allows you to drag the object around the screen with the mouse. This is sometimes called Panning.

Using Tool Icons to Change View
In the Toolbar window on the lower part of the screen there are a number of tools that will help you get just the view you want. The tools are arranged in groups.

 Autoscale – Clicking on this tool will make the object fill the Design Window. You can also use the keyboard shortcut Shift+A.

 Autoscale Selection – If you have something selected, whether it is a line, a feature or an entire object, clicking on this tool will make the selection fill the screen.

 Zoom In Tool – Click on this tool and the cursor turns into this shape:
To use the *Zoom In Tool*, you will create a box with the mouse that will become the full screen. In most programs you create a box by starting in a corner and dragging the cursor to make the box. With the Pro/DESKTOP zoom tool you place the cursor in

the center of the place you are interested in enlarging. The smaller you make the box the more you will zoom in. The larger you make the box the less you will zoom in. This tool takes a bit of getting used to.

Zoom Out Tool – When you click on this tool you zoom out so the image is one-half of its original size. You can make more than one click and zoom way out.

Tumble – Clicking on the "happy face" tool makes the object tumble around randomly on the screen. To stop the tumble command, click in the Design window or press the keyboard space bar once. Use this command on one of your more complex designs to impress visitors.

Automatic Views

These icons are located in a sub-menu. Clicking on one of the icons changes your view of the object.

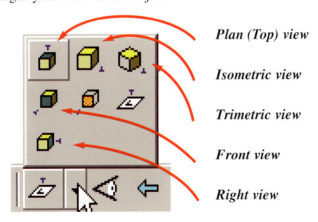

Plan (Top) view

Isometric view

Trimetric view

Front view

Right view

Understanding the CAD Environment

Computer-aided design software is different than other kinds of programs that allow you to draw images on the screen. To understand how CAD software works let's look at a simplified example: drawing a square.

Although it is not required, if you can start Pro/DESKTOP on your computer, you can see on the screen what is being described in this next section.

- Start **Pro/DESKTOP** and begin a **New Design** by clicking on the **File** pull-down window and selecting **New Design** from the list.
- Expand the design window by clicking on the **Maximize** icon in the upper right corner of the design window.
- Use the keyboard shortcut **Shift+W** (hold down the Shift key while pressing the W key once). This will change your view so that you are looking directly down at the active workplane and sketch.
- Select the **Straight Line** tool in the Design Toolbar on the right side of the screen.

When looking at a new sketch in a Pro/DESKTOP design window, you will see the origin as a point where the bases of the two green arrows meet. If you place a drawing tool at that point, in the top menu you will see 0,0 as this location (**Figure 1.48**).

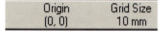

Figure 1.48
New Image

Moving around the drawing tool will give you an idea of the meaning of the two numbers. Move the tool to the right and you will see the first number increase while the second number remains zero. Move the pointer up and the second number increases while the first number remains at zero. Move the pointer either to the left or down and a negative number appears for the first or second number accordingly.

The Pro/DESKTOP program is keeping track of the location of the cursor. You can use the information displayed in these two numbers as a guide as you draw.

The x-axis is horizontal and the y-axis is vertical, so the location of the cursor can always be described as these two numbers. There will be more about this in Chapter 4 where the screen is described as an x-y grid.

Summary

CAD, short for Computer-Aided Design, is used by most design professionals because it makes the process of design more efficient and helps companies reduce the time it take for a product to reach the market. Pro/DESKTOP, developed by PTC, Incorporated, is a 3D design and modeling software program intended for engineers and product designers.

The Pro/DESKTOP program has three environments: the Design Interface, the Drawing Interface and the Album Interface. Creating 3D objects is usually done in the Design Interface.

01. *Getting to Know Pro/DESKTOP®*

Two-dimensional sketches on Workplanes are drawn first. Then Features are used to create 3D solids from the sketches.
The Design Interface contains the Design Window, the Browser, the Design Toolbar, and the Top and Bottom Toolbar Areas. The Browser keeps a running account of workplanes and sketches, and of features applied to sketches. The toolbars contain icons for performing various operations, such as drawing and changing views. Many operations in Pro/DESKTOP can be accomplished with pull-down menu commands, keyboard shortcuts, and icons.

CAD programs keep track of the geometry of two-dimensional sketches by locating points on X-Y axes. Typically, when you are looking at these axes on the computer screen the X-axis runs horizontally and the Y-axis runs vertically. However, if you rotate your drawing, the axes will rotate as well.

Test Your Knowledge

1. What does CAD stand for?

2. Name three different kinds of designers that might use CAD:

3. What does CAM stand for?

4. Name one reason a company might use to justify installing an industrial robot. Name one reason the union representing the workers at that company might use to argue against installing an industrial robot.

5. What are some of the factors that a designer must consider when developing a product?

6. What is the difference between design and drafting?

7. What is the purpose of drafting drawings?

8. What are the three Pro/DESKTOP interfaces?

9. Most design work is done in which interface?

10. What is the name for the 2D lines that are used by Pro/DESKTOP to make 3D solids?
    a. drawing
    b. sketch
    c. rendering
    d. drafting

11. When you are designing in Pro/DESKTOP, where on the screen is the Design Toolbar containing the Drawing and Select Tools located?
    a. top center
    b. left side
    c. right side
    d. bottom center

12. When you are designing in Pro/DESKTOP, where on the screen is the Browser Window located?
    a. top center
    b. left side
    c. right side
    d. bottom center

13. How does Pro/DESKTOP turn 2D sketches into 3D solids?
    a. with Interfaces
    b. with Features
    c. with Workplanes
    d. with Constraints

14. In what window does Pro/DESKTOP keep track of the workplanes, sketches and features you have used to create a solid model?
    a. Browser window
    b. Design window
    c. Toolbar window
    d. History window

test your knowledge 38

01. Getting to Know Pro/DESKTOP®

activity:

Form two groups. One group will represent a company named DinoTeck that designs and manufactures plastic parts for the aerospace industry. DinoTeck has 350 employees, 300 of which are employed in the company factory. The company has a profit-sharing plan that means that increased company profits puts more money in the pockets of each employee.

The second group represents the people who work in the company factory – the workers who run the machines and make the parts.

DinoTeck is considering the installation of 17 new industrial robots. The robots will be expensive, but the company will realize quite an increase in profit as a result. Estimates have been made that indicate that 63 workers will lose their jobs as a direct result of the new industrial robots.

The company management has called a meeting of the two groups to discuss the advantages and disadvantages of installing the new industrial robots. What is the best course of action?

02

extrude profile feature & round edges command

In this chapter you will learn how to:

- Create valid sketches to extrude
- Add and subtract material in an extrusion
- Round edges
- Use the Thin option

Introduction

In this chapter you will learn about two Pro/DESKTOP® features, the **Extrude Profile** feature and the **Round Edges** command. For every project in this chapter, almost every step is described in detail to allow you to follow along. In further chapters, the steps introduced here will become less detailed because you will have gained experience and knowledge about how to use the program and perform these operations.

Figure 2.1 This model of a computer tower was developed in Pro/DESKTOP using only the Extrude Profile and Round Edges features.

Should you have difficulty with a certain command or operation, you can always refer back to this chapter. This text would get very long and boring if each step was spelled-out in detail in every chapter.

As in any computer software program, there is a lot to learn just to get "up and running." The previous chapter introduced you to some of the general information you will need to use Pro/DESKTOP®. In this chapter, many of the concepts you have already read about will be reinforced and new information will be introduced that will allow you to create basic designs.

Your teacher may ask you to save all or some of the projects in this book. You should decide where your work will be saved and then save everything to that location so you can easily find your files again. Some choices are: My Documents, a folder on the Desktop; a floppy disk (you will only be able to save a limited number of files on a floppy); a removable drive disk, such as a Zip disk; a USB "pen drive"; or in a folder on a network drive. Check with your teacher to find out where you should save your files.

Throughout this book you will be directed to save files in the format "*name.des*." Pro/DESKTOP will automatically put the extension *.des* at the end of a design file, but to make it clear that you are being asked to save a file name, the *.des* is shown in the text. You do not need to put this extension on a file name when saving.

Important Terms

When you are drawing, whether it is on paper or on a computer screen, you are drawing in two-dimensions: ***length*** and ***width***. The term *2D* refers to these two-dimensions. Although artists and designers can make very realistic 3D pictures of objects, if they are on paper, an artist canvas, or a computer screen, they are still 2D.

Objects we see around us are three-dimensional objects. That is, they have length and width, but they also have depth, or a third dimension. The term *3D* refers to these three-dimensions. Objects created in Pro/DESKTOP® appear as 3D even though they are viewed on a computer screen. Pro/DESKTOP is called a 3D design program because the information stored about the design you have created contains data about all three dimensions. This information can be used to actually create the object, or a model of the object. Only the real objects, however, are actually 3D.

In computer-aided design language, a ***solid model*** is a 3D object that contains all the information to describe it mathematically. A solid model is much more than just a picture of the object. The solid model file contains the information to actually make the model on computer-driven machines, such as CNC milling machines, lathes and rapid prototyping machines. Often, solid model is shortened to just the word *solid* by designers and engineers.

The Extrude Profile Feature

The ***Extrude Profile Feature*** is probably the most basic and most used 3D feature in Pro/DESKTOP. It is easy to use and will allow you to develop all kinds of interesting models. With this feature you can also remove material from a model and create fairly complex forms from both closed sketch shapes and open-ended lines.

Extrusions (what you get from applying the Extrude Profile feature) are like toothpaste. The shape of the toothpaste that comes out of the tube is based on a round hole through which the toothpaste is "extruded." Imagine what the shape of the toothpaste would be if the hole in the tube was square, or oval, or star-shaped. A cookie press functions in the same way. Most cookie presses come with a variety of nozzles that will make different shaped cookies when the dough is "extruded" through the nozzle (Figure 2.2a and Figure 2.2b).

The Sketch

To make a 3D model, you must start with a 2D sketch. A sketch contains lines that are used by Features, such as Extrude, to create the solid. Pro/DESKTOP® has six drawing tools that will allow you to create almost any kind of line. More about sketches will be introduced in Chapter Four (Figure 2.3).

Figure 2.2a Cookie Press

Figure 2.2b Cookie dough extrusion

Figure 2.3

Valid Sketch Profiles

Most extrusions are applied to closed sketch shapes, that is, lines drawn in a sketch that form a continuous outline of a shape. Any extra lines that are not necessary to form this closed shape will cause an error message.

Figure 2.4 shows a series of valid sketch profiles that can be extruded. Although some shapes are geometric and some are organic, all shapes 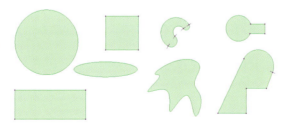 **Figure 2.4** have a continuous outline with no crossed lines and no extra lines anywhere on the sketch. Of course there are countless other valid sketch profiles you can create. Just remember that if your sketch does

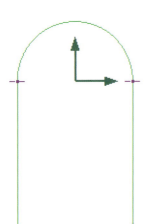

Figure 2.5a

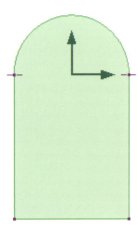

Figure 2.5b

not fill, it is probably because there are stray lines, or lines that do not meet, or lines that cross. Throughout his book there are hints about troubleshooting problem sketches.

The Toggle Sketch Filled Command

Pro/DESKTOP® helps you to determine if the sketch you create is valid. It does this by filling the sketch with a color. If the sketch is invalid, no color will fill the sketch. **Figure 2.5a** shows a sketch that has not filled because there is a very small space where the bottom and left side lines should meet. In **Figure 2.5b** the sketch has filled because the left line has been re-drawn to make it meet the bottom at the corner. There are times when you will want to turn off the Sketch Filled command. For example, if you create a sketch that will be used to remove material from an object, the filled sketch may prevent you from seeing the hole. Also, when you want the model to look more realistic for printing or creating an animation, a filled sketch may detract from the realism of the object. The default mode (which means the way Pro/DESKTOP is set up when you install it) is for sketches to fill when they are valid.

You can turn off and turn on sketch filling. To turn off this command, go to the ***Line*** pull-down menu and select ***Toggle Sketch Filled***. You turn on the sketch filled command by going back to the ***Line*** pull-down menu and selecting ***Toggle Sketch Filled*** again (**Figure 2.6**).

Figure 2.6

02. Extrude Profile Feature & Round Edges Command

the extrude profile feature 45

Exercise 2.1 Create Your First Sketch

To get the feel of Pro/DESKTOP® try drawing a sketch. You will use the drawing tools located on the Design Toolbar on the right side of the screen. There are six drawing tools, straight line, circle, rectangle, ellipse, arc, and spline (Figure 2.7).

Figure 2.7
The six drawing tools

Here is how to create the sketch.
Start a New Design file
- Move the cursor to the upper left corner of the screen and click on the design icon (Figure 2.8). A new design window appears.

- Enlarge the design window by clicking on the *Maximize* icon in the upper right corner of the design window (Figure 2.9). You are looking at the *initial sketch* on the *base workplane* in 3D in the *Trimetric View* (Figure 2.10).

Figure 2.9

Figure 2.8

Make sure you are working in inches

- Move the cursor to the top of the screen and click on the *Tools* pull-down menu. Choose *Options*, which is at the bottom of the menu list (Figure 2.11a).

- Click on the *Units* tab in the floating window.

- If the word *inches* does not appear under both Model dis-

Figure 2.11a

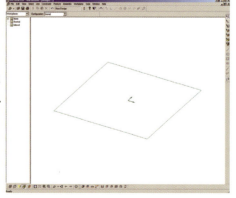

Figure 2.10

tances and Paper distances change them to inches (**Figure 2.11b**).

• Click **OK** to close the Options window.

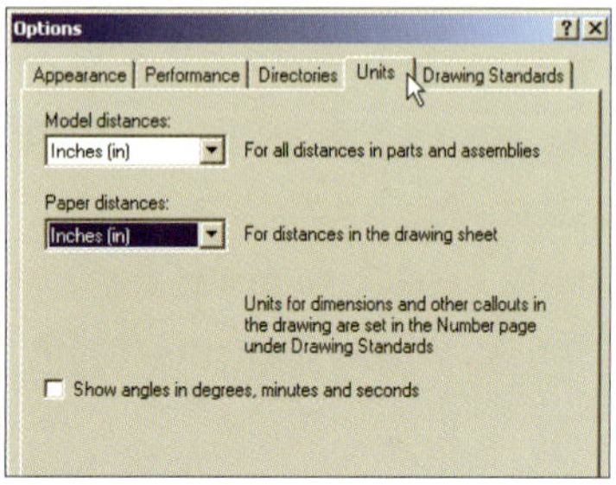

Draw a rectangle

• Click and release on the **Rectangle** tool located on the Design Toolbar found on the right side of the screen. The cursor will change to "cross-hairs" as you move it onto the Design window. If you look just above the Design window you will see the words **Snap to Grid**. Below that you will see two numbers separated by a comma.

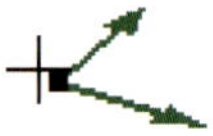

Figure 2.11b

Figure 2.12

• Move the cursor over the **Origin** point where the two green arrows meet (**Figure 2.12**). A small black square will appear where the two arrows intersect. This means that the drawing tool has "snapped to" the Origin. Also, the words **Snap to Grid** changes to **Origin** and both numbers are zero (0,0).

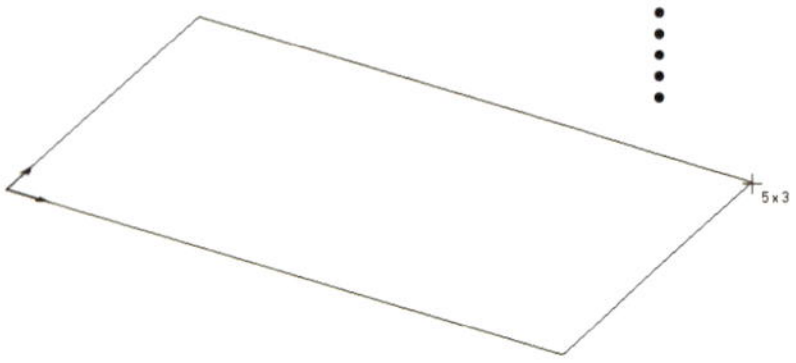

Figure 2.13

• Click and drag the cursor to the upper right until the "read-out" window attached to the cursor reads about 5 x 3 (**Figure 2.13**). If you have trouble drawing the rectangle exactly 5 x 3, don't worry. It may be the mouse. A little practice will help you get the feel for the drawing tools.

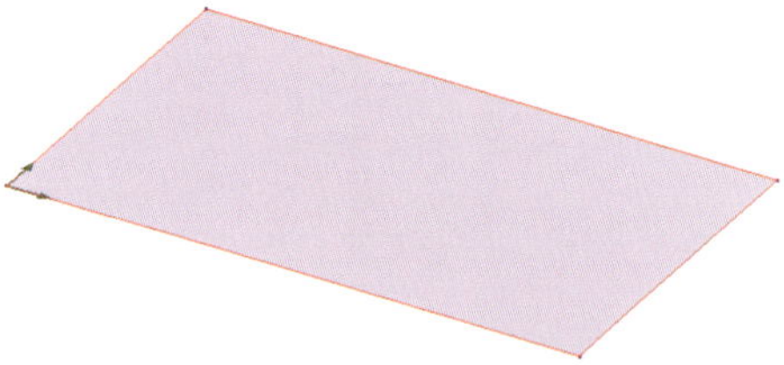

• When you release the mouse button, the sketch will fill with a color, as shown in **Figure 2.14**. The filling means the sketch is valid.

Figure 2.14

Pre-highlighting

A handy feature of Pro/DESKTOP® is pre-highlighting. Pre-highlighting occurs when the cursor moves over a line and that line changes color (usually to bright blue) even though you haven't used the mouse button. This way, you know which lines you are selecting.

- Click on the **Select Lines tool** on the Design Toolbar.
- Move the arrow cursor across the lines of the rectangle. You will notice the lines turning bright blue (**Figure 2.15**).

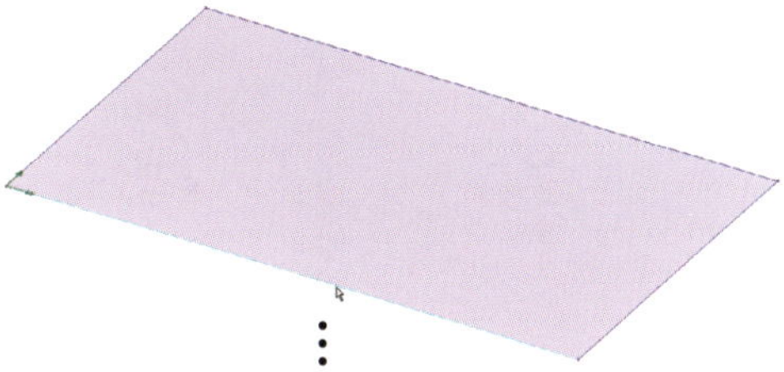

Figure 2.15

Draw a circle

- Click on the **Circle tool** located on the Design Toolbar. The cursor will again change to "cross-hairs."
- Move the cursor inside the upper right corner of the rectangle and click and draw away until the circle overlaps (extends outside) the rectangle. Notice that the filling inside the rectangle has disappeared. This is because the sketch is no longer valid (**Figure 2.16**).

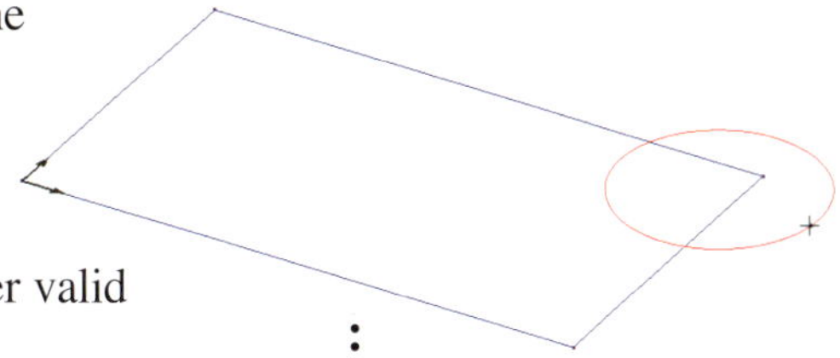

Figure 2.16

Modify the sketch to make it valid

- Click on the **Delete Line Segment tool** at the bottom of the Design Toolbar. The cursor changes to scissors.

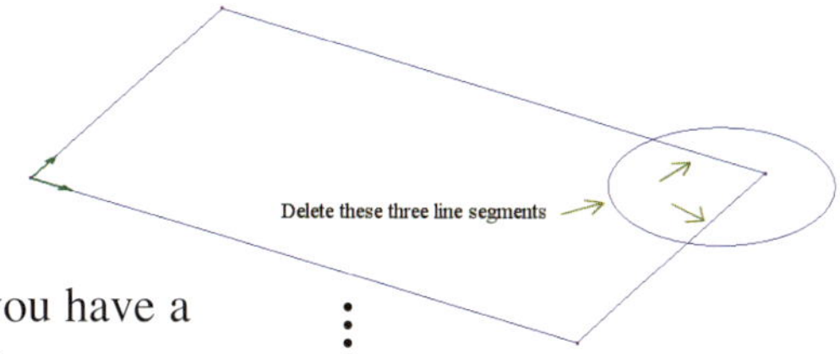

Delete these three line segments

- Identify the lines that you want to delete so that you have a closed shape of one continuous line (**Figure 2.17**).

Figure 2.17

- Move the cursor over the lines you want to delete – make sure they pre-highlight in blue – and click to delete them.

48 the extrude profile feature

02. Extrude Profile Feature & Round Edges Command

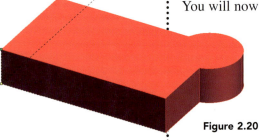

Figure 2.18

- When you have deleted the last invalid line, the sketch will fill with a color. This indicates that the sketch is now valid (**Figure 2.18**).
- Save the file as ***sketch1.des***

You are now ready to ***Extrude*** the sketch profile you have created.

Extrude the sketch

- Go to the top of the screen to the ***Features*** pull-down menu and select ***Extrude Profile*** from the list. A floating dialog box appears.
- In the ***Distance box*** enter the value 1, for one inch (**Figure 2.19**). Leave the other options as they are.
- Click ***OK*** to close the dialog box.

The solid object you have created is red (**Figure 2.20**) because it is still selected. You will now deselect it.

Figure 2.19

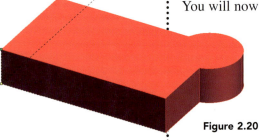

Figure 2.20

the extrude profile feature

- Click off the object on a blank part of the design window to deselect the object. The active tool is the **Select Features** tool (**Figure 2.21a**).
- Click on the **Select Lines** tool on the Design Toolbar. Notice that you can now see the sketch lines you created (**Figure 2.21b**).

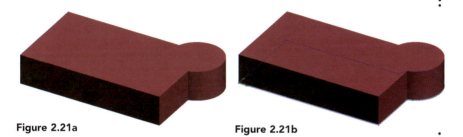

Figure 2.21a   **Figure 2.21b**

Pro/DESKTOP® makes visible only the information appropriate for the active tool. You did not see the sketch lines when the Select Features tool was active because the tool is only used to select features, such as extrusions. The sketch lines appeared when you switched to the tool used to select lines.

Exercise 2-2 Toy Block

The first project will involve creating a child's toy block. First, you will create a square and then extrude it into a cube. Then you will place letters on the sides and use the extrude command again, only this time you will subtract material. The letters will then be indented into the side of the block. This project will involve using the Extrude Profile feature to both add material and to subtract material.

Figure 2.22

50 the extrude profile feature

Figure 2.23

Begin a New Design

- Open a *New Design* File.
- *Maximize* the Design window.
- Use the keyboard shortcut *Shift+W* so that you are looking directly at the *base workplane* and *initial sketch*. This shortcut will always change the view to look directly at the active workplane.
- The *Green Square* you are seeing is the base workplane. The green arrows in the center indicate that there is a sketch on that workplane (*Figure 2.23*).

Make sure your design will be in inches.

- Click on the *Tools* pull-down menu at the top of the screen.
- Select *Options* at the bottom of the menu list.
- Click on the *Units* tab.
- In the two pull-down lists select *inches* for both *Model distances* and *Paper distances*
- Click *OK* to close the Options window.

Draw the Toy Block Sketch

- Select the *Rectangle Tool* from the Design Toolbar on the right side of the screen.

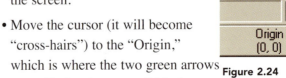

Figure 2.24

- Move the cursor (it will become "cross-hairs") to the "Origin," which is where the two green arrows meet. Notice that a small black square appears where the arrows meet when the cursor is near this point. In the toolbar above the Design window the word *Origin* appears and (0,0) appears underneath (*Figure 2.24*).

the extrude profile feature

- Hold down the *Shift* key while dragging the cursor up and to the right to make a square. Notice the "read-out" window attached to the cursor as you draw. When the cursor read-out window reads *2 x 2* release the mouse button (**Figure 2.25**). If you released the mouse button at the wrong time and your block is not the right size, go to the Edit pull-down menu and select Undo, then try again.
- *Save* the file as *toyblock1.des*

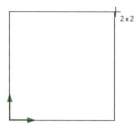

Figure 2.25

When you held down the shift key as you drew the square, Pro/DESKTOP® constrained the rectangle into a square with equal sides. When you constrained the length of one side to 2 inches, Pro/DESKTOP automatically changed the length of the other side to 2 inches.

Extrude the Block

- Use the keyboard shortcut *Shift+T* to change the view in the Design window to *Trimetric View*. This will allow you to see the block in 3D.
- Click on the *Features* pull-down menu.
- Select *Extrude Profile* from the list. A floating window or dialog box appears in the lower right corner of the screen.
- In the dialog box, make sure *Add material* and *Above workplane* are selected and then enter *2* in the *Distance (in):* window (**Figure 2.26**).

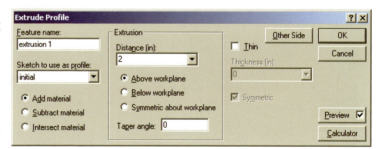

Figure 2.26

52 the extrude profile feature

02. Extrude Profile Feature & Round Edges Command

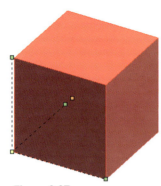

Figure 2.27

Figure 2.28

Figure 2.29

- Click *OK* to close the Extrude Profile window. You will see the square sketch become a red 3D cube (Figure 2.27). The red color means that the Extrude feature is still selected.
- Click the cursor in a blank part of the screen to de-select the cube.
- Save your work.

Create a New Workplane and Sketch on the Top Face of the Block

It is often necessary to select the face of an object to tell Pro/DESKTOP® where you want to place a new workplane and sketch. A new sketch is always necessary to create a new feature. A new workplane is often necessary to make a place for the sketch.

- Click on the *Select Faces Tool* in the Design Toolbar on the right side of the screen.
- Move the cursor arrow across the block without clicking the mouse. Notice that the edge lines of the block pre-highlight as you move across them (Figure 2.28).

- Move the cursor across the top face near the corner that appears closest to you until the four lines that make up the top face pre-highlight in blue – then click once. The top surface of the block will turn red, which indicates you have selected that face (Figure 2.29). If one of the other block faces turns red, click once off the block to de-select that face and try again.

- With the top face of the block selected, click on the *Workplane* pull-down menu at the top of the screen and select *New Sketch* from the list (Figure 2.30). Because you have a face of an object selected, Pro/DESKTOP creates both a new Workplane and a new Sketch at the same time.

the extrude profile feature

- Change the name of the sketch to *A* and the name of the workplane to *top* (**Figure 2.31**) and close the dialog box by clicking *OK*.

Figure 2.30

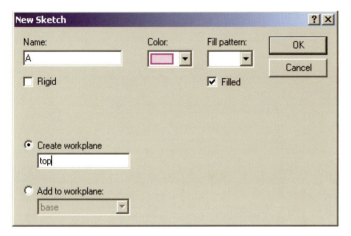

Figure 2.31

- You are still in the select faces mode (because the Select Faces tool is still active). To see the workplane and sketch, click on one of the drawing tools in the Design Toolbar (Line, Circle, Rectangle, etc.). Pro/DESKTOP only shows information related to the tool selected. Now you will see the new workplane and sketch on the top of the block (**Figure 2.32**).

- Use the keyboard shortcut *Shift+W* to change the view so you are looking directly at the new sketch and workplane you created (**Figure 2.33**).

Figure 2.32

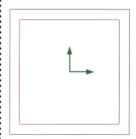

Figure 2.33

Create a Letter Outline on the Top Face of the Block

- Click on the *Line* pull-down menu at the top of the screen.
- Select *Add Text Outline* from the list. A small *Text Outline* window appears (**Figure 2.34**).

54 the extrude profile feature

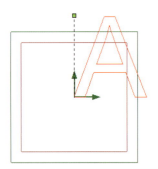

Figure 2.34

Figure 2.35

- Type the capital letter *A* in the Text box; Choose **Arial** for the Font; select **Regular** as the Style; and enter the value *1.5* for the height; click on **Preview** to see if the size of the letter is the appropriate size for the block (**Figure 2.35**).

- Click *OK* to close the dialog box.

- While all the lines of the letter *A* are selected in red, move the cursor slowly over it until you see the cross-hair arrows (**Figure 2.36**).

- Click and hold and drag the *A* until it is positioned in the center of the block, then release (**Figure 2.37**).

- *Save* your work.

Figure 2.36

Figure 2.37

Extrude the Letter A

This time you will remove material when you extrude.

- Use the keyboard shortcut **Shift+T** to change the view in the Design window to **Trimetric View**. This view will help you to see what is happening in the following steps (**Figure 2.38**).

- Click on the **Features** pull-down menu.

- Select **Extrude Profile** from the list. The Extrude Profile dialog box appears in the lower right corner of the design window.

Figure 2.38

- In the dialog box, make sure **Subtract material** and **Below workplane** are selected and then enter **0.125** in the **Distance (in):** window (**Figure 2.39**).

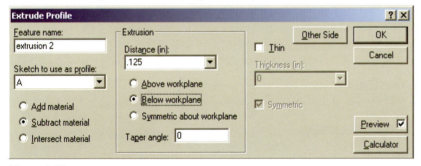

Figure 2.39

- Click **OK** to close the Extrude Profile window. The letter A is now recessed into the block 1/8th inch (**Figure 2.40**).

Note: If all the lines of the letter are not selected, the letter will distort. If this happens, delete all the letter lines and start again.

Note: This is a good example where the Toggle Sketch Filled command might give you problems. If you click on a drawing tool, or the Select Lines tool, you will no longer see the letter recess because the sketch of the letter A is filled. You can turn off Sketch Filled on the Line pull-down menu.

Figure 2.40

Note: If you have drawn a figure, such as a square or letter, on a face of your block and cannot move it because no crosshairs appear, you can select the figure two ways. You can *Shift click* to select each line segment of the figure, or you can click off the figure and then click and drag a box around it, using your *Select Line* tool. If you click & drag a box around your figure, stay close to the figure. A box that is too large may encompass some part of a figure on another sketch, and prevent you from moving or deleting the figure you were attempting to select.

Extrude the Letters B, C, D, E, F

- Using the same method, extrude the letters B, C, D, E and F on the other faces of the block (Figure 2.41). Here are abbreviated steps:
- Select a face of the block.
- Create a *New Sketch* on that face.
- *Add Text Outline* of the Letter 1.5 inches high on the sketch and drag it into position.
- *Extrude* letter outline below the workplane 1/8th inch, subtracting material.
- *Save* your work.

Figure 2.41

Exercise 2-3 Another Toy Block Challenge

Many toy blocks have more detail and look like the one in Figure 2-42. Your challenge is to create the more realistic toy block in a 3-inch cube. The recess in each side is done by creating a slightly smaller square sketch and extruding it, subtracting material, to a depth of one-eighth inch (0.125-inches). Figure 2.43 shows the sketch for the recess, which is 2.5-inches square. You can refer back to the previous toy block steps if you need to.

Figure 2.42

Figure 2.43

Figure 2.44

To create the raised letters, you must select the face of the recessed surface and create a New Sketch there (Figure 2.44). The letters are added as before by using the Add Text Outline command and extruding the letter sketch one-eighth inch *Above the workplane*. Save this new toy block as *toyblock2.des*

The Thin Option

The Extrude Profile dialog box has the option **Thin**. When you use this option, you do not need a closed shape sketch to extrude. The Thin option works on lines, not closed shapes. For example, if you would like to create a shallow slot in a solid object, you could draw the shape of the slot with the line, arc, or spline tool, and use the extrude profile feature, subtracting material, and the thin option (Figure 2.45).

Figure 2.45

Figure 2.46 shows the Thin option checked. Notice that the Thickness box (which is normally grayed out) appears and you are required to enter a value for the width of the extrusion, something unnecessary for a simple extrude.

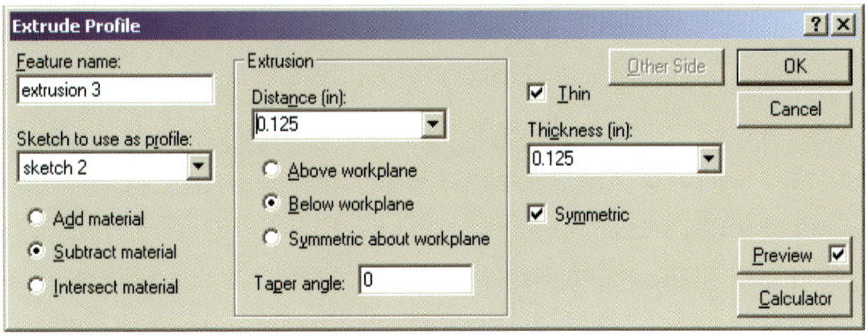

Figure 2.46

You also have the option of defining the Thin command to subtract or add material with a different amount on one side of the line than the other. Removing the check next to **Symmetric** gives you these options. You also have a taper option you can use to angle the extrusion generated by the line.

Exercise 2-4 A Simple Thin Extrusion

Create a line sketch

- Start a *New Design*. Maximize the window.
- Make sure the units you are working in are *inches*.

You will be working on the initial sketch on the base workplane.

- Click on the *Straight Line* tool in the Design Toolbar.
- Move the cursor to the *Origin* point, click and drag a line up and to the right.
- Make a zig-zag sketch with three additional lines (four total), similar to Figure 2.47. Make sure the end of each line is connected to the others.

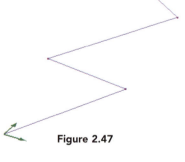

Figure 2.47

Extrude the line sketch

At the bottom center of the screen are a number of icons. They are shortcuts for Pro/DESKTOP® operations. The group of icons on the right is for Features.

- Click on the *Extrude Profile* icon
- Enter a Distance of *1* (inch).

02. Extrude Profile Feature & Round Edges Command

round edges command   59

- Click on the *Thin* button.
- Enter a Thickness of *0.2*
- Click on the *OK* button.
- Save this file as *zigzag.des*

The extruded "zig-zag" line should now look like Figure 2.48.

Round Edges Command

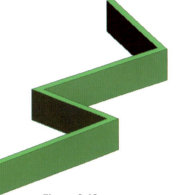

Figure 2.48

The round edges command is simple to use and will make the models you develop look realistic. Most real products have rounded edges, such as the toolbox in Figure 2.49.

Edges are rounded for a number of reasons: safety, durability, efficiency of manufacturing and appearance. A sharp edge on a product is only useful if it is intended to cut. Otherwise, edges are "softened" (the expressions "to break an edge" or a "broken edge" are also used when referring to the process of eliminating sharp edges and corners).

Figure 2.49

There are good reasons to soften edges. Sharp edges or corners are damaged easily and look worn very quickly. Paint and other finishes chip rapidly at sharp edges. Rounded edges stay looking good longer.

In addition, some industrial processes, such as injection forming, rely on a liquid material forced into a mold. Sharp internal corners are sometimes difficult to fill, so rounding internal edges on a mold results in rounded external edges on the product. Strength of a material is increased where two planes meet if the internal corner is rounded instead of a sharp 90-degree corner. A rounded internal corner is called a *Fillet*.

The Round Edges command can be accessed three ways: The Features pull-down menu; the Round Edges icon at the bottom of the Design window; and by a right mouse click after you have selected an edge with the Select Edges tool.

The following digital camera project will help you learn how to use the Round Edges command.

Exercise 2-5 Create a Simple Digital Camera Model

In this next section you will use the Extrude Profile Feature to create a simple digital camera model, like the one in Figure 2.50. The Round Edges command will be used to make the model more realistic. When the model is completed you can add additional details as you like.

Figure 2.50

Create the sketch for the camera body and Extrude

- Start a *New Design*. Maximize the window.
- Make sure the units you are working in are *inches*.
- Use the keyboard shortcut *Shift+W* to look directly at the initial sketch on the base workplane.

02. Extrude Profile Feature & Round Edges Command

round edges command 61

- Using the **Rectangle** drawing tool (found in the Design Toolbar on the right side of the screen), place the cursor over the Origin point until you see a small back square where the two green arrows meet (Figure 2.51).

- Click and hold, and drag up and to the right until the cursor "read-out" indicates 4 x 1 inches (Figure 2.52).

Figure 2.51

Figure 2.52

- **Extrude** this sketch **3 inches** high by clicking on the Extrude Profile icon on the bottom of the Design window (Figure 2.53). Use the options **Add material** and **Above the workplane**.

- **Save** the file as **camera-1.des**

Figure 2.53

Create a new sketch for the lens and Extrude

- Using the **Select Faces** tool found on the Design Toolbar, select the front face of the camera body (Figure 2.54).

- Right mouse click and select **New Sketch** from the menu. The New Sketch dialog box appears.

- Change the name of the sketch to **lens** and the name of the workplane to **camerafront** (Figure 2.55).

- Use the keyboard shortcut **Shift+W** to look directly at the new **camerafront workplane**.

Figure 2.54

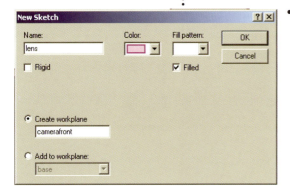

Figure 2.55

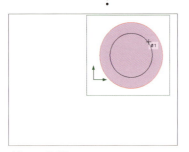

Figure 2.57

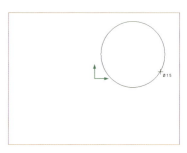

- Use the ***Circle*** drawing tool (found in the Design Toolbar on the right side of the screen) to make a circle about ***1.5 inches*** in diameter near the upper right corner (**Figure 2.56**).

Figure 2.56

- Use the ***Circle*** drawing tool to create another circle 1-inch in diameter concentric and inside the first. To do this, move the cursor near the inside edge of the first circle (you may want to zoom in) until you see a small black square in the center of the first circle. When you see the small square, click and drag in toward the center of the circle (**Figure 2.57**). The area between the two circles should now be filled, which tells you that this is the area that will be extruded (refer back to the image of the camera in **Figure 2.50**).

- ***Extrude*** the circles sketch ***0.25*** (one-quarter) inch. Use the options ***Add material*** and ***Above the workplane***. Notice that only the area between the inner and outer circles has been extruded (**Figure 2.58**).

- ***Save*** your work.

Figure 2.58

Create another New Sketch on the camerafront workplane.

This time you will create a New Sketch in a different way than you have done before. You will find that you will use this technique often in your design work.

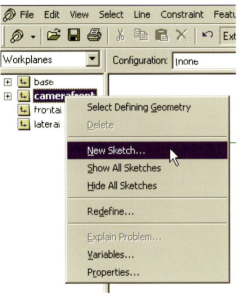

Figure 2.59

- Move the cursor to the Browser window on the left side of the screen. Make sure the word Workplanes is in the small window above the Browser. If not, click on the down arrow next to the window and select ***Workplanes*** from the list.

- Right mouse-click on the yellow icon next to the ***camerafront*** workplane and choose ***New Sketch*** from the floating list (**Figure 2.59**).

- When the New Sketch dialog box appears, change the name of the new sketch to ***viewfinder*** and click ***OK***. You have created a new sketch on the ***camerafront*** workplane.

Draw the sketch for the viewfinder

- Using the ***Rectangle drawing tool*** (found in the Design Toolbar on the right side of the screen) draw a small rectangle (about ***0.7 x 0.5*** inches) to the left of the lens (**Figure 2.60**). This will form the viewfinder.

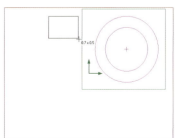

Figure 2.60

Figure 2.61

- *Extrude* the rectangle 0.1-inch, but this time use the options *Subtract material* and *Below workplane* (Figure 2.61). The viewfinder is now a shallow depression in the front of the camera (Figure 2.62).

Figure 2.62

Round the edges of the model

In this section you will need to make sure that the lens and viewfinder do not interfere with the rounded corners. Remember, you can always move the circle sketches used to make the lens and the viewfinder. If you do, you will probably need to *Update* the design by clicking on the green "traffic light" button at the top of the screen.

Round the vertical edges:

- Use the keyboard shortcut *Shift+T* to change the view to *Trimetric*.
- Click on the *Select Edges tool* on the Design Toolbar.
- Select the near vertical edge on the camera (Figure 2.63).

02. Extrude Profile Feature & Round Edges Command

round edges command

- Right mouse-click and choose **Round Edges** from the menu. The Round Edges window appears. Right clicking after you have selected an edge gives you short-cuts to several features.
- Enter a value of **0.25** in the **Radius (in.)** window in the Round Edges dialog box (Figure 2.64).

Figure 2.63

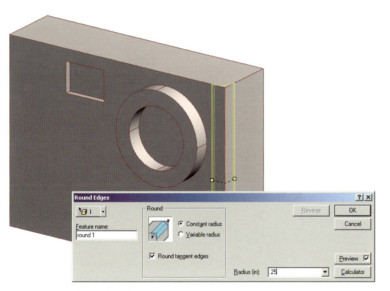

Figure 2.64

In Pro/DESKTOP® the tools are still active when the dialog window is open. You will select the remaining three vertical edges so the Round Edges command will apply to all four edges. Although you can round each edge separately, by doing all four as a group it will make it possible to change all four edges in one step.

- Hold down the **Shift** key and use the **Select Edges** tool to select the other three vertical edges of the camera (Figure 2.65). Rotate the camera with the keyboard arrow keys if necessary.

Figure 2.65

Figure 2.66

Figure 2.68

Tip: If you have entered a value for the radius of a round that is too large, and it interferes with another feature, you will get an error message. Try to redefine a smaller radius value.

- Click **OK** to close the **Round Edges** window (**Figure 2.66**).
- **Save** your work.
- If you get an error message, **Undo** the previous step and round the edges again using 0.15-inches as the radius.

Round the top and bottom edges:

- Using the **Select Edges tool**, select the top front edge of the camera and the bottom front edge of the camera (**Figure 2.67**). Remember to hold down the **Shift key** to select more than one edge at a time.

Figure 2.67

- Right mouse-click and choose **Round Edges** from the menu. This is a shortcut to get to the Round Edges command.
- Enter a value of **0.1** in the **Radius (in.)** window. Notice that the side edges and the curved edges on both the top and the bottom are automatically selected (**Figure 2.68**).
- Click **OK** to close the Round Edges window.
- **Save** your work.

Round the lens:

- Using the **Select Edges tool**, select both the outer and inner edge of the lens (**Figure 2.70**). Remember to hold down the **Shift key** to select more than one edge at a time.

Figure 2.70

round edges command

- Right mouse-click and choose **Round Edges** from the menu.
- Round the edges of the lens to **0.05-inches**. The radius should now look like Figure 2.71.

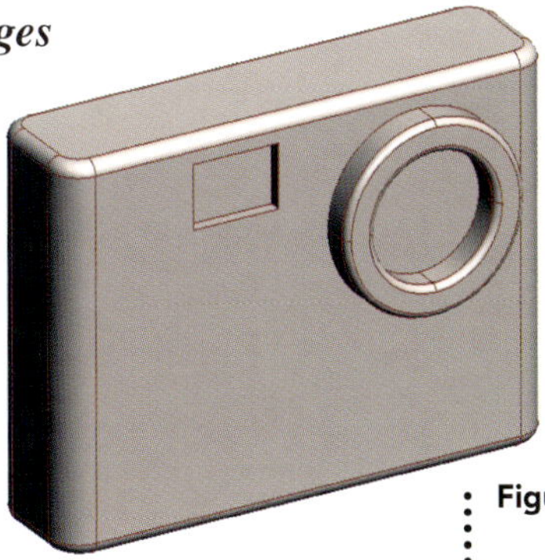

Round the edges of the viewfinder:

- Using the same procedure you have used to round the edges of the camera body and the lens, round the outer edges of the viewfinder recess to a radius of 0.04-inches (Figure 2.72).
- *Save* your work.

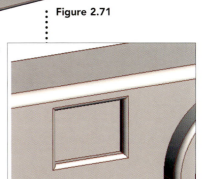

Figure 2.71

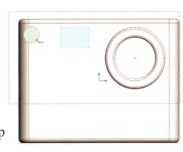

Figure 2.72

Create a button on the front of the camera

A button to take a picture should help make the camera more realistic. It will be placed on the front of the camera in the upper left corner.

- Create a new sketch called **button** on the **camerafront**. Go to the Browser window and right-click on the yellow icon next to the **camerafront** workplane and choose **New Sketch** from the list. Change the name of the sketch to **button** and click **OK**.
- Use **Shift+W** to look directly at the new sketch.
- Draw a circle **0.4-inches in diameter** in the upper left corner of the camera. Make the circle stick out over the left round a bit (Figure 2.73). Try to align the top

Figure 2.73

68 round edges command

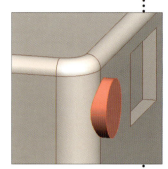

Figure 2.74

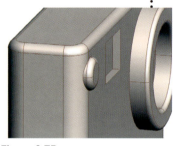

Figure 2.75

of the circle with the top of the viewfinder. Alignment of elements is good design practice.

- ***Extrude*** the circle 0.15-inches using the ***Add material*** and ***Symmetric about workplane*** options. Figure 2.74 shows the extruded circle hanging over the round edge just a bit. The Symmetric workplane option makes the extrusion grow both above and below the workplane, so as you are looking at the camera, the extrusion has added material from the workplane out in front toward you, and from the workplane toward the back of the camera away from you. You would not notice the extrusion below the workplane except for the fact that the circle sketch overlaps where the round left edge is located. Use the arrow keys to turn the camera to get a better look.

- ***Round*** the edges of the button by selecting the circle edge of the extrusion and using the ***Round Edges feature*** with a radius of ***0.07-inches*** (Figure 2.75).

Detail Features

Now you will make three narrow grooves in the bottom of the camera to add a little design detail to the model.

- Create a new sketch called ***detail*** on the ***camerafront*** workplane.

- Use ***Shift+W*** to look directly at the new sketch.

- Using the ***Rectangle drawing tool***, draw a narrow rectangle starting on the left edge of the camera body and running to the right edge of the lens (Figure 2.76). In this case the rectangle is 3.66-inches by 0.04-inches but your sketch

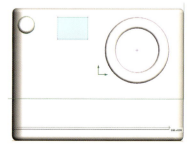

Figure 2.76

may have slightly different dimensions. Note the dimensions of your rectangle.

- ***Draw*** a second rectangle using the same dimensions and also starting on the left edge of the camera body.
- ***Draw*** a third rectangle the same size.
- Evenly space the rectangles (Figure 2.77). Remember, all four lines of a rectangle must be selected (red) in order to move it without distorting its shape.

Figure 2.77

- ***Extrude*** the three rectangles (you can do it all at once because they are on the same sketch) using the ***Subtract material*** and ***Below workplane*** options. Figure 2.78 shows what your camera should look like.
- ***Save*** your work.

Modify the camera

The digital camera model you have constructed can be made to look more realistic if other features are added, such as a flash, rear LCD screen, battery compartment hatch, manufacturer's name, etc. Modify your design to include some or all of these additional details.

- ***Save*** the modified camera as ***camera-2.des*** using the ***Save As*** command in the ***File*** pull-down window.

Note: Another way to add these details is by using a line and the Thin option.

Figure 2.78

Figure 2.79a

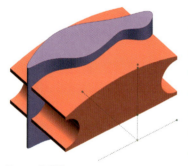

Figure 2.79b

Intersect Material Option

The Extrude Profile dialog box has an option that will help you create solids (or remove material from a solid) that would be difficult or impossible to accomplish with the other feature commands. With the Intersect Material Option, two Extrude Profile sketches are required on two different workplanes. The first Extrude is done normally. The second Extrude must intersect the first. Figure 2.79a shows the result of using the Intersect Material option. Figure2.79b shows the result of the two extrusions done normally, without the Intersect Material option selected.

Exercise 2-6 Using the Intersect Material Option: Telephone Handset

Figure 2.80 shows the telephone handset you are going to develop in this exercise. You are going to estimate the distances using the "Snap to Grid" in the top toolbar on the screen. By starting your sketch at the Origin point, you will be able to figure out the location of the drawing cursor anyplace on your drawing. The dimensions are to the nearest one-half inch so you can easily estimate distances, as each dimension will be either in whole inch (1, 2, 3, etc.) or half inch (0.5, 1.5, 2.5, etc.) increments.

Create the sketch for the telephone handset body and Extrude

Figure 2.80

- Start a *New Design*. Maximize the window.
- Make sure the units you are working in are *inches*.

- Use the keyboard shortcut **Shift+W** to look directly at the initial sketch on the base workplane.
- **Save** the file as **handset.des**
- Starting at the Origin point and using the **Rectangle tool**, draw a rectangle 2.5-inches wide by 8-inches long, as in Figure 2.81.

Figure 2.81

- Using the **Rectangle tool**, draw a rectangle inside the first rectangle 0.5-inches from the top and bottom edges and 2.5-inches from each end, as in Figure 2.82. Use the **Snap to Grid** as a guide.

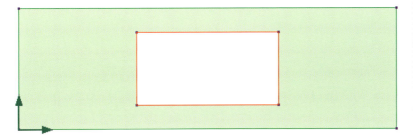

Figure 2.82

- **Draw** lines across the narrow width of the larger rectangle 2-inches from each end using the **Straight Line tool**

Figure 2.83

(**Figure 2.83**). Hold down the **Shift** key as you draw to keep the lines straight. Also, make sure these lines touch the top and bottom but do not overlap.

- **Draw** diagonal lines with the **Straight Line** tool from the edges of the inside rectangle to the place where the lines you drew in the previous step intersect the outside rectangle (**Figure 2.84**).

Figure 2.84

- With the **Line Segment Delete** tool, clip away all the lines that do not appear in **Figure 2.85**. When the sketch fills with color you will know that you have deleted all the necessary lines.

- **Extrude** the sketch profile you have drawn 3-inches (Add material, Above workplane). The model should look like **Figure 2.86**. Change the view to **Trimetric (Shift+T)**.

- **Save** the file.

02. Extrude Profile Feature & Round Edges Command

round edges command 73

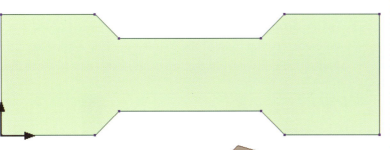

Figure 2.85

Create the sketch for the intersecting profile

First, you will need to create a new Sketch on the frontal workplane. The frontal workplane is the one running along the bottom of the first rectangle you drew.

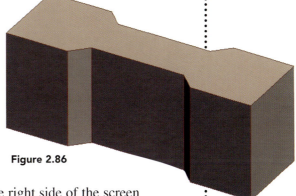

Figure 2.86

- Go to the **Design** Toolbar on the right side of the screen and click on the **Select Workplane** tool (the third tool from the top).

- Find the **frontal workplane** by moving the cursor across the two vertical workplanes (Figure 2.87). Select the frontal workplane.

- With the **frontal workplane** selected, right mouse-click and choose **New Sketch** from the floating menu. **Rename** the new sketch **intersection**.

- Use the keyboard shortcut **Shift+W** to look directly down on this new sketch on the frontal workplane.

- Use the keyboard shortcut **Shift+A** to **Autoscale** the screen so the handset extrusion fills the screen.

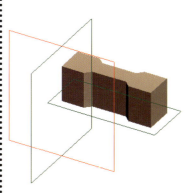

Figure 2.87

- Use the ***Straight line tool***, and starting to the left of the extrusion and ending to the right of the extrusion, draw a horizontal line about 1-inch down from the top of the extrusion (**Figure 2.88**).

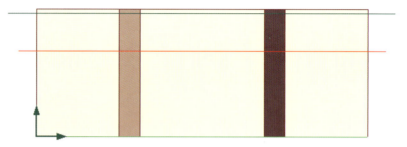

Figure 2.88

- Choose the ***Arc or Fillet tool*** on the Design Toolbar on the right side of the screen. Select the straight line you just drew by clicking once and releasing. Move the cursor over the selected line and the cursor will change. Click and drag up to make the straight line into an arc. Drag up until the arc is almost to the top of the extrusion but not touching the top edge (**Figure 2.89**). If you have trouble with making the arc, use the ***Undo*** command

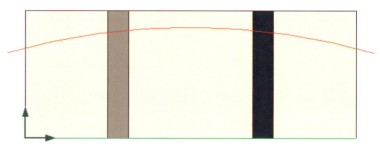

Figure 2.89

and try again. Remember to first deselect the line, then click on it once with the ***Arc or Fillet*** tool, and then click and drag it up.

- Using the ***Straight Line tool*** draw a second straight line near the bottom of the extrusion (**Figure 2.90**). If you have trouble with the line "snapping" to the extrusion, zoom in and try again.

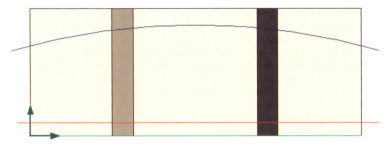

Figure 2.90

- Use the ***Arc or Fillet tool*** to create an arc with the second straight line, trying to make the arc radius about the same as the arc on the top line (**Figure 2.91**).

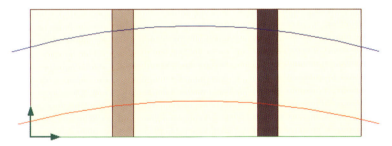

Figure 2.91

- ***Draw*** two straight vertical lines close to the edge but not touching the edge, one on either side of the extrusion (**Figure 2.92**).

- Use the ***Line Segment Delete*** tool to clip away all crossing lines so the sketch fills with color (**Figure 2.93**). Sometimes the sketch will not fill even though the sketch is valid, so try the next step.

76 round edges command

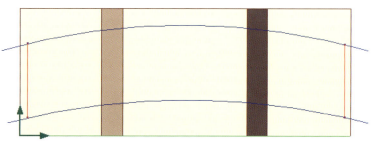

Figure 2.92

- Go to the *Features* pull-down menu and select *Extrude Profile*. Use the following options: Intersect material; Below workplane; 3-inches distance. Also, you might need to click on *Other side* if the wrong part of the solid is left after you click *OK*. If that happens, go to the *Edit* pull-down menu and select *Undo* and use the *Extrude Profile* feature again.

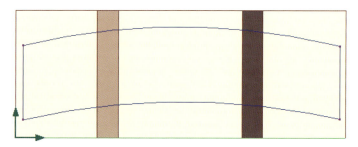

Figure 2.93

- With the *Select Faces* tool, select the back of the handset. Sometimes you can select a face and round all the edges instead of using the *Select Edges* tool and Shift+clicking all the edges.

- Using the *Round Edges feature*, round all the back edges to 0.7-inch radius (Figure 2.94). If you get an error message try *Undo* and use 0.6-inch radius.

- *Select* the front face of the handset and round those edges to 0.25-inch radius.

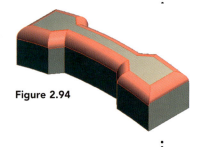

Figure 2.94

- With the **Select Edges tool** select the four outside edges and round those to 0.2-inches. The handset should look like Figure 2.95.
- **Save** your work.

The **Intersect Material** option can produce some interesting results. When you are designing, or when you are reverse-engineering components to develop in Pro/DESKTOP®, keep this option in mind.

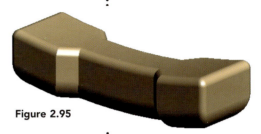

Figure 2.95

Summary

In this chapter you learned how the Extrude Profile feature may be used to create 3D solids from valid sketches. The Extrude Profile feature has a number of options that will let you add or subtract material, extrude the profile above or below the active workplane, or both above and below the workplane equally with the "symmetrical about workplane" option. You can create 3D models by entering exact values for the extrude distance.

The Thin option will permit you to create extrusions from lines, as opposed to valid sketches of closed figures. Using the Thin option you can also add or subtract material.

The Round Feature creates smooth, rounded edges on 3D objects. This feature is used to "break" sharp edges in a way that reflects how real products are made. Rounded edges are used to increase the strength of a material, as a way to make products look better longer, and as a way to make certain the product is appropriately manufactured. Both internal corners – called fillets - and external corners can be rounded.

02. Extrude Profile Feature & Round Edges Command

test your knowledge **78**

Test Your Knowledge

Project 2.1 USB Pen drive

USB pen drives have a number of advantages over floppy discs and zip disks. They are smaller, have no moving parts to wear out, and they can hold a lot of information.

design brief Design and develop a model of a 256MB USB pen drive. Show the drive with the dust cap removed, so the USB plug is exposed.

Research several existing USB pen drives and sketch out their sizes and shapes.

Specifications

- Use millimeters as the dimension units;
- Round the corners of the drive where appropriate;
- Use the Text Outline command to inscribe – **256MB** – on one side of the drive and – **USB 2.0** – on the other side.
- Save the file as **usbpen.des**

Project 2.2 Plasma TV

Plasma televisions are rapidly increasing in popularity despite their very expensive price tags. They have many advantages over conventional televisions: they are larger and easier to see, they are thin and can be mounted on the wall, hung from the ceiling or sit on a table; they are considerably lighter than large conventional large screen televisions, which can weigh as much as two hundred pounds.

design brief Design and develop a model of a 42-inch plasma television that incorporates speakers, one on either side of the screen.

Research the sizes, shapes, and looks of several 42-inch plasma televisions made by at least three different manufactures. Write down this information and draw simple sketches of each that captures their dimensions, including overall size and screen size.

Specifications

- Use inches as the dimension units.
- Use only the Extrude Profile and Round Pro/DESKTOP® features;
- Use the Extrude Profile feature to either create holes for the speaker grills or the thin option to create lines for the speaker grills;
- Incorporate a table stand so the TV can rest on a table or platform;
- Save the file as **plasmatv.des**

02. Extrude Profile Feature & Round Edges Command

design link — who are designers?

designers are people who like challenges.

They take problems and turn them into opportunities. They create something that did not exist before, or they improve something that already exists.

designers are employed in a wide range of businesses and industries.

Landscape designers create outside environments with plants, trees, walkways, and structures. **Interior designers** create inside environments with textiles, furniture, art objects and other artifacts. **Architects** create human habitats, including houses and commercial buildings. **Graphic designers** work with the printed or electronic page to create two-dimensional products, such as posters, magazine advertisements, and web pages. **Industrial designers** create products, from tractors and kitchen appliances, to hip replacement joints. Most engineers are also designers: the **civil engineer** may design bridges, towers or roads; **industrial engineers** may design manufacturing facilities; **computer engineers** design the circuits for computers used in cars and microwave ovens as well as the computer that sits on your desk.

designing is challenging and rewarding work.

Good designers are in high demand and they make good salaries. Most companies recognize that if their products are well-designed, they will sell more of them. Consumers recognize that well-designed products last longer and are easier to use.

80

03

modeling challenge using extrude feature

In this chapter you will learn how to:

- Create Sketches and Workplanes
- Create valid Sketch Profiles
- Use Constraints to dimension a sketch
- Use the Extrude feature to add material
- Use the Round command to contour edges
- Use the Album to render a simple object

Introduction

Consumer electronics products are continually changing as the technology improves. These products seem to get smaller, lighter, and have more features every year. Consumers expect next year's model to be better, so to be competitive companies have to continuously improve their products.

An example of a product that is continuously changing is the pager. Because the new, smaller cell phones are cutting deeply into the pager market, pager manufacturers are adding new features and making their product look "cool." Some of the new pagers are only slightly larger than a credit card.

The project you will tackle is to create a 3D model of a pager.

Design Challenge: The Pager Model

This unit will take you through a step-by-step procedure to create a pager model. Because you will only use two Pro/DESKTOP® features, the pager you will model will be very simple and will not have some of the interesting shapes of some of the newest pagers on the market. As you learn more features of Pro/DESKTOP you will be able to create more elaborate designs.

Figure 3.1 Examples of several different pagers

A real pager would be made from many parts, such as front and back shells that snap together to hold all the electronics inside, plus buttons, battery and other components. You will be making a model of a pager to learn how to use the Pro/DESKTOP program and it will only look like a pager case.

pager model

The Big Picture – what you will do

In this project you will use Pro/DESKTOP® to model a pager. You will learn how to use the basic operations of the program and become familiar with some techniques to render the model. This project will provide you with detailed instructions to reinforce what you have learned in the previous chapter. Although you may be comfortable with many of the procedures here, the detail will allow you to complete the project by yourself.

- First, you will draw a rectangle sketch outline (**Figure 3.2**).

Figure 3.2

- Then you will extrude the sketch into 3-Dimensions (**Figure 3.3**).
- Round the four corners (**Figure 3.4**).

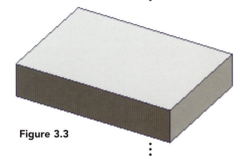

Figure 3.3

Figure 3.4

03. Modeling Challenge Using Extrude Feature

pager model 85

Rounding the edges gives the mode a more realistic appearance (**Figure 3.5**).

- Create a ***workplane*** and ***sketch*** on the top surface of the pager to form the buttons (**Figure 3.6**).

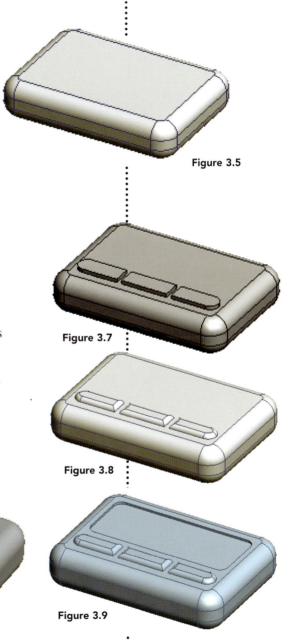

Figure 3.5

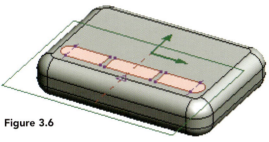

Figure 3.6

- ***Extrude*** the button sketch into 3-Dimensions (**Figure 3.7**).
- Round the edges of the buttons (**Figure 3.8**).
- Add the screen (**Figure 3.9**).
- Render the model in the Album Interface (**Figure 3.10**).

Figure 3.7

Figure 3.8

Figure 3.10

Figure 3.9

- Change the color and add screen color (Figure 3.11).

Figure 3.11

Getting Started on The Pager

New Design icon

Begin a New Project
- Start a *New Design File*. Do this by clicking on *New Design* icon located in the upper left corner of the screen.
- *Maximize* the design window so it will fill the screen.
- Use the keyboard shortcut *Shift+W* to look directly at the initial sketch on the base workplane (Figure 3.12). This shortcut will always take you to the *active sketch*. At this point it is a good idea to check and see what units you will be working in. The most common units for product design are inches and millimeters. For this project you will use inches.

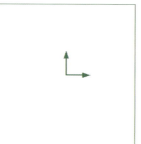

Figure 3.12

Select Inches as the Units
- Go to the top of the screen and click on the *Tools* pull-down menu.
- Select *Options*, the last item on the list.
- Click on the tab that reads *Units*.
- Change both Model and Paper distances to *inches*.
- Click *OK* to close the Options dialog box.
- *Save* the file as *pager-1.des*

Draw a 3-inch by 2-inch rectangle
- Use the *Rectangle tool* to draw a rectangle beginning at the *Origin Point*. Draw the rectangle by holding the left mouse button while moving the cursor up and to the right. The small "read-out" window attached to the cursor tells you the dimensions (length and width) of the rectangle. Make the rectangle about *3 x 2* (Figure 3.13).

Figure 3.13

Although you could have drawn the rectangle to the final dimensions in the previous step, we wanted to show you how to change the dimensions to make them exact. The next steps will show you how.

Constrain the length of the rectangle sketch to 2.5-inches
You will constrain the length and width of the rectangle to 2.5-inches by 1.75-inches. This size will make a nice, small pager.

- Choose the *Sketch Dimension Tool* (Figure 3.14) from the Constraints toolbar above the design window.
- Using the *Sketch Dimension Tool*, move the cursor over the left vertical line, but don't click on the mouse. Notice

Figure 3.14

03. Modeling Challenge Using Extrude Feature

that the line turns bright blue (cyan color) as the cursor moves over the line (Figure 3.15). This is called ***pre-highlighting***.

Pre-highlighting is a very handy feature of Pro/DESKTOP®. You will use it often as you design.

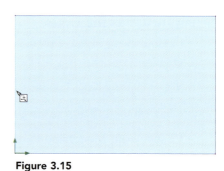

Figure 3.15

- Click on the left vertical line and release the mouse button. Notice that as you click, the line turns from blue to orange.

After you have released the mouse button the line turns bright red. A bright red line means that the line is selected.

In Pro/DESKTOP, when lines, surfaces or objects are bright red it means they are selected.

- Now move the cursor over the right vertical line. Click and hold the mouse button.
- With the mouse button still pressed, move the cursor down. You should now see a horizontal line with arrows on each end – this is a dimension line (Figure 3.16).

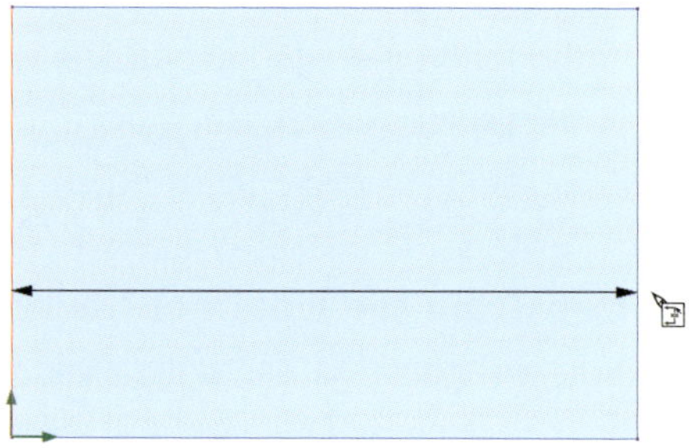

Figure 3.16

- Keep dragging the dimension line until it is below the sketch.

- Release the mouse button. You will now see a number value of the distance between the two vertical lines (**Figure 3.17**). You have just constrained the distance between the two lines to this distance. **When you constrain a distance in this way, the only way the lines can be moved closer together or further apart is to change this number.**

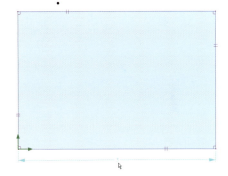

Figure 3.17

The pager will be designed so it will be small enough to fit in a pocket. You will change the distance between the two vertical lines to 2.5-inches.

- Click on the **Select Constraints Tool** in the Design Toolbar on the right side of the screen.

- Move the cursor over the dimension constraint. Notice that the constraint lines pre-highlight (**Figure 3.18**).

- Double click on the constraint value (the number 3). A floating Properties dialog box appears with the value in the box (**Figure 3.19**).

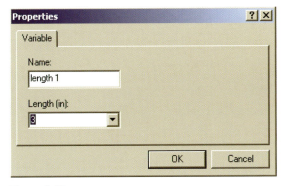

Figure 3.19

03. Modeling Challenge Using Extrude Feature

Figure 3.20

- Change the value to **2.5** (for two and one-half inches) in the dialog box (**Figure 3.20**).
- Click on the **OK** button to close the **Properties** dialog box.

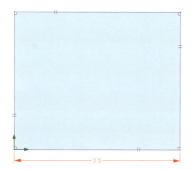

Figure 3.21

Your sketch should now look something like the one in **Figure 3.21**, but don't worry if it is taller or shorter than the illustration. What is important is that you have constrained the width to 2.5-inches.

You have just learned how to make a sketch the length you want. Now you will constrain the width.

Follow the same procedure to constrain the width of the rectangle sketch to 1.75-inches

Figure 3.22

- With the **Sketch Dimension Tool**, click and release on the top line of the sketch. It should turn bright red (**Figure 3.22**).
- Click and hold the mouse button on the bottom sketch line.
- While still holding down the mouse button, move the cursor to the right and the dimension line will appear (**Figure 3.23**).

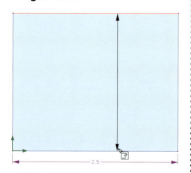

Figure 3.23

- Move the dimension line to the right until it is outside the sketch lines (**Figure 3.24**).
- With the mouse cursor, click on the **Select Constraints** tool.

Figure 3.24

- Double-click on the width constraint. The *Properties* dialog box will appear.
- In the box *Length (in)*: type in the new value of 1.75 for the height of the pager.
- Click on the *OK* button to close the *Properties* dialog box.

Your sketch should look like the illustration in Figure 3.25.

Now is a good time to save your work!

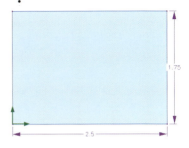

Figure 3.25

Extrude the rectangle sketch

So far, you have only drawn in two dimensions. Now you will make a three-dimensional solid from that sketch. To do this, you will use the *Extrude Feature*.

You are now looking directly down on the sketch you have drawn on the base workplane. To see how the Extrude feature works, change your point of view.

- Use the keyboard shortcut *Shift+T* to change to *View Trimetric*. There are two other ways to change the view to *Trimetric*: from the *View* pull-down menu at the top of the screen (*View>Go To> Trimetric*), and an icon on a *View* sub-menu at the bottom of the screen. The keyboard shortcuts are the easiest method to change views.

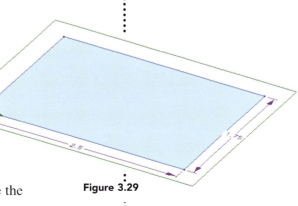

Figure 3.29

Now you are looking at the sketch at an angle, like the illustration in Figure 3.29.

- Click on the ***Extrude Icon*** on the bottom menu. There are four of the most commonly used ***Feature*** commands together and the Extrude icon is the first. The command to Extrude is also available from the ***Feature*** pull-down menu at the top of the screen. The pull-down menu contains all the feature commands including other, less frequently used features.

You will see a floating dialog box appear (**Figure 3.30**). Pro/DESKTOP® allows you to sketch your ideas quickly. In the next step you will learn a technique for sketching a 3D solid with the ***Extrude Profile*** feature.

Figure 3.30

- ***Move the cursor over the yellow box*** in the center of your sketch. Notice that the box turns green and the shape of the arrow changes (**Figure 3.31**).

The box is a "handle" that you can use to drag your sketch into a 3D solid.

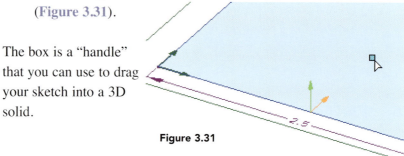

Figure 3.31

- With the cursor over the box, **click and hold the mouse button**.
- **Drag the "handle"** up and down. Notice that the number in the cursor "read-out" window changes as you move the mouse cursor (**Figure 3.32**).
- **Release the mouse button when that number reaches 0.5** (one half inch).

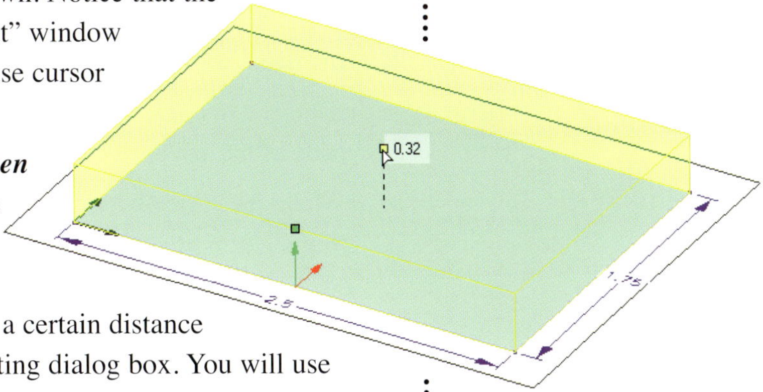

Another way to extrude a sketch to a certain distance is to type in the distance in the floating dialog box. You will use this method for another extrusion later.

Figure 3.32

- If the **Extrude Profile** dialog box has disappeared, move the cursor over the collapsed **Extrude Profile** window. It will reappear.

Notice that there are options in the **Extrude Profile** dialog box that you didn't have to worry about this time. Know that they are there for future projects.

- Click **OK** to close the dialog box. The pager model should now look like **Figure 3.33**.
- **Save** your work.

Try using the arrow keys on the keyboard to turn the pager around.

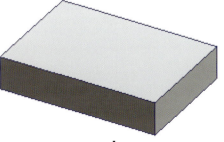

Figure 3.33

Another way to rotate an object in Pro/DESKTOP is to click the center button or wheel on the mouse. (You need a 3-button mouse to do this.) Click and hold and move the mouse and you will be able to manipulate the object.

03. Modeling Challenge Using Extrude Feature

If you hold the **Shift** key while in the **Manipulate** mode, you can drag an object around the screen. This is called **Panning**.

Round the Corners

Select Edges tool

- Click on the **Select Edges tool** in the Design Toolbar on the right side of the screen.

- Move the cursor over the pager. Notice that edges of the solid pre-highlight in bright blue when the cursor passes over them.

- When one of the four vertical edges pre-highlights, click to select it. Hold down the **Shift** key and select the remaining three edges (Figure 3.34).

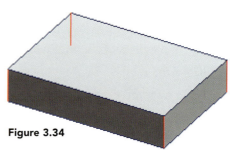

Figure 3.34

Right mouse-click and select **Round Edges** from the floating menu. This is a handy shortcut for getting to the **Round Edges** command. A floating dialog box appears, as well as the yellow "handle" you first saw with the extrude feature. You will type in a radius for the round because it is often difficult to make small radius edges by dragging the handle. On other projects with larger radius rounds you may want to use the yellow handles and drag a round on the edges.

Tip: Once you have applied a feature (such as **Extrude**) to a sketch, you cannot apply a new feature to that sketch. The only way you can change a feature is to redefine it. Right mouse-click on the feature name in the Browser window and select **Redefine**.

- Enter a value of **0.25** inches for the radius of the round.

- Click **OK** to close the Round Edges dialog box.

Figure 3.35

Round the Edges

The pager still doesn't look much like a real pager. It's flat and has sharp edges on the top and bottom. Next, you will round over the edges.

To round edges you again need to tell the software what edges you want to round. To do this you will again use the **Select Edges** tool.

- Click on the **Select Edges tool.**

Here is where pre-highlighting really helps you to identify the line you want to select.

- **Move the cursor** over the top edge (don't click). Notice that only a portion of the line pre-highlights in blue (**Figure 3.36**).
- **Click on the edge** and that line will turn red.

Figure 3.36

Now select the remaining lines on the top edge by holding down the shift key and clicking the rest of the lines on the edge until the entire top edge is selected (red) (**Figure 3.37**).

Figure 3.37

This time, you will use the **Feature** pull-down menu to access the **Round Edges Feature**.

- Move the cursor to the top of the screen and click on the **Feature** pull-down menu. Move the cursor down to the **Round Edges** feature. Notice that many other Features can be accessed from this menu (**Figure 3.38**).

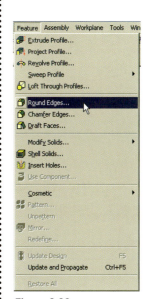

Figure 3.38

Select Faces tool

- Type in *0.18* for the **Radius** of the round in the window and Click *OK* to close the dialog box (Figure 3.39).

Figure 3.39

Now that you have rounded the top, you will use a different technique to select edges to round the bottom. Often, you can round all the edges on a face of an object by selecting that face instead of selecting each edge of the face.

- Click on the **Select Faces tool** on the Design Toolbar on the right side of the screen.
- Use the arrow keys to turn the pager upside down.
- Move the cursor arrow until all the bottom edges turns bright blue, then mouse-click. The underside will turn red, which means it is selected (Figure 3.40).

Figure 3.40

- Use the **Round Edges feature** and enter *0.18* for the radius of the round in the floating window, just as you did before to round the top edges. (*Features* pull-down menu, then select *Round Edges*)

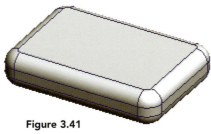
Figure 3.41

The pager should now look like Figure 3.41.
- *Save* your work.

You have been looking at the pager in the "enhanced" mode. Let's view the pager in a few different modes.

View pager in different view modes

To see different views of the pager, click on the icons on the bottom toolbars located just under the Design Window. These icons are shown next to the view mode each creates in **Figures 3.42a, 3.42b, 3.42c** and **3.42d**. You can use these different modes as you design but you will probably find the enhanced view the most useful. There are times when it helps to visualize edges and surfaces that are hidden in the enhanced mode and that is when you might find the other modes useful.

Pager Buttons

Pagers have several buttons to access different functions. In an actual pager the buttons would be connected to switches on a printed circuit board inside. In this model pager, the buttons will only be used to show what the actual pager would look like, but they will not function.

In order to create buttons on the top surface of the pager it is necessary to create a new workplane and sketch on that surface.

Create a new workplane and sketch on the top face of the pager

- Click on the **Select Faces** tool from the Design Toolbar.
- Move the cursor over the flat surface of the pager near one of the round edges. The edges that make up the square top

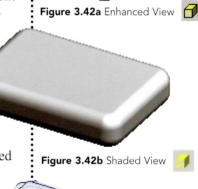

Figure 3.42a Enhanced View

Figure 3.42b Shaded View

Figure 3.42c Transparent View

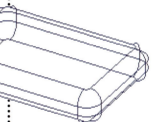

Figure 3.42d Wireframe View

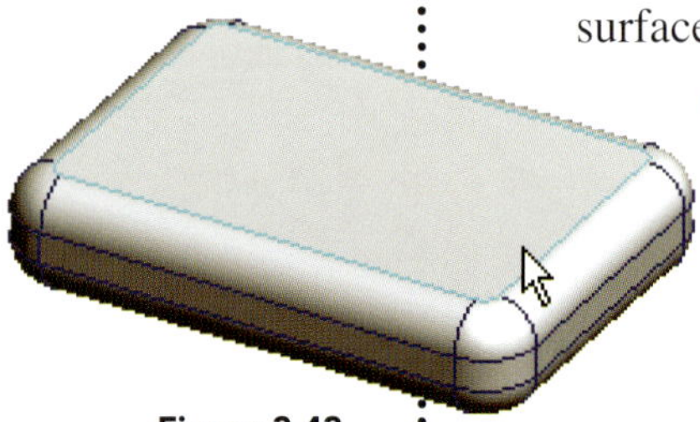

surface will pre-highlight in bright blue. When all four edges pre-highlight, click on the mouse button (Figure 3.43).

The flat surface of the pager will turn red (Figure 3.44). If it does not, click once off to the side of the pager and try again.

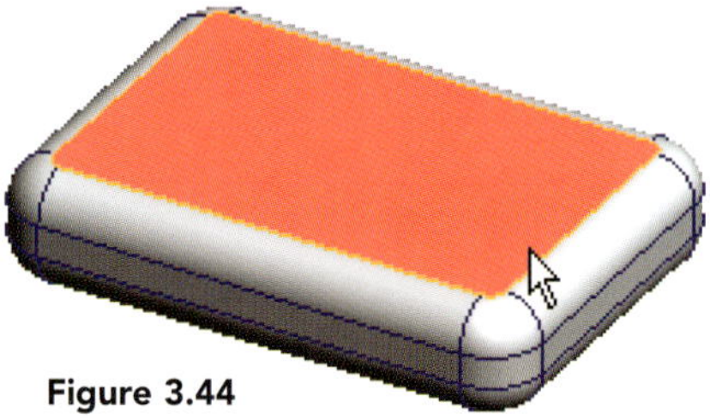

Figure 3.43

Figure 3.44

- With the top surface selected, right mouse-click. A new, floating menu appears (Figure 3.45). Select *New Sketch* and left mouse-click. Pro/DESKTOP® automatically creates both a new workplane and a new sketch when you select New Sketch, but it does this only when you have selected a face.

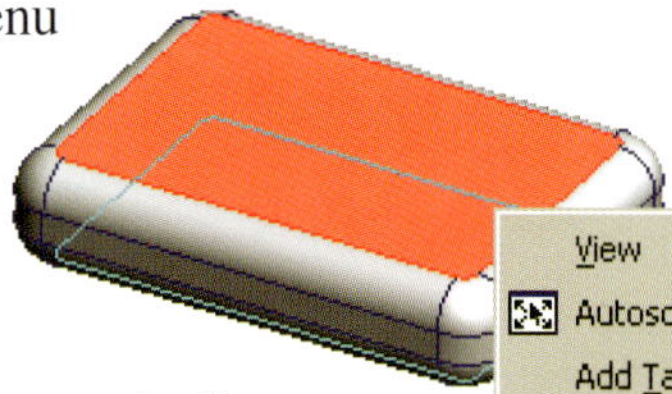

A new dialog box appears (Figure 3.46). Notice that it has given the name of the new sketch as *sketch 1*. It has also given the name of the new workplane as *workplane 1*. You will change the names of both the sketch and the

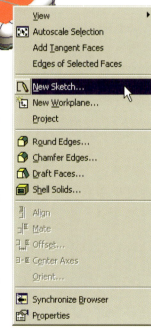

Figure 3.45

Figure 3.46

workplane so that you will be able to go back later and find a specific sketch or feature.

- Click in the *Name* box and type in *buttons*.
- Click in the *Create Workplane* box and change the name to *top* (**Figure 3.47**).
- Click on the *OK* button.

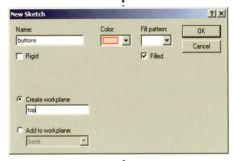

Figure 3.47

You probably do not see any new workplane or sketch. This is because you are still in the Select Faces mode. Pro/DESKTOP® only displays information appropriate to the mode you are in.

- Click on the *Select Lines* tool.

Notice that you can now see a new workplane and sketch on the top surface of the pager. The green rectangle is the workplane and the two green arrows in the center represent the sketch (**Figure 3.48**).

- Using the keyboard, type *Shift+W*. This changes the view so that you are looking directly down on the top face.

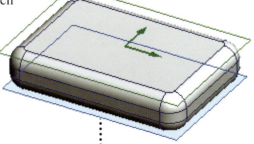

Figure 3.48

Pro/DESKTOP has quite a few keyboard shortcuts. You will use some of them on this project but a complete list appears at the end of this book.

Now you are going to draw the sketch that will create the buttons. The steps you will take to draw the sketch will ensure that the buttons are centered and have an interesting shape.

Make a construction line

- Using the *Straight Line* tool draw a vertical line from the origin point down and running off the bottom of the pager.

100 pager model

03. Modeling Challenge Using Extrude Feature

- Right mouse-click and choose **Toggle Construction** from the list to make the line a construction line (**Figure 3.49**).

- Go to the **Constraints** pull-down menu and select **Toggle Fixed** from the list. This will ensure that the construction line will not move from the center of the sketch. A small triangle on the line indicates the line is fixed and cannot move.

Did you know?

TIP: A **construction line** is a dashed line that does not affect the validity of a sketch, so it can be used to line up shapes or as a center line.

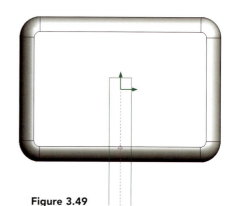

Figure 3.49

Start the button sketch

- Using the **Rectangle Drawing** tool, draw a rectangle about the size of the one in the illustration in **Figure 3.50**.

- Use the **Sketch Dimension tool** to constrain the length of the bottom line of the rectangle. To do this, click, hold and drag down on the bottom line (**Figure 3.51**).

- Click on the **Select Constraints tool** found on the Design Toolbar. Double-click on the sketch dimension. In the floating Properties box, change the **length** to **1.8**. Click **OK** to close the box.

- **Save** your work.

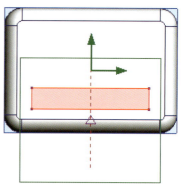

Figure 3.50

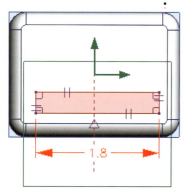

Figure 3.51

Use the **Sketch Dimension tool** to constrain the other rectangle dimension. This time you will be constraining the distance between the top and bottom line of the rectangle.

- Click and release on the top line of the rectangle to select it.
- On the bottom rectangle line click, hold and drag to the right.
- Change this dimension by using the **Select Constraints tool**.
- Double-click on the dimension. In the floating **Properties** box, change the length to *0.25*.
- Click **OK** to close the box (Figure 3.52).

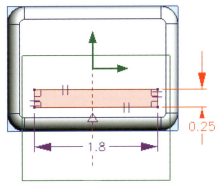

Figure 3.52

Center the sketch

You will center the rectangle on the pager using the construction line you drew earlier. You made the construction line run down the center of the pager, so we want the rectangle sketch to "straddle" the centerline. The distance from the center to either the left or right side of the rectangle is half the length of the rectangle, or equal to *1.8 divided by 2*, or *0.9*.

- Using the **Sketch Dimension tool**, click once and release on the *center construction line*.
- On the left side of the rectangle, click, hold and drag up to display the distance from the center to this edge (Figure 3.53).

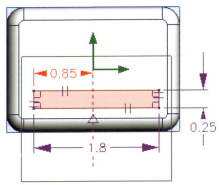

Figure 3.53

Did you know?

If you find you cannot access a part you want to work on, you may be in the wrong sketch. There are 2 ways to return to the desired sketch.

1. Double-click on any of the sketch lines in the sketch you want to make active.
2. Go to the Browser window and double-click on the pencil icon next to the name of the sketch you want to make active. An active sketch is always in **bold** type.

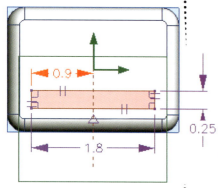

Figure 3.54

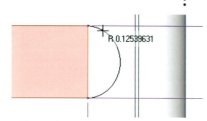

Figure 3.56

- Click on the **Select Constraints tool** found on the Design Toolbar. Double-click on the sketch dimension. In the floating Properties box, change the length to **0.9**. Click **OK** to close the box. The rectangle is now centered (**Figure 3.54**).

Round Button Ends

Next, you will round the ends of the rectangle to make the button shape a little more interesting.

- Click on the **Arc / Fillet** tool.

- Click once and release on the right side of the rectangle sketch. The line will turn red and the small box icon along side of the cursor will change (**Figure 3.55**).

Figure 3.55

- Click again on the same line but this time hold the mouse button down and drag to the right. You will see that the straight line has now become an arc. Drag the arc out until you have a nice rounded end. If you want to use the cursor "read-out" window as a guide, try to get close to a reading of **R 0.125**. (**Figure 3.56**). Release the mouse button.

- If you have trouble with the last step, **Undo** and try again.

Make sure that the arc line is not selected (not red). If it is, click on the **Select Lines tool** and click once on the screen off to the side of the pager.

- Use the keyboard shortcut **Z** to access the **Sketch Dimension tool**.

- With the cursor, click and hold on the arc and drag to the upper right. Release the mouse button (**Figure 3.57**).

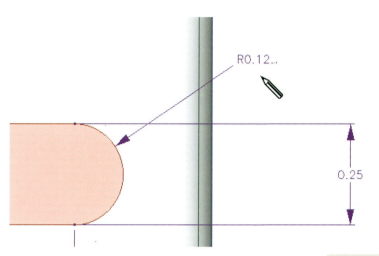

Figure 3.57

- Click on the *Select Constraints tool*. Double-click on the sketch dimension.

- Change the radius of the arc to *0.125* (Figure 3.58).

- The sketch should now look like (Figure 3.59).

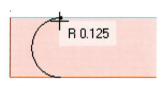

Figure 3.59

- For the arc on the left side, we will use a different method.

- With the arc or fillet tool selected, move the crosshair cursor over the lower horizontal line until it pre-highlights. Click once and release to select it. The cursor will change to a box with a part of a circle in it and the line will turn red.

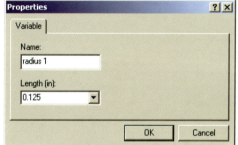

Figure 3.58

104 pager model

03. Modeling Challenge Using Extrude Feature

- Move the cursor to the top horizontal line until the line pre-highlights. A small black square appears on the pre-highlighted line. Click and drag to the left: an arc should form (**Figure 3.59**). Slide the cursor along the pre-highlighted line. Drag the left end of the top line. The cursor will read RO.125. Release the mouse button. If the arc goes the wrong way, click undo and try again. Be sure to delete the original left line of the rectangle.

If you have trouble with making the arcs, just use the Undo command and try again. Sometimes it may take several tries to get it just right.

Next, you will divide the sketch you have just made into three parts, so that you end up with three buttons.

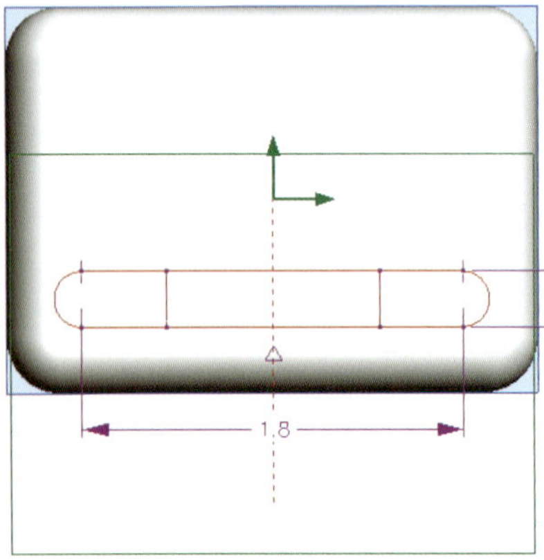

- Click on the **Straight Line tool** from the menu on the right side of the screen.
- *Draw* two vertical lines as illustrated in **Figure 3.60**. Use the shift key to keep the lines straight and make sure they snap to the top and bottom lines (a small square will appear where the two lines intersect). Try to keep the lines about the same distance from the curved ends.
- *Save* your work.

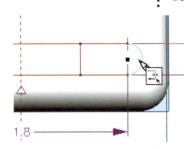

Figure 3.60

Next, you will constrain the lines so that the right and left buttons will be the same size.

- Click on the **Sketch Dimension tool** from the tool menu on the top menu.
- Move the cursor over the arc on the right side of the sketch until a black square appears in the center of the arc (**Figure 3.61**). Click once and release. You have now selected the center of the arc as one side of the constraint.

Figure 3.61

- Now click once on the vertical line closest to the arc, hold and drag up. You will get a dimension line. When you release, the distance from the center of the arc to the line will be shown, as in **Figure 3.62**.

- Change the dimension to one-half inch (0.5) by using the **Select Constraints tool** and double-clicking on the constraint. Type in *0.5* in the floating **Properties** dialog box.

- Click on the **OK** button to close the **Properties** dialog box.

- Repeat this process on the left side by constraining the distance from the center of the left arc to the other vertical line to 0.5 inches (**Figure 3.63**).

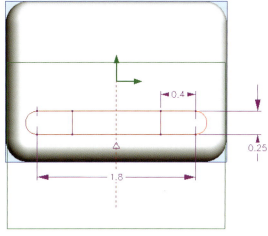

Figure 3.62

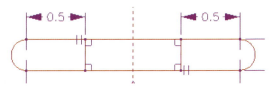

Figure 3.63

In the next section you will complete the buttons sketch by drawing two additional vertical lines and then deleting four short lines.

- Draw two more vertical lines next to the ones you have just constrained (**Figure 3.64**).

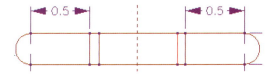

Figure 3.64

In the next steps you will constrain the distance between each line and the line next to it to *0.07-inches*.

- Click on the **Sketch Dimension tool** on the top menu.
- Click once and release on one of the vertical lines.
- On the line next to the one you just selected, click, hold and drag up.
- Change the dimension to *0.07-inches* by using the **Select Constraints tool** and double-clicking on the constraint. Type in *0.07* in the floating **Properties** dialog box.
- Click on the **OK** button to close the **Properties** dialog box (**Figure 3.65**).

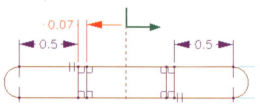

Figure 3.65

- Constrain the distance between the other two vertical lines in the same way (**Figure 3.66**).

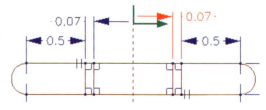

Figure 3.66

The last thing we need to do with the button sketch is to delete the short lines between the vertical lines.

- Click on the ***Delete Line Segment tool***, found in the Design Toolbar on the right side of the screen.
- Move the "scissors" cursor over the four short lines and click to delete them. The three parts of the sketch should fill and should look like Figure 3.67.

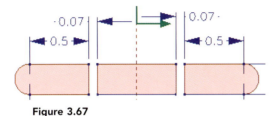

Figure 3.67

Extrude the buttons

When a feature like Extrude is applied in Pro/DESKTOP®, everything in the active sketch is extruded. If you draw two circles and apply the Extrude feature, you will get two cylinders (as long as the lines of the two circles do not touch each other). You have drawn three shapes that will extrude as three separate buttons. Now you are ready to extrude them.

- Change the view to ***Trimetric*** (***Shift +T***).
- Click on the ***Extrude Icon*** on the bottom menu.
- In the floating dialog box, click on the following options:
  ▸ *Add material*
  ▸ *Above workplane*
- In the ***Distance (in):*** window type in ***0.05*** (five one-hundredths of an inch) for the extrude distance (Figure 3.68).
- Click on the ***OK*** button to close the ***Extrude Profile*** dialog box.

Extrude Icon

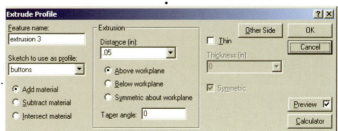

Figure 3.68

108 pager model

03. Modeling Challenge Using Extrude Feature

Your pager should now look like Figure 3.70. The buttons are still selected after closing the extrude dialog box. Click once off the model to deselect the button extrusion.

Figure 3.70

• Click on the *Save* icon.

To make the buttons more realistic, you will round the edges. Each button needs to be rounded separately. You will make a round with a 0.06-inch radius.

TIP: There are three ways to access the **Round Edges** feature: the **Feature** pull-down menu at the top of the screen; the **Round Edges** icon on the bottom menu; and right mouse-click when edges are selected.

Round Top of Buttons

• Click on the *Select Edges tool*.

• **Click on the top edges** of one of the buttons. Remember to hold down the shift key to select all the top edges of one button. There are four edges on the left button: the arc, top, bottom, and end (Figure 3.71).

Figure 3.71

• Right mouse-click. A floating menu appears (Figure 3.72).

• Move the cursor arrow down to **Round Edges** and left mouse-click.

• In the **Round Edges** dialog box, type in the radius of the round edge in the window: *0.06*

• Click on the *OK* button to close the **Round Edges** dialog box.

• Click on *Save* the icon

Figure 3.72

Your pager should now look like **Figure 3.73**.

- Use the same procedure to round the other two buttons. Remember, each button needs its own Round Edges command.

Figure 3.73

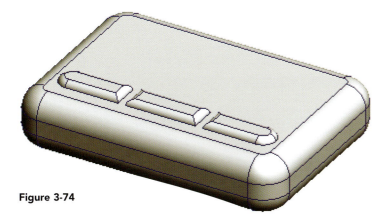

Figure 3-74

Change the Color of the Pager

It might be a bit difficult to see all the edges and surfaces of the pager, so in the next operation you will change its color.

Select Parts icon

- Click on the *Select Parts icon* from the Design Toolbar on the right side of the screen.

- Move the cursor over the pager until the edges of the pager pre-highlight in blue (**Figure 3.75**).

- Click the mouse button once and release. The pager will turn bright red, which means the whole part is selected.

Figure 3-75

110 pager model

03. Modeling Challenge Using Extrude Feature

Figure 3.76

- Right mouse-click and a floating menu will appear (**Figure 3.76**).
- Select **Set Component Color** and left mouse-click.

The **Color** floating menu will appear (**Figure 3.77**). If you set the color too dark it will be difficult to see details of the pager, so you will set the color a light blue.

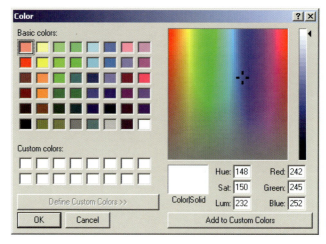

Figure 3.77

- Type in these numbers for the values of:

    Hue   **134**
    Sat   **135**
    Lum   **188**
    Red   **169**
    Green **209**
    Blue   **231**

- Click on the **OK** button to close the dialog box. Click off the sketch. The color of the pager has now been changed to a light blue (**Figure 3.78**).

Figure 3.78

Making the Screen

Most pagers have a Liquid Crystal Display (LCD) screen that allows the display of phone numbers and text messages. Your pager will have a screen above the buttons.

Earlier, you created a new workplane called *top* on the top face of the pager. This workplane was created so you would have a place to create a sketch for the buttons. You will use this same workplane but create another, *New Sketch* for the LCD screen. Because you will use the *Extrude* feature to create the LCD screen, a new sketch is required.

IMPORTANT Every new feature requires a new sketch.

On the left side of your computer screen there is a vertical, skinny window called the *Browser*. The browser is the place where Pro/DESKTOP® keeps track of workplanes, sketches, and features. The browser is very useful because it allows you to easily make changes to your design. The browser also helps you to find out important information about your design, such as, in which sketch certain lines are located. In this case, you will use the browser to help you create a new sketch.

The Browser has three parts: *Workplanes*; *Features*; and *Components*. You will be working in Workplanes.

The yellow box with the arrows represents a workplane, and the pencil represents a sketch. You will create a new sketch on the top workplane.

Create the Screen Sketch
Go to the *Browser Window*.

- First Click on the **+** next to the *top* workplane. You will see the sketch called **buttons** you created earlier (**Figure 3.79**).

Figure 3.79

- Move the cursor over the yellow workplane icon next to the *top* workplane and **Right mouse-click**. A floating dialog box will appear. Select *New Sketch* from the list. This will add a new sketch to the *top* workplane.

- Name the new sketch *screen* (**Figure 3.80**).

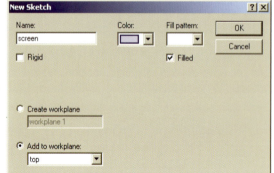

Check to make sure that the *Add to workplane* box is checked and *top* is in the window.

- Click on the *OK* button to close the dialog box.

Figure 3.80

Notice that the sketch you just created called *screen* now appears in the Browser window under the *top* workplane (**Figure 3.81**).

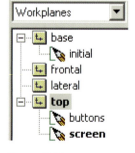

Figure 3.81

- Use the shortcut Command **Shift+W** to change the view. You will be looking directly down on the workplane and the top of the pager.

Create the Screen Profile

- Click on the **Rectangle** drawing tool.
- **Draw** a rectangle on the top face of the pager. Try to get the left and right sides about even with the outer edge of the left and right buttons (Figure 3.82). Notice that some of the constraints/dimensions for the buttons have been deleted. You may delete the constraints to remove some of the clutter from the model.

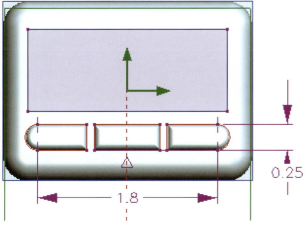

Figure 3.82

Note: The screen sketch will be drawn by "eye" and not constrained, so try to center it and make it look as close as you can to the illustration.

- Select the **Arc or Fillet Tool** from the tool menu on the right side of the screen.
- Move the cursor so that the two intersecting lines of the rectangle pre-highlight in blue, like Figure 3.83.

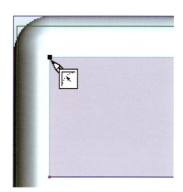

Figure 3.83

- Click and drag in toward the center of the rectangle. While still holding down the mouse button, move the cursor to one of the rectangle lines (**Figure 3.84**). Move the cursor back and forth along the line until the cursor readout reads 0.12. Release the mouse button. The radius increments are matched to the Snap to Grid scale when you move the cursor to one of the edge lines.

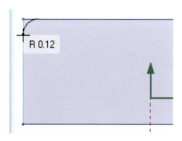

Figure 3.84

- Use the same procedure to round the other three corners of the screen sketch to the same radius. You now have a sketch that can be used to create the screen (**Figure 3.85**).

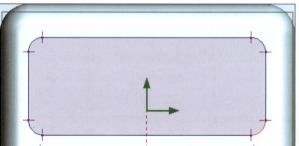

Figure 3.85

Extrude the Screen

You will use the Extrude feature to create the screen. But this time, instead of adding material you will subtract material. The screen will be slightly indented into the top of the pager.

- Click on the ***Extrude*** icon on the bottom menu. A floating dialog box will appear.

- Select: ***Subtract material***, and ***Below workplane*** and enter ***0.03*** as the distance for the extrusion.
- Click on the ***OK*** button to close the ***Extrude Profile*** dialog box.

Because you are looking directly down on the pager, it will be difficult to see the result of the last operation.

- Use the keyboard shortcut ***Shift+T*** to switch to ***Trimetric view*** (Figure 3.86).
- Click on the ***Save*** icon.

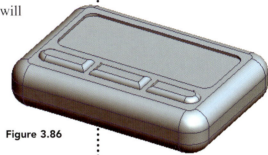

Figure 3.86

The Pro/DESKTOP® Album

The Album interface of Pro/DESKTOP will create realistic renderings of the objects you create. In this next section, you will take the pager you have created and add textures and spot color to give it a more realistic appearance.

If you have closed the pager design file, you must open it again to work in the Photo Album.

Start a New Album File

- Start in the Design Interface with the pager file open.
- Click on the lower "wheel and axle" icon in the upper left corner of the computer screen. Choose ***Photo Album*** from the sub-menu (Figure 3.87).

Figure 3.87

116 pager model

Figure 3.88

The first step is to tell the Album which image you want to work with.

Choose a File to work with
- Click on the *Image* pull-down menu at the top of the screen.
- Select *New Image* from the menu.

A floating dialog box will appear.
- Select *pager-1.de*s (Figure 3.88).
- Click on the *OK* button to close the dialog box.
- *Save* file as *pagerrender.alb*.

The pager will now appear in the Album window. Notice that the pager is in *perspective* view. A perspective view is more realistic looking to the eye than a trimetric or isometric view because distances appear shorter the farther away they appear to be from you. In other words, the back of the pager appears shorter than the front of the pager. Use the arrow keys to rotate the pager and you will see how some of the edges are angled.

Perspective would not be appropriate in the Design interface because accuracy in distance is needed, but in the Album interface, the realism of the graphic image is enhanced by the use of the perspective view.

Render the image
Notice that the *Update* button near the top center of the computer screen is green.

- Click on the *Update button*.

The Album now renders the pager image (Figure 3.89).

The first thing that you will do will be to specify the material for the pager. Then, you will change the color of the buttons.

Figure 3.89

Set a Material

- Go to the Browser window on the left side of the screen. The word *Images* appears in the box above the Browser.
- Click on the down arrow next to this box and choose *Materials* (**Figure 3.90**).
- A new Browser menu appears with a number of material choices: metal, non-metal, special, custom and default.
- Click on the + to the left of *non-metal*. You will now see a long list of materials you can apply to the pager (**Figure 3.91**).

Figure 3.90

There are two ways to set a material for an object: Set the material for the *whole object* or set the material for a *selected face*.

Set the material for the whole object

- Click on the *Select Parts* icon on the right menu.
- Move the cursor down across the pager until blue pre-highlight lines appear.
- Without moving the cursor, click once and release. The pre-highlight lines will turn orange indicating that the part is selected. When you move the cursor, the lines will turn to red (**Figure 3.92**).

Now that you have selected the object, you can apply materials.

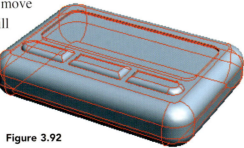

Figure 3.92

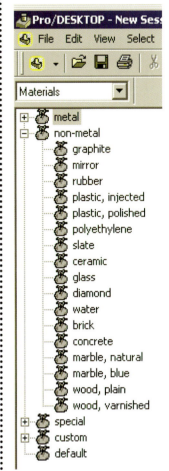

Figure 3.91

03. Modeling Challenge Using Extrude Feature

- Go to the Browser window and right mouse-click and release on *plastic, injected*.
- Select *Apply Material* from the sub-menu and left mouse-click.
- Click on the *Update button*. The pager model is rendered (Figure 3.93). Note that the color applied in the Design Interface has been lost when the model is rendered. You can re-apply a color to the injection molded plastic, or other materials, if desired.

Figure 3.93

Change Image Properties

Next, you will change the lighting on the pager. Depending on the object shape and position, some lighting options show more or less detail than others. It is a good idea to try out the alternatives when you want to present your work.

- Click on the *Image* pull-down menu and select *Image Properties* from the list. A floating dialog box will appear (Figure 3.94).
- Click on the *Studio* tab. You will see that the Lighting is set to Default.
- Click on the down arrow next to the word *Default*.
- From the lighting choices, select *Day Light* (Figure 3.95).
- Click on the *OK* button to close the dialog box.
- Click on the *Update* icon to see how the change in lighting has affected the view of the pager (Figure 3.96).

Experiment with the other lighting modes to see what happens. Don't forget to *Update*.

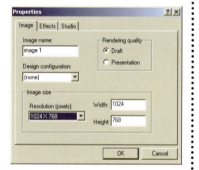

Figure 3.94

Figure 3.95

03. Modeling Challenge Using Extrude Feature

pager model   **119**

- Set the lighting back to *Day Light*.

Set the Image Background

- Click on the *Image* pull-down menu and select *Image Properties*. A floating dialog box will appear.
- Click on the *Effects* tab. You will see that both the Foreground and Background are set to *None*.

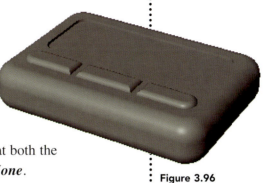

Figure 3.96

- In the *Background* box, click on the down arrow next to *None*.
- Select *Clouds* from the menu (**Figure 3.97**).
- Click on the *OK* button to close the dialog box.
- Click on the *Update* icon to see how the change in background has affected the view of the pager (**Figure 3.98**).
- Experiment with the other backgrounds to see what these effects do. Don't forget to *Update*.

Figure 3.97

Figure 3.98

03. Modeling Challenge Using Extrude Feature

Set Color of Pager

- Click on the *Select Parts* icon in the top menu.
- Select the entire pager as you did before. Move the cursor down across the pager until blue pre-highlight lines appear.
- Click once and release. While the object lines are still orange, right mouse-click. A floating menu appears (**Figure 3.99**).
- Choose *Set Material Properties* and left mouse-click. A Materials Properties dialog box appears.
- Click on *Set Color*.

A floating menu appears for the *Color Pallet*.
- Enter the following numbers to set the pager to a dark gray (**Figure 3.100**):

Figure 3.99

Hue	**160**
Sat	**0**
Lum	**120**
Red	**128**
Green	**128**
Blue	**128**

- Click on the *OK* button to close the color pallet.

Figure 3.100

- Click on the *OK* button to close the *Material Properties* dialog box.
- Click on the *Update* icon to see how the change in color has affected the pager (**Figure 3.101**). The color is only a little darker than that produced by the injection plastic material color alone.

Set Color of a Face

The screens of some pagers are a bright blue. You will set the color on the screen of your pager a similar color.

- Click on the ***Enhanced*** view icon on the right menu. In this view mode Pro/DESKTOP® will react more quickly because it does not need to render and re-render the model.

- Click on the ***Select Faces*** icon on the right menu.

- Move the cursor over the pager, just inside the screen until the bottom edge of the screen pre-highlights in blue (**Figure 3.102**).

- Click once and release. The screen will turn red to show it is selected (**Figure 3.103**). If you select the wrong surface, just click once outside the model and try again.

- Right mouse-click and release. You will get a floating menu.

- Select ***Material Properties*** and left mouse-click. Another floating menu appears.

- Click on ***Set Color***. A floating menu appears for the Color Pallet.

Figure 3.101

Figure 3.102

Figure 3.103

03. Modeling Challenge Using Extrude Feature

- Enter the following numbers:

Hue	**140**
Sat	**200**
Lum	**153**
Red	**86**
Green	**163**
Blue	**239**

- Click on the ***OK button*** to close the color pallet.
- Click on the ***OK*** button to color the ***Material Properties*** dialog box.
- Click on the ***Update*** icon to see the new screen color (**Figure 3.104**).

Figure 3.104

You have completed the first major Pro/DESKTOP® project. At this point you may see possibilities for improving on the design.

You may want to challenge yourself to see if you can come up with a more creative design.

Test Your Knowledge

Figure 3.105

Now that you have had a little experience with the Album Interface, apply what you have learned to create a realistic model of the toy block you created in Chapter 2 (**toyblock1.des** or **toyblock2.des**). **Figure 3.105** shows what a rendered block might look like.

Here are some specifications to guide your rendering:
- Make the Block look like wood.
- Make the face of the letter a solid color, using a different color for each letter.
- Make the background textured.
- Make the lighting: daylight.
- Save the file as **toyblockrender1.alb**.

Open the toy block file
- Go to the **File** pull-down menu and find the toy block file you want to use.
- The file will be open in the Design Interface.
- Leaving the file open, go to the **File** pull-down menu and choose **New**…

then choose **Photo Album** from the sub-menu.
- In the Album Interface go to the Image pull-down menu. Select **New Image** from the list. In the sub-menu select the file name you opened in the Design Interface.

How to make the block look like wood
The Album Interface allows you to both color objects and to apply graphics that simulate textures, such as wood or rubber. You can also apply bitmap images from files or from digital pictures you have taken. To apply a texture in the Album, you need to first select either the entire object, or a face of the object.

Apply a texture to the whole object
To apply the texture to the entire object use the **Select Part** tool, located on the Vertical Toolbar on the right side of the screen.
- Click on the **Select Part** tool and move the cursor over the object until lines in the object pre-highlight in blue. While the lines are pre-highlighted, click once with the mouse and release. The lines will turn orange.

- Just above the Browser Window click on the down arrow next to the word **Images**. Now select **Materials** from the list (the list only includes Images and Materials).
- Click on the plus signs (+) and you will see a list of textures in each of the categories: metal, non-metal, special and custom. Several woods appear in the non-metal and custom categories.
- Right mouse-click over **maple, wood**. A short menu appears.
- Select **Apply Material** and left mouse-click.
- To see the rendering with the material applied, click on the green **Update** button at the top of the screen.

Apply a texture to a face
- Use the **Select Faces** tool and move the cursor over the object until the lines that form the edges of that surface pre-highlight in blue.
- Click once and release.
- Go to the Browser Window and right mouse-click over the material you want to apply.
- Select **Apply Material** from the short list.
- Click on the **Update** button to view the rendering.

Note: When some materials are applied, the **Album** will not let you change the color of a face. To work around this problem, you will need to first apply a different material to the face and then change the color of the face. For example, you cannot change the color of the face of a letter on the toy block when the material of the block has been changed to wood. To overcome this problem, first select the face of a letter and apply the material plastic, injected. Now the face of the letter can be changed because the **Album** permits you to color plastic.

design link
why is 3D design software so important?

People who use 3D design software, like Pro/DESKTOP®, usually work for companies that make products or individual parts for products. In the last few years, 3D design software has made the process of designing a product much quicker. You have most likely heard the expression that "time is money" and this is very true for business. Companies that can bring a product to the marketplace more quickly save money and are more competitive.

Old ways of designing and making products required designers to make sketches and pass these sketches to people who would draw plans for how to make the product. Drafting is the development of the drawings that describe how to make the product and the drawings are called **orthographic drawings**. Although some companies still use these drawings and employ people to draw them, many businesses have changed to 3D design software that create orthographic drawings automatically from the 3D computer designs. In addition, 3D design software can export files that can be used to automatically create models or prototypes of the product. Some companies have almost eliminated paper drawings by doing all the work on the computer.

Another advantage of CAD is that several people can share the design files at the same time, and the design process becomes one of a team effort. Instead of a process where one person passes ideas and designs to the next, like links in a chain, CAD allows the design to develop more efficiently. If a person in the old "chain" asked to have a change made, the design went back "to the drawing board" and the draftsperson made the changes. Then the design worked its way back up the chain for approval. Now with CAD all the people who must approve of the design, and those who have skills and knowledge that must be considered in the design, can participate in the design process. This approach takes less time and makes for better products.

04
sketches

04. Sketches

In this chapter you will learn:

- How to create new Workplanes and Sketches
- How to use Pro/DESKTOP® drawing tools
- The characteristics of valid sketch profiles
- How to find and correct sketch problems
- To duplicate a sketch to create an X-Y matrix of copies
- To duplicate a sketch to create a number of copies around a center point
- To mirror lines around an axis
- How to use the Text Outline command

Introduction

Producing 3D objects in Pro/DESKTOP requires that you understand how to create sketches and use the drawing tools. Occasionally, sketches will be simple and contain only a straight or curved line. Most sketches, however, are more complex and require knowledge about appropriate tools and techniques. This chapter will help you to learn a number of fundamental concepts that you will use over and over again as you create more complex designs.

introduction

Chapter One provided an overview of the Pro/DESKTOP® design environment. In Chapter Two you learned how to create 3D solids with the Extrude Profile feature using only basic sketches. In this chapter you will learn more about how to use the tools and commands that create more sophisticated sketches. Sketches are the foundation of any 3D object.

Here are a few things to keep in mind as you create sketches:

- It is worthwhile to *use the Origin point* when creating sketches. In some cases this means starting a corner of a square or rectangle on the origin point. In other situations it means using the Origin point as the center of a circle or ellipse. It is difficult to provide a more specific rule-of-thumb, just try to use the Origin point as a beginning when sketching.

- *Zoom-in, zoom-out* and *change views* to get a better view of what you are trying to sketch. Those new to using CAD have a tendency to try to draw sketches with the screen view as it is. The mouse wheel (if you have one) is very handy for zooming in and out. Place the cursor over the area you want to zoom in on before you use the wheel. Otherwise, the image will move to the side as it becomes larger.

- *Get used to the keyboard shortcuts*, such as **Shift+Z** (to zoom-in), **Shift+H** (zoom-out half scale), and **Shift+W** (change view to look directly at the active workplane). These will greatly improve your ability to create what you want to draw. There are other keyboard shortcuts that may be handy. A list of these shortcuts appears in the Appendix.

- *Use the Snap to Grid* information and cursor "read-out" to estimate sizes and distances. If you have used the Origin as a starting point in your sketch, you will always know the distance a drawing tool is from the origin, so you can create sketches about the right size. This can help you create fast sketches without the need to constrain them with dimensions. Later, when you have gotten your ideas out of your head and "onto the page," you can go back and add dimensions.

- ***Save your work often!*** You only have to loose an hour's worth of work once and you realize that saving often is very timesaving. Shortly after you begin a new design, save and name the file. Then, use the keyboard shortcut ***Ctrl+S*** to re-save often.

Creating New Sketches on Existing Workplanes

Sketches are located on Workplanes. Pro/DESKTOP® begins each new Design file with three Workplanes and one sketch. In Chapter One you learned that new design files begin with the ***base***, ***frontal*** and ***lateral Workplanes***. You also learned that the base workplane always has a sketch called ***initial*** on it when you begin. Unless you create new sketches, you can only draw on the ***initial*** sketch.

New sketches can be attached to any existing Workplane. This is handy when you want the object you create to have a particular orientation. An object's orientation is the position it takes when you open the object file. For example, if you create the sketch for a clock face on the ***base workplane*** and then Extrude it, the clock will be modeled in a flat position, as if it is lying down on a table. Creating a new sketch on the frontal (or lateral) workplane for the clock face

04. Sketches

new sketches on existing workplanes   **131**

sketch will result in a clock that is oriented upright, just like a clock would appear when hung on the wall. **Figure 4.1** shows two clock faces that have been created in different orientations. This may not seem like a "big deal," but when you develop more complex products that have a number of different parts that need to be assembled, building the individual parts in their natural orientation will save you time and effort when assembling.

The best way to learn about creating workplanes and sketches is to go through the steps of creating them yourself. In this section you will create workplanes and sketches using a variety of techniques.

Exercise 4.1 Create a New Sketch on an Existing Workplane

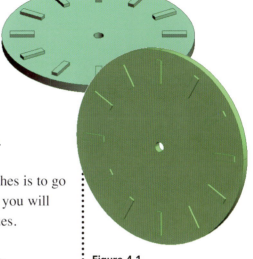

Figure 4.1

In this exercise you will create a new sketch on an existing workplane. This is a technique you will use often.

- Start a *New Design*.
- Check to see if the *Units* you are working in are *inches* (*Tools > Options > Units > inches*).
- Click on the *Select Workplanes* tool on the *Design* Toolbar. By selecting this tool, you will see the three existing Workplanes (**Figure 4.2**).

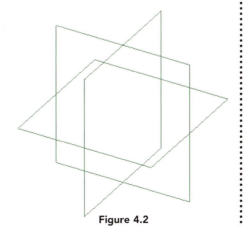

Figure 4.2

04. *Sketches*

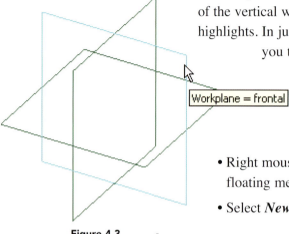

Figure 4.3

- Find the ***frontal workplane*** by moving the cursor arrow over one of the vertical workplanes (don't mouse-click yet) until it pre-highlights. In just a moment you will see a yellow box that tells you the name of the workplane (**Figure 4.3**). If it is not the frontal workplane, move the cursor until you find the frontal workplane.
- Select the ***frontal workplane*** by clicking on it once. It will turn red.
- Right mouse-click on the now selected frontal workplane. A floating menu appears (**Figure 4.4**).
- Select *New Sketch* from the menu.

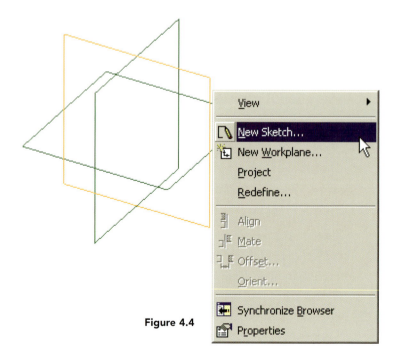

Figure 4.4

- Name the sketch *clock face* in the *New Sketch* dialog box.
- Click on the *OK* button in the dialog box to close it.
- Use the keyboard shortcut *Shift+W* to look directly at the new sketch.
- *Draw* a 6-inch diameter circle using the *Origin* point as the center.
- *Draw* another circle 0.35 inches in diameter, again using the *Origin* point as the center.
- *Extrude* the sketch one-quarter inch (0.25-inches). Your design should look like Figure 4.5.
- *Save* the file as *newsketch-1.de*s. You will use this design file in **Exercise 4.13** later in this chapter.

Figure 4.5

Any time you want a new sketch on an existing workplane you can use this technique. Remember, it is just a matter of finding and selecting the workplane using the *Select Workplane* tool; right clicking on the selected workplane; and choosing *New Sketch* from the floating menu.

Creating a New Workplane and Sketch on the Face of an Object

New workplanes and sketches can be attached to any flat face of a 3D object. This is especially handy when you want to create a sketch to make a hole or add material in some shape to a 3D form you have already created. In fact, this particular technique for creating workplanes and sketches is the one you will use most often in your design work.

04. Sketches

134 new workplane/ sketch on face of an object

You used this technique for creating a new workplane and sketch in Chapter 3 when you created the pager. Try this technique again in the following exercise.

Exercise 4.2 Create a New Workplane and New Sketch at the Same Time

When you select the flat face of a 3D object and then choose New Sketch, Pro/DESKTOP® assumes that you want to place that sketch on the face of the object, which will also require a New Workplane.

- Start a *New Design*.
- Change the *Units* you are working in to *millimeters* (*Tools > Options > Units >* change both model distances and paper distances to *millimeters*).
- On the *initial* sketch on the *base workplane*, draw a square about 80mm on a side. Use the *Rectangle* tool while holding down the *Shift* key to draw the square (Figure 4.6).

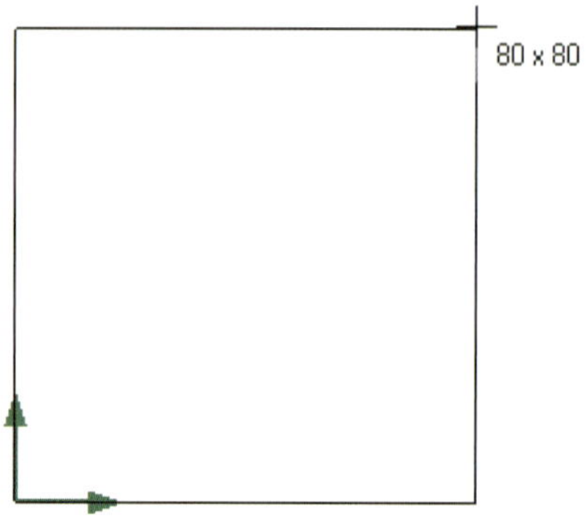

Figure 4.6

- Use the keyboard shortcut *Shift+T* to change the sketch to *Trimetric* view.
- *Extrude* the square to 80mm thick. Remember to click *OK* in the *Extrude Profile* dialog box. It often disappears and it is easy to forget this step (Figure 4.7).

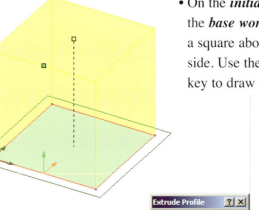

Figure 4.7

04. Sketches

new workplane/ sketch on face of an object 135

- Use the ***Select Faces*** tool to select the right face of the cube (**Figure 4.8**).

There are two places in Pro/DESKTOP® where you can find the New Sketch command. The first is in the ***Workplane*** pull-down menu. The second is a very handy shortcut. For this exercise you will use the right mouse-click shortcut.

- Right mouse-click and select ***New Sketch*** from the menu. Because you have selected a face before you chose ***New Sketch***, Pro/DESKTOP assumes you want to create a new workplane on that face and will add a ***New Sketch*** at the same time.

- Change the name of the New Sketch to ***hole***. Change the name of the New Workplane to ***side*** (**Figure 4.9**).

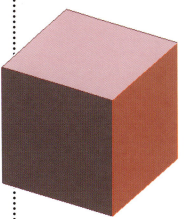

Figure 4.8

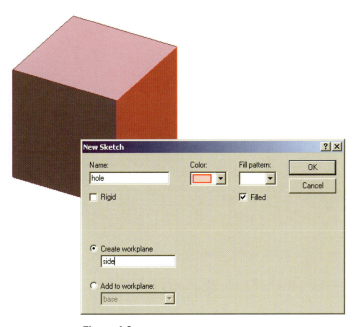

Figure 4.9

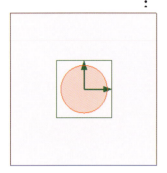

Figure 4.10

- Click **OK** to close the New Sketch dialog box.
- Use the keyboard shortcut **Shift+W** to view directly down on the new sketch.
- Use the **Circle** tool to draw a 25mm diameter circle on the side of the cube (Figure 4.10), using the origin point as its center.
- Use the keyboard shortcut **Shift+T** to change the view to **Trimetric**.
- **Extrude** the circle 40mm using the **Subtract** material, and **Below Workplane** options (Figure 4.11).

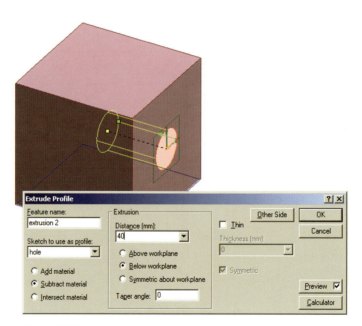

Figure 4.11

- Click **OK** to close the **Extrude Profiles** dialog box.
- Click on the **Select Faces** tool. Now you can see the hole in the

side of the cube. Use the keyboard shortcut **F10** to change to *Transparent* view so you can see that the hole goes halfway though the cube (Figure 4.12). Type **F12** to return to "normal" *Enhanced* view. If you click on the *Select Lines* tool the circle sketch becomes filled and you may not see the hole, only the circle sketch. You can turn off the sketch filled option by going to the *Lines* pull-down menu and choosing *Toggle Sketch Filled* from the list. Be sure to toggle it on again so that sketches will fill in the next exercises.

• *Save* the file as *newsketch-2.des*.

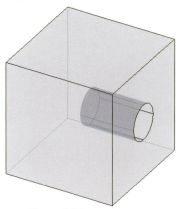

Figure 4.12

In this exercise you have created a new sketch (and a new workplane) on the face of a 3D object by using the right mouse-click short cut.

Creating Tangent Workplanes

Pro/DESKTOP® will allow you to create a new workplane that is tangent to a round surface, such as a cylinder. This may be useful when you want to put a hole through the center of a rod or pipe, such as pictured in Figure 4.13. The following exercise will show you how to do this.

Exercise 4.3 Create a New Workplane Tangent to a Cylinder

• Start a *New Design*.

• Change the *Units* you are working in to *inches* (*Tools > Options > Units >* change both model distances and paper distances to inches).

• On the *initial* sketch on the *base* workplane, draw a circle 2-inches in diameter.

Figure 4.13

04. *Sketches*

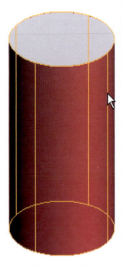

Figure 4.14

Figure 4.15

- ***Extrude*** the circle to 4-inches.
- ***Save*** the file as ***newsketch-3.des***.
- Using the ***Select Faces*** tool, select the outer surface of the cylinder (Figure 4.14).
- Right mouse-click and select ***New Workplane*** from the floating menu.
  - In the ***New Workplane*** dialog box, make sure that ***Tangent*** is selected on the left side. If you need to, drag the dialog box out of the way so you can see the cylinder you created.
    - Move the cursor to the small yellow box on the cylinder in the middle of the yellow plane that represents the new workplane. When the cursor is over this box the small box will turn blue.
    - Click and drag the box around the cylinder. As the workplane follows the box around the cylinder the cursor "read-out" gives you the angle in degrees from the original workplane location. Note that you can also change the position of the workplane by entering the ***Angle*** in the dialog box (Figure 4.15).
    - Return the workplane to its original location by typing in 0 (zero) in the ***Angle*** window in the dialog box. Also, type in ***tangent*** in the ***Name:*** window to re-name the workplane (Figure 4.16).

04. Sketches

creating tangent workplanes   139

- Click **OK** to close the Workplane dialog box.

You have created a new workplane but you will have to create a **New Sketch** on that workplane in order to draw. In certain situations, it takes two steps to create a new sketch and new workplane. This is one of those situations.

- Move the cursor to the browser window. Make sure that the word **Workplanes** appears in the small window directly above the Browser. If not, click in the small window and select **Workplanes** from the list. Note that the new workplane (named *tangent*) that you just created appears in the list of workplanes (**Figure 4.17**).

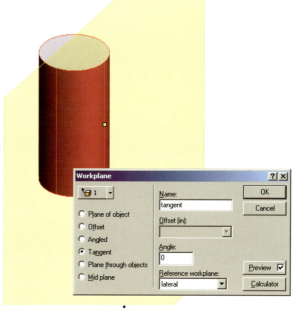

Figure 4.16

- Move the cursor over the yellow icon to the left of the word tangent in the **Browser** and right mouse-click. Choose **New Sketch** from the floating menu (**Figure 4.18**).

- Name the new sketch *hole* and click **OK** to close the **New Sketch** dialog box.

Figure 4.17

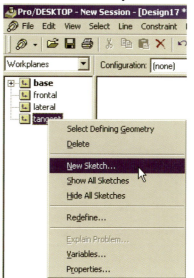

Figure 4.18

- Use the keyboard shortcut **Shift+W** to look directly down on the new sketch.

Figure 4.19

- *Draw* a small circle, about 1-inch in diameter with its center on the origin point (Figure 4.19).
- Use the *Extrude Profile* feature to make a hole halfway through the cylinder. Use the following options in the *Extrude* dialog box: *Subtract material*; *Below workplane*; Distance = 0.5-inches.
- Click *OK* to close the Extrude dialog box.
- *Save* the file.
- The cylinder should now look like the one in Figure 4.20.

Creating Offset Workplanes

Figure 4.20

Selecting the face or surface of an object works well for creating a new workplane and sketch. But sometimes, the place you want to draw does not have a flat or cylindrical face that you can select. For example, if you want to create a feature on a 3D object that has an irregular shaped side, such as the object in Figure 4.21, Pro/DESKTOP® will not be able to create a new workplane from that irregular face. However, Pro/DESKTOP can create a new workplane using an existing workplane as a reference, and that will allow you to create a new workplane almost anyplace you need one.

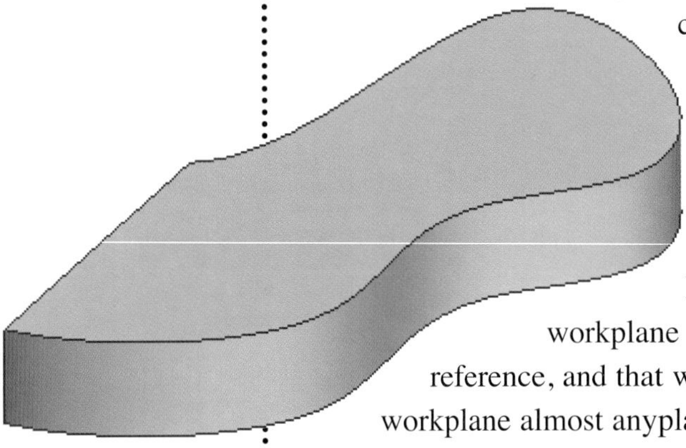

Figure 4.21

04. Sketches

creating offset workplanes 141

In **Figure 4.22** you see the 3D solid with a new, offset workplane/sketch created on the right side.

Exercise 4.4 Create A New Offset Workplane

In this exercise you will create a new workplane that is offset from an existing workplane.

- Start a *New Design*.
- Check to see if the *Units* you are working in are *inches* (*Tools > Options > Units > inches*).
- Click on the *Select Workplanes* tool on the *Design* Toolbar. You will see the three existing *Workplanes*.
- Move the cursor and pre-highlight one of the *Workplanes* and keep it pre-highlighted a moment until a small yellow box appears. The box will tell you which workplane you have pre-highlighted.
- Find the *Lateral Workplane* and select it. It will turn red (**Figure 4.23**).
- While the *lateral workplane* is selected, right mouse-click and select *New Workplane* from the floating menu.

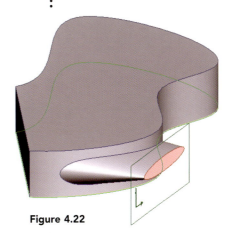

Figure 4.22

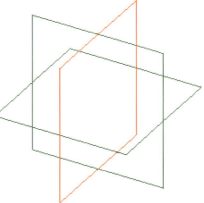

Figure 4.23

142 creating offset workplanes

- You will see a small yellow box (called the "handle") in the center of the **Lateral** workplane and a floating dialog box called **Workplane**. Notice that the **Offset** option has been chosen. Because you selected the **Lateral** workplane before you chose the command "New Workplane," the program thought that you probably wanted to create a new workplane that was offset to the one you selected (**Figure 4.24**).

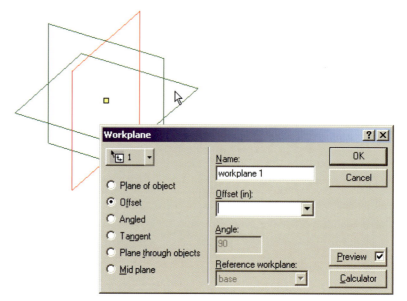

Figure 4.24

- While you can enter a value for the offset distance, Pro/DESKTOP® allows you to drag the yellow handle to visually offset the workplane. A "read-out" next to the yellow handle will indicate the distance from the new workplane to the **Lateral** workplane.

- Move the cursor over the yellow handle and it will turn green. Click and drag it to the right until the "read-out" indicates a 3-inch offset (**Figure 4.25**). Notice that the workplane is in yellow. Release the mouse button.
- Use the ***left*** and ***right arrow keys*** to rotate the view so you can see the offset of the workplane you have created.
- Move the cursor over the blue panel of the ***Workplane*** dialog box, which probably disappeared when you were dragging the handle. The dialog box will re-appear.
- Change the name of ***workplane 1*** to ***3in offset*** (**Figure 4.26**). It is a good idea to get into the habit of renaming Workplanes and sketches to names that relate to their position and their purpose. Complex designs can have dozens of Workplanes and many, many sketches.

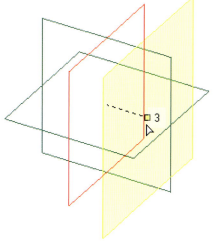

Figure 4.25

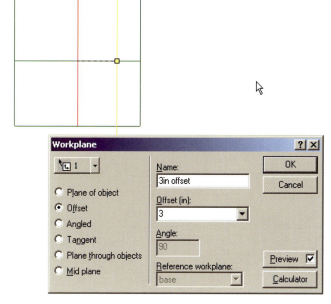

Figure 4.26

04. Sketches

- Click **OK** to close the dialog box.
- While the new offset workplane is still selected right mouse-click and choose **New Sketch** from the menu.
- Re-name the new sketch *circle*.
- Click **OK** to close the **New Sketch** dialog box.
- **Draw** a circle 2-inches in diameter in the center of the new sketch.
- Click on the **Select Lines** tool. You can now see the offset workplane and sketch.
- Go to the **Browser** window and find the new offset workplane. Click on the "+" sign to the left of it and you will see the sketch *circle* (Figure 4.27).
- **Save** the file as *offsetworkplane-1.des*

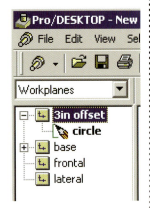

Figure 4.27

Creating Angled Workplanes

As you move to more interesting and sophisticated designs, you will notice that the products you see around you are not just cubes, cylinders and other very basic geometric shapes. Many of these products incorporate angles, as well as curves and organic forms. Figure 4.28 is a model of a skateboard truck, designed to hold wheel axles. The angled cylinder is created using an angled workplane.

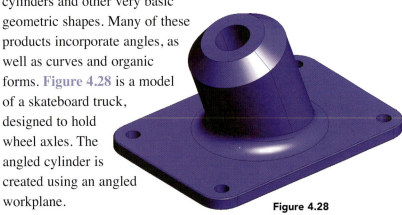

Figure 4.28

04. Sketches

creating angled workplanes   145

Exercise 4.5 Create a New Angled Workplane

In this exercise you will create a cube. Then you will create a new angled workplane and place a sketch on it. Then you will draw a sketch and extrude it.

- Start a *New Design*.
- Check to see if the *Units* you are working in are *inches* (*Tools > Options > Units >* change both *model distances* and *paper distances* to *inches*).
- On the *initial* sketch on the base workplane, draw a square about 2-inches on a side (Use the *Rectangle* tool while holding down the Shift key).
- *Extrude* the square to 2-inches. Remember to click *OK* in the *Extrude Profile* dialog box. It disappears and it is easy to forget this step (Figure 4.29).
- Use the *Select Edges* tool to select the upper left edge of the cube (Figure 4.30).

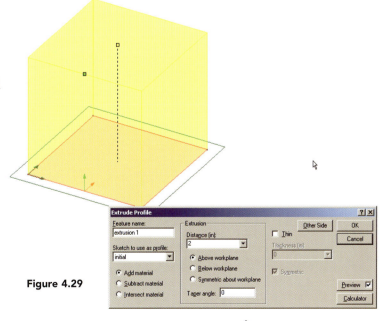

Figure 4.29

146 creating angled workplanes

Figure 4.30

- Right mouse-click and choose **New Workplane** from the menu. The Workplane dialog box appears. Notice that the **Angled** option has been chosen. Because you selected an edge before you chose the command **New Workplane**, the program thought you probably wanted to create a new workplane that was angled to the edge. Also notice that the new workplane is in yellow and there is a handle that can be dragged to change the angle.

- Instead of using the handle, enter the value **45** for the angle in the dialog box window. The workplane angle will change (Figure 4.31).

- Re-name the workplane to **45 angled workplane**.

- Click **OK** to close the Workplanes dialog box.

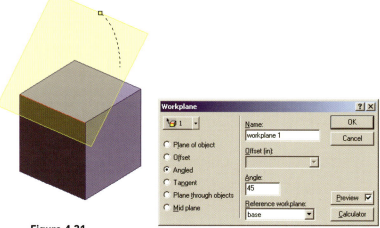

Figure 4.31

You need to create a **New Sketch** so you can draw sketch lines on the new angled workplane.

- While the new workplane is selected, right mouse-click and choose **New Sketch** from the menu. Rename the sketch to **circle**.

04. Sketches

creating angled workplanes 147

- Click **OK** to close the New Sketch dialog box.

Draw a circle on the new angled workplane.

- Use the keyboard shortcut **Shift+W** to look directly down on the new workplane.
- Use the **Circle** tool to draw a circle with the **Origin** point as the center (Figure 4.32).
- Use the keyboard shortcut **Shift+I** to change to a Isometric view.
- **Extrude** the circle through the cube. Drag the handle down through the cube (Figure 4.33).
- Move the cursor over the blue stripe to make the **Extrude Profile** dialog reappear.
- Make sure the **Add material** option is chosen.
- Click **OK** to close the Extrude Profile dialog box.
- Click on the **Select Lines** tool to de-select the object.
- **Save** the file as **angledworkplane-1.des**.

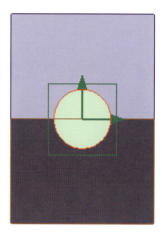

Figure 4.32

Figure 4.34 shows what the model will look like. The angled workplane allows you to create more complex solid models.
Another way to create an angled workplane is to draw a construction line on a sketch. The line can be either a regular sketch line or a construction line. Select the line with the **Select Lines** tool and use the same procedures as in the exercise above. That is, with the construction line selected, go to the

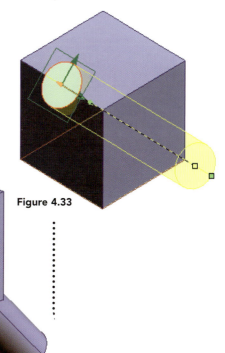

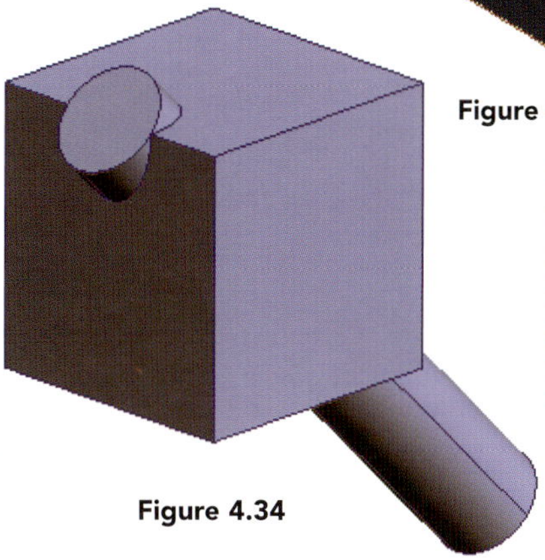

Figure 4.33

Figure 4.34

Workplanes pull-down menu and select *New Workplane*. Make sure that *Angled* is selected and enter the number of degrees for the workplane angle or drag the handle on the workplane in the Design window.

Angled Workplanes can be created from edges on solid objects or from sketch lines. You may need to experiment to find the most appropriate method for the object you want to model.

Create a New Sketch in the Browser Window

When you would like to add a sketch to a particular workplane it is very easy. Move the cursor to the *Browser* window and make sure that *Workplanes* appears in the small box above it. If not, click on the down arrow in the window and choose *Workplanes* from the list.

Find the name of the workplane you want to add a new sketch to, then move the cursor over the name of the workplane or the icon next to it, and right mouse-click. Choose *New Sketch* from the menu (Figure 4.35). Re-name the sketch and click *OK*. To confirm you have created a new sketch on the correct workplane you can click on the "+" sign to the left of the workplane icon. A list of all the sketches on that workplane appears (Figure 4.36).

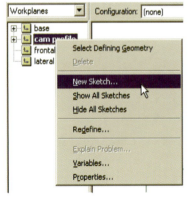

Figure 4.35

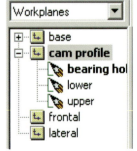

Figure 4.36

Drawing Sketch Lines

The Snap to Grid

When looking at a new sketch in a Pro/DESKTOP® design window, you will see the origin as a point where the base of the two green arrows meet. If you place a drawing tool at that point, in the top menu you will see the words **Snap to Grid** with the numbers *0,0* appearing in parenthesis underneath (Figure 4.37).

Figure 4.37

Moving the drawing tool around will give you an idea of the meaning of the two numbers. Move the tool to the right and you will see the first number increase while the second number remains zero. the first number represents the *x-axis*, or horizontal position. Move the pointer up and the second number increases while the first number remains at zero. The second number represents the *y-axis*, or vertical position. Move the pointer either to the left or down and a negative number appears for the first or second number accordingly. In fact, the design window is actually a grid. If you could see it, the grid would look something like Figure 4.38.

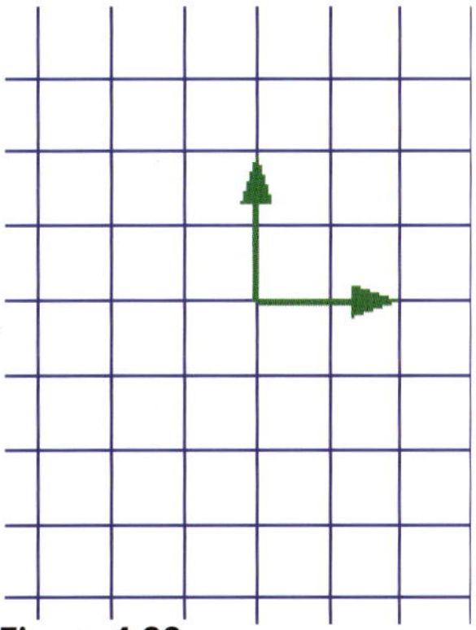

Figure 4.38

The location *0,0* would be in the center, where the horizontal zero line and the vertical zero line meet.

The location *2, -1* is shown by the center of the red circle in Figure 4.39. In other words, the location of the center of the circle is two increments of the grid in the positive direction (to the right) on the *x-axis*, and one increment in the negative direction (below the zero line) on the *y-axis*.

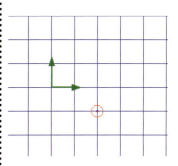

Figure 4.39

The horizontal line is usually called the *X axis*, while the vertical line is called the *Y axis*. You can see that any location on this grid can be identified with two numbers. This is the principle behind identifying a location on a map using latitude and longitude.

Changing the Snap to Grid Resolution

As you move a drawing tool around on the screen you will see the *Snap to Grid* numbers change. Often, when you start a New Sketch, the numbers change rapidly, skipping some numbers. This is especially evident when using millimeters because one millimeter is quite a small distance.

The resolution, or how small the increments are that change in the Snap to Grid, depends upon the zoom factor. If you *zoom in* the Snap to Grid numbers change in smaller increments. If you *zoom out*, the numbers change in larger increments (Figure 4.40).

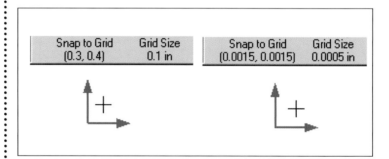

Figure 4.40

The Drawing Tools

There are six drawing tools: **Straight Line tool**, **Rectangle tool**, **Circle tool**, **Ellipse tool**, **Arch/Fillet tool**, and the **Spline tool**. Using a combination of these tools, you can draw almost any shape. Figure

4.41 shows the drawing tools (plus the **Delete Line Segment** tool) in a horizontal orientation, although you will probably see it most often located in a vertical position on the right side of the screen in the Design Toolbar.

Figure 4.41

Drawing Straight Lines

Straight lines are drawn with the **Straight line** tool. Click and hold the mouse button while you draw. Pro/DESKTOP® will tell you both the length of the line and its angle from the horizontal (Figure 4.42). Holding down the Shift key while you draw a straight line snaps it to either a vertical or horizontal line.

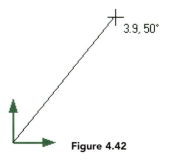

Figure 4.42

Drawing Arcs

Arcs are drawn with the **Arc or Fillet** tool. Arcs are segments of a circle so all arcs have a radius, the distance from any point on the arc to a center point. The longer the radius, the more gradual the arc; the shorter the radius, the more curved the arc.

The Arc or Fillet tool is used most often to create a round corner where two lines intersect. In Figure 4.43 you see an arc on one corner of a rectangle sketch. An arc can generally be created with lines that intersect at any angle, but the maximum radius of the arc will be affected by that angle.

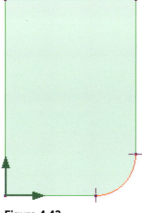

Figure 4.43

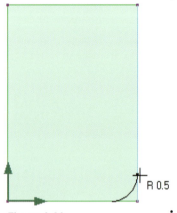

Figure 4.44

Figure 4.45

When creating an arc on two intersecting lines, begin the arc at the intersection point, *making sure that both lines pre-highlight*. When both lines pre-highlight, the cursor will change to an arc icon. Click and drag the tool inward, between the intersecting lines.

In cases where the lines intersect at 90-degrees, move the cursor to the point where the two lines intersect and pre-highlight, and move the cursor along one of the lines (instead of the space between the two intersecting lines). This will force the arc radius to change in increments of the current Snap to Grid (**Figure 4.44**). If you drag between the intersecting lines, the radius will change in a value up to 8 or 9 decimal places (**Figure 4.45**). If you find it difficult to make an arc to an exact radius with the tool, drag the cursor until the radius is close, then use the **Sketch Dimension** tool to constrain the arc to the radius you want.

Drawing Circles

The **Circle** tool is used to draw circles. Place the cursor where you want the center of the circle to be located, then click and drag until you have the diameter you want. The small numbers next to the cursor while you are dragging (cursor "read-out") indicate the diameter of the circle. The

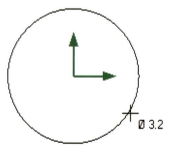

Figure 4.46

diameter symbol Ø is used to show the value is a diameter instead of a radius (**Figure 4.46**).

To create a second circle the same size as the first, make sure the existing circle is selected, then click on the Circle drawing tool, hold the Shift key and move the cursor to the center point where you want to draw the second circle, and click and drag the mouse. Holding down the Shift key with the first circle selected forces an ***Equal Radius*** constraint on the second circle. If you have a number of circles that need to be the same size this is a handy shortcut.

Drawing Ellipses

An ellipse is a shape that results when you slice a cylinder at an angle. For example, when you cut a salami with a knife on an angle the result is an ellipse. The greater the angle the longer the ellipse (Figure 4.47a and 4.47b).

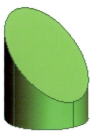

Figure 4.47a

A circle is defined as a shape made from a series of points that lie the exact same distance from one point called the center. This distance is called the radius of the circle. Mathematically, an ellipse has two "center points" called the foci (plural of focus) and is defined as a shape made from a series of points such that the sum of the distances from "centers" is the same. Because ellipses have these two "centers" they have two diameters, the major diameter and the minor diameter. The major diameter is an imaginary line drawn through the longest part of the ellipse (Figure 4.48).

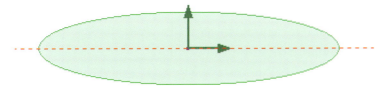

Figure 4.48

Figure 4.47b

In Pro/DESKTOP® ellipses are drawn with the ***Ellipse*** tool. You can only draw an ellipse horizontal or vertical, that is, with the major axis along the horizontal axis of the sketch or along the vertical axis of the sketch. If you need an ellipse with the major axis at some other angle than horizontal or vertical, you can do one of two things: The first method is to draw the ellipse with the major axis either vertical or horizontal and then, while the ellipse is still selected, go to the **Edit** pull-down menu and choose **Transform**. In the Transform dialog box click on the **Rotate** tab and enter a value in the **Angle** window.

The second method is to rotate the sketch axes before you draw the ellipse. Go to the **Workplane** pull-down window and choose **Transform Axes** from the list. In the Transform Axes dialog box click on the **Rotate** tab and enter a value in the Angle window. The green arrows will rotate showing that the sketch axes have changed.

Drawing Rectangles

Rectangles are four-sided figures with 90-degree angles between the sides. The **Rectangle** tool is used to draw rectangles (surprise!). While drawing a rectangle, the cursor "read-out" will show you the length and width (**Figure 4.49**).

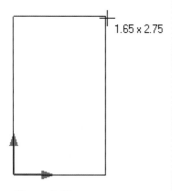

Figure 4.49

The square is a special case of rectangle, where all four lines are the same length. To draw a square with the **Rectangle** tool, hold down the Shift key while dragging the cursor. The cursor "read-out" will show you the size of the square (**Figure 4.50**).

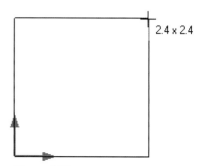

Figure 4.50

Drawing Organic Shapes

The **Spline** tool draws squiggly lines. This tool is more difficult to use than the other drawing tools because it does not create simple geometric shapes. However, Pro/DESKTOP® must store the mathematical information from all sketch lines in order to allow the program to create files that can be used to make a part, so geometric coordinates are used.

To use the Spline tool click the mouse where you want the line to start, then drag to another location where you want the line to bend. At this point, release and click the mouse button again and drag in a different direction (**Figure 4.51**). You can do this as many times as you want. Each time you release the mouse button and click again, the program stores that point, called an ***Attraction point***. If a spline line is selected with the ***Line Select*** tool, moving the cursor over the line reveals the ***Attraction Points***, which appear as small black squares on the line. You can click and drag on any of these points to modify the shape of the spline line (**Figure 4.52**).

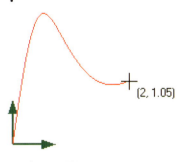

Figure 4.51

If you want to make sharp corners (angles) with the ***Spline*** drawing tool, deselect the line you are drawing by clicking once away from the line. Then move the Spline cursor back to the end of the line and click and drag. The line will continue from that intersection at the angle you drag the cursor (**Figure 4.53**). The geometric information Pro/DESKTOP keeps on spline lines is shown in **Figure 4.54**.

Figure 4.52

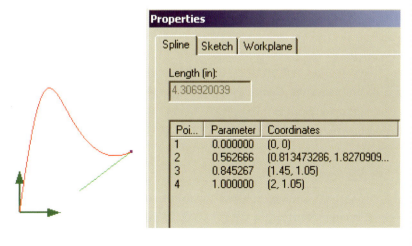

Figure 4.54

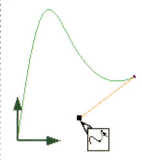

Figure 4.53

In **Exercise 4.11**, several pages ahead, you will practice using the Spline tool along with the **Mirror** command.

Creating Basic Shapes

Creating rectangles, squares, circles and ellipses are easy with the drawing tools in Pro/DESKTOP®. But you will want to create shapes that are more interesting than these. In the following section, you can try some of the more unusual shapes. When you have practiced some of these, you can try your own variations.

Exercise 4.6 Combining Geometric Shapes

Combine two simple geometric shapes to make more complex geometric shapes. Begin with a rectangle and an elipse.

- Start a *New Design* File.

- Make sure the *Units* are in *inches* (*Tools* pull-down menu > *Options* > *Units* > inches).

- Use the keyboard shortcut *Shift+W* to look directly down on the workplane and sketch.

- *Draw* a rectangle starting at the *Origin* point using the *Rectangle* tool. Make the rectangle about 2-inches by 3-inches. (Figure 4.55). The sketch will fill with a color.

Figure 4.55

- Using the *Ellipse* tool, start the ellipse on the inside of the right side of the rectangle. Make the ellipse about 4-inches in its major diameter. Notice that the fill color has disappeared. The sketch is no longer valid because you have crossed lines (Figure 4.56).

Figure 4.56

04. Sketches

drawing sketch lines   **157**

- Use the ***Delete Line Segment*** tool to clip out the four lines in the sketch that cross (Figure 4.57). The sketch will fill with a color when the last invalid line is deleted.
- Use the keyboard shortcut ***Shift+T*** to change to ***Trimetric*** view.
- ***Extrude*** the sketch to 1-inch. Be sure to close the ***Extrude Profile*** dialog box by clicking ***OK***.
- ***Save*** the file as *ellipsesquare.des*.

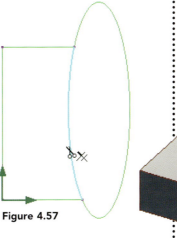

Figure 4.57

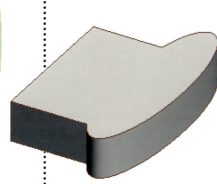

Figure 4.58

Modifying Sketch Lines

It is often necessary to change the sketch lines you have drawn. There are a few important tools that let you do this.

The Arc/Fillet Tool

The ***Arc/Fillet*** Tool can be used to create sketch lines and to modify sketch lines. The tool is located on the Design Toolbar located on the right side of the Design Window. The term ***Fillet*** is commonly used to describe a round on the corner where two lines intersect. The use of this tool was described in the previous section, although there are some interesting tricks you can do with it.

For example, if you want to create an arc to join two lines that are next to each other, use the Arc or Fillet tool and click once and release on select one line, then move the cursor to the other line and click and drag (Figure 4.59). When you release the mouse button, a neat arc joins the two lines (Figure 4.60).

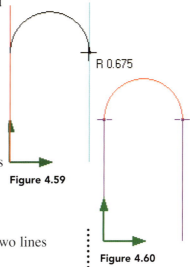

Figure 4.59

Figure 4.60

Delete Line Segment Tool

Deleting lines is done with the *Delete Line Segment* tool, found on the Design Toolbar. You can only delete lines in the active sketch, even though you can see lines in other sketches.

With the *Delete Line Segment* tool selected, move the scissors cursor over sketch lines until the line you want to delete pre-highlights in blue (Figure 4.61), then click the mouse.

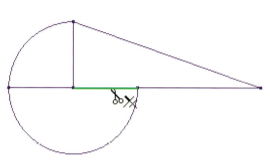

Figure 4.61

Select Lines tool

Most sketch lines can be modified with the *Select Lines* tool. The lines you want to modify must be on the active sketch.

Here are some simple ways lines can be modified:

Straight lines – Select the line, and the length of the line can be changed and the angle of the line can be changed. Select the line first by clicking and releasing, then move the cursor to one end until the cursor changes and the black square (attraction point) appears (Figure 4.62). Click and drag the line to lengthen or shorten it.

Figure 4.62

Circles – Select the line and the diameter of a circle can be changed (Figure 4.63). Note that the cursor changes to a small square with two concentric circles.

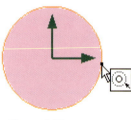

Figure 4.63

Rectangles – Select one line only and move the cursor across the selected line until you see the four arrow "cross hairs." Click and drag the line to change the rectangle in one dimension. If you want to rotate the rectangle, select one line and move the cursor to the corner at either end. Click and drag to rotate (Figure 4.64).

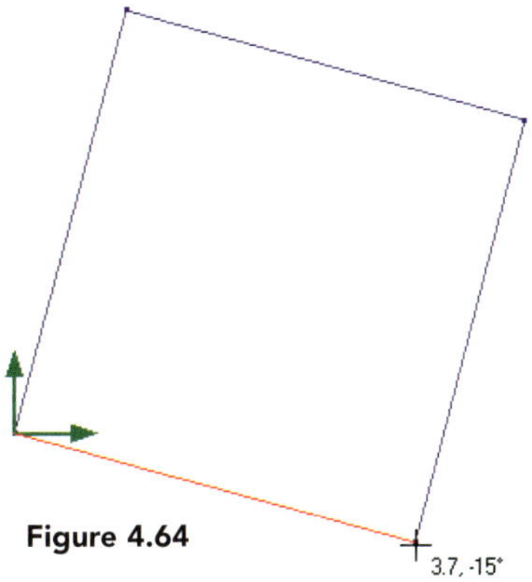

Figure 4.64

Arcs – Select the arc and the radius of the arc can be changed. Clicking on the middle of the arc changes its radius in place (Figure 4.65).

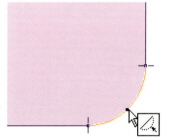

Figure 4.65

Ellipses – Select the ellipse and click and move the cursor over the line until a small black square (attraction point) appears. There are four attraction points, one on each end of the minor diameter and one at each end of the major diameter, although you can see only one at a time (Figure 4.66). Click and drag an attraction point and you can change the minor and major diameters as well as the angle of the ellipse to the origin axes.

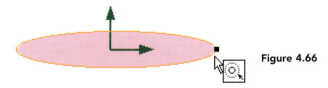

Figure 4.66

Valid Sketch Profiles

Most features are applied to closed sketch shapes, that is, lines drawn in a sketch that form a continuous outline of a shape. Any extra lines that are not necessary to form this closed shape will cause an error message when a feature is applied.

04. Sketches

160 valid sketch profiles

Figure 4.67 shows a series of five valid sketch profiles. Although some shapes are geometric and some are organic, all of these shapes have a continuous outline with no crossed lines and no extra lines anywhere on the sketch. For clarity, the sketches are shown unfilled (***Toggle Sketch Filled – off***).

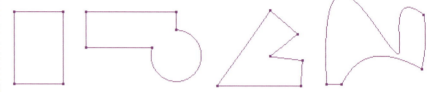

Figure 4.67

> **Did you know?**
>
> **Organic shapes** are similar to shapes you might find in nature, such as the shape of a leaf or a butterfly wing.

Notice that in each of the valid sketches each corner has a small dark red square. This square indicates that the two lines have joined correctly. If you do not see that square you will know that there is a problem where the two lines join.

One of the most common problems with sketch profiles is crossed lines. When drawing sketches using several Pro/DESKTOP® drawing tools, there is always the chance that two lines will not meet exactly, but instead one line or both will cross. Figure 4.68 shows several examples of lines that have crossed. Notice that in each case where lines cross there is no small square at the intersection. Sketch profiles that contain any of these conditions are not valid and an error message

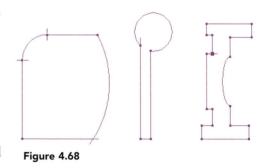

Figure 4.68

will appear when you attempt to Extrude. To correct this problem, use the **Delete Line Segment** tool to cut out the extra lines.

A second common problem with sketch profiles is lines that do not meet at all. Figure 4.69 shows two sketches. In the one on the left it is obvious that the lines in the lower part of the sketch do not meet. The sketch on the right, however, appears to be a valid sketch with all lines connected. Notice, however, that the lower left corner does not have the tiny square that appears at the other corners. Figure 4.70 is a view zoomed in on that corner. When magnified, you can see that the lines do not quite meet, making the profile open and invalid. To correct his problem, either use the **Select Lines** tool to extend the line or add a short line with the **Straight Line** tool.

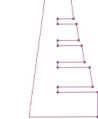

Figure 4.69

Sometimes you will need to zoom way in on a corner, or other place where lines join, to find a problem. Use the keyboard shortcut **Shift+Z** to activate the **Zoom** tool. If you are comfortable zooming in and out, and moving around the design screen, it will be much easier for you to find problems with sketches. If you have a "wheel mouse," rotating the mouse wheel will change the view to zoom in or zoom out.

Figure 4.70

Another cause of sketch problems is stray lines. These are lines that you did not intend to draw but are there because you accidentally clicked the mouse while you were moving it. This happens to everyone. If you have stray lines you must look carefully at the screen to find them and then delete them. One thing you should look for is the green workplane lines that surround a sketch. If stray lines exist outside the boundaries of your drawing, the workplane will be larger than necessary to simply contain your sketch lines. Figure 4.71 shows the green lines of the workplane boundaries around a sketch.

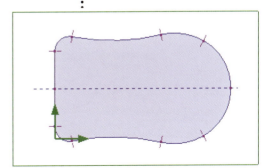

Figure 4.71

162 valid sketch profiles

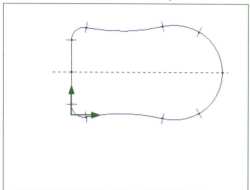

Figure 4.72

Figure 4.72 shows what the workplane boundaries might look like with a stray line.

Construction Lines

Construction lines are used primarily for layout. They appear as dashed lines in Pro/DESKTOP®. In **Figure 4.73** you will see a complex sketch that has a number of elements that have been accurately placed with the use of construction lines. The construction lines allow the designer to locate sketch elements with great accuracy, such as the center of circles, ellipses, notches, and others.

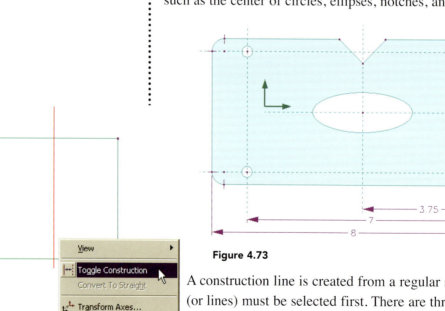

Figure 4.73

Figure 4.74

A construction line is created from a regular sketch line. The line (or lines) must be selected first. There are three ways to create construction lines: (1) use the **Line** pull-down menu and select **Toggle Construction** from the list; (2) right mouse-click and select **Toggle Construction** from the floating menu (**Figure 4.74**); (3) use the keyboard short-cut **CTRL-G**.

valid sketch profiles

"Toggle" means that the regular sketch line is changed to a construction line when the command is applied, and may be changed back to a regular line when the command is re-applied.

Exercise 4.7 Construction Lines

In this exercise you will use construction lines to help you place the sketches for holes in a plate.

- Start a *New Design* file.
- Make sure the *Units* are in *inches* (*Tools* pull-down menu > *Options* > *Units* > inches).
- Use *Shift+W* to look directly down on the initial sketch on the base workplane.
- Starting at the origin point, and using the *Rectangle* tool, *draw* a rectangle up and to the right 5-inches wide by 4-inches high (Figure 4.75).
- Using the *Arc/Fillet* tool, make a 1.5-inch arc on the upper right corner (Figure 4.76).

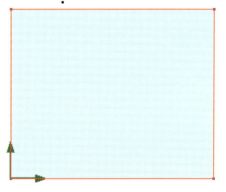

Figure 4.75

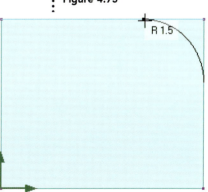

Figure 4.76

- With the *Line* tool, and starting from a point below the bottom line of the rectangle and 0.75-inches to the right of the origin point (Snap to Grid: 0.75, -0.4), draw a vertical line through the rectangle, ending above the top line (Figure 4.77). Note that the rectangle sketch has lost its filling. This is because the sketch is now not a valid sketch profile.

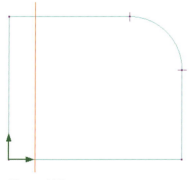

Figure 4.77

Remember that a valid sketch profile is a closed figure with no crossing or "stray" lines. You have just made a crossed line.

- While the new line you just created is still selected, right mouse-click and choose **Toggle Construction** from the floating menu list. The sketch should now be filled again because it is again a valid sketch profile.

- Repeat the process above to make another vertical construction line 0.75-inches from the right side of the rectangle (Snap to Grid: 4.25, -0.4). Your sketch should look like **Figure 4.78**.

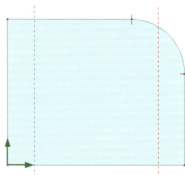

Figure 4.78

- *Draw* a horizontal line starting 0.75-inches above the origin and to the left of the left side of the rectangle (so you again cross the rectangle line) and ending the line past the right side of the rectangle. Use the **Toggle Construction** command on this line.

- Repeat the process to make another horizontal construction line 0.75-inches below the top rectangle line. Your sketch should now look like **Figure 4.79**.

- Use the **Circle** tool to make four 0.5-inch diameter circles where the construction lines cross (**Figure 4.80**).

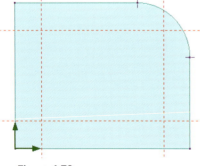

Figure 4.79

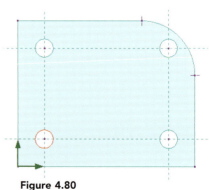

Figure 4.80

- **Extrude** the sketch to 0.5 inches.
- **Save** the file as **constructline-1.des**.

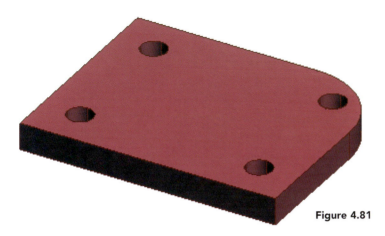

Figure 4.81

Using the construction lines allowed you to accurately locate the four holes. If you wanted to change the shape of the rectangle, you could fix the position of the construction lines (select the lines, go to the **Constraints** pull-down menu, select **Toggle** Fixed) and then make the changes. The holes would stay in the same locations.

Drawing Sketches

There is no one right way to draw a sketch. In fact, for most sketch profiles there are a number of ways that you can get to the same sketch result. When you are thoroughly familiar with the drawing tools and how to create construction lines, then the act of drawing becomes one of choice.

valid sketch profiles

04. Sketches

Let us say that you would like to create a sketch similar to the one in **Figure 4.82**, which is an isosceles trapezoid with a 4-inch top, 2-inch bottom and a height of 3-inches. You could create a 3" x 4" rectangle and then *Draw* two construction lines 1-inch from each end. Connect the top corners with the bottom of the construction lines and delete the extra lines to form the trapezoid (**Figure 4.83**).

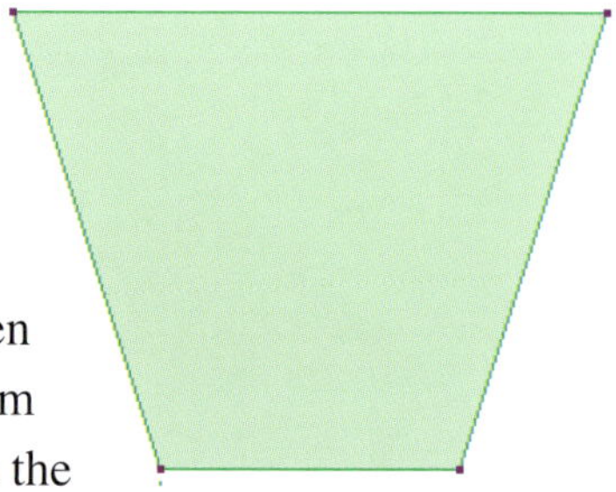

Figure 4.82

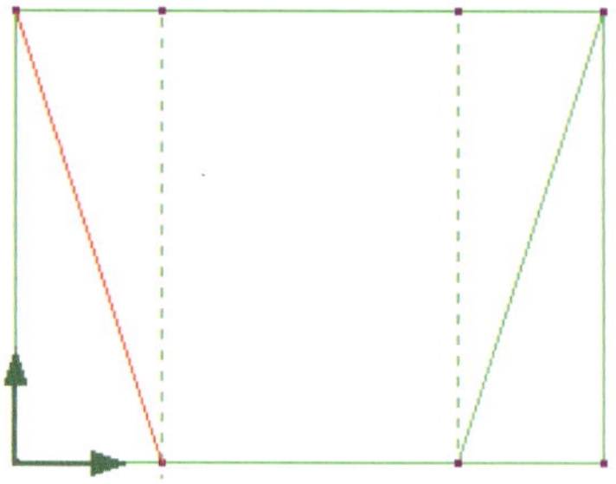

Another method you could use to create the sketch is to draw one half of the sketch and use the *Mirror* command to fill in the other half (**Figure 4.84**).

Figure 4.83

Sometimes it may take you a few tries to figure out the best way to draw what you have in mind. It is always a good idea to sketch out your plan on paper first, before you begin to draw sketches in Pro/DESKTOP®.

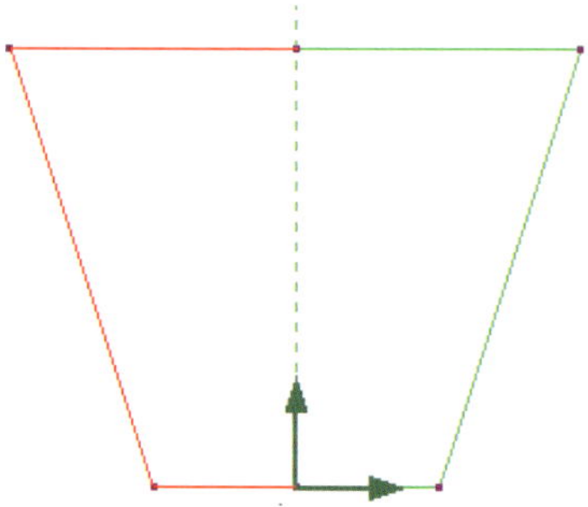

Figure 4.84

Duplicating Lines

When you would like to copy lines on a sketch, Pro/DESKTOP gives you several choices. First, you can select the lines and use the *Copy* command in the *Edit* pull-down menu (shortcut: *Ctrl+C*). The lines or sketch can then be pasted elsewhere on the sketch. Of course the *Copy* and *Paste* icons in the Standard

Toolbar can also be used to achieve the same results. If your design requires several identical copies of the lines, you may paste the lines you have copied a number of times. Often in a design, however, you must position each copy by one or more constraints. When you need to duplicate lines so that they fall in a precise location Pro/DESKTOP® provides you with other options.

Duplicate Command - Rectangular

The ***Duplicate*** command copies a sketch, or individual sketch lines, and duplicates multiple copies in either an *X-Y* grid or around a circle. Figure 4.85 shows a telephone keypad. The keys are laid out in an *X-Y* grid, with 3 keys across (*X*-Direction) and 4 keys down (*Y*-Direction) for 12 keys total. Figure 4.86 shows a clock face with 12 rectangular "bumps" spaced evenly in a circular pattern. Both of these patterns were created with the ***Duplicate*** command.

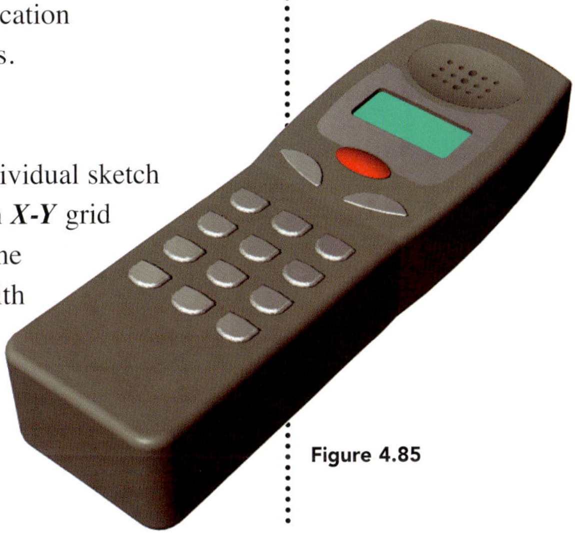

Figure 4.85

In Figure 4.87 you can see the ***Duplicate*** command dialog box used to create the telephone keypad. Note that the ***Rectangular*** option is chosen. Only one shape was drawn for the bottom left key, and the remaining shapes were produced using the ***Duplicate*** command.

Figure 4.86

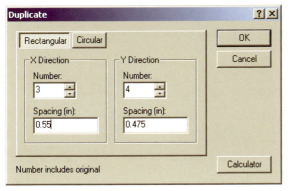

Figure 4.87

Note that number of copies of the shape in the **X**-direction (axis) and **Y**-direction (axis) were chosen and the spacing was different for the two axes.

Spacing

Spacing for the ***Duplicate*** command can seem confusing, but it is actually very logical. Figure 4.88 shows a 1" x 1" sketch shape that will be duplicated. In Figure 4.89 you can see the shape duplicated once along the **X**-Direction with a spacing of 0.5-inch. Notice that the copied shape is overlaid on the first shape. Figure 4.90 shows the copied shape duplicated in the **X**-direction with a spacing of 1.5-inches.

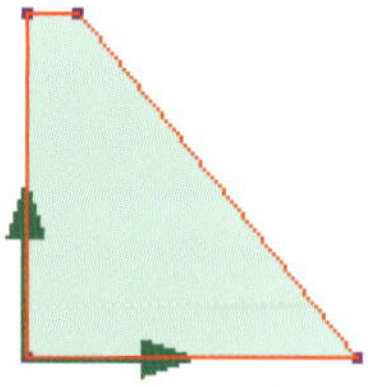

Figure 4.88

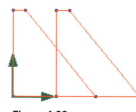

Figure 4.89

The spacing is not the distance between duplicated shapes. Instead, it is the distance that the copied shape is offset from the original shape. Figure 4.91 shows the result when the selected box is duplicated and offset by 1.5-inches, two in the **X**-Direction and two in the **Y**-Direction.

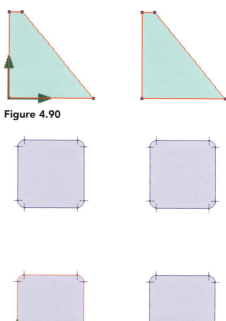

Figure 4.90

Figure 4.91

The distances entered into the *Spacing* boxes for the *X*- and *Y*-Directions will make copies to the right and above the original sketch lines. However, if you enter negative distance values, like –1 or –2.25, then the copies will appear to the left and below the original sketch lines. Depending on where you would like the duplicate lines to appear, you can enter positive or negative values for the *X*- and *Y*-Directions. In the telephone keypad example, in Figure 4.85, notice that the original sketch was located in the lower left corner of the phone, so the positive values entered duplicated the key shape above and to the right of the original.

Exercise 4.8 Duplicate Assignment One: Simple Calculator Design

For this project you will develop a simple calculator model like the one in Figure 4.92.

- Start a *New Design* file.
- Make sure the *Units* are in *inches*.
- *Draw* a rectangular sketch 2.4-inches wide by 4.2-inches long on the initial sketch on the base workplane (Figure 4.93).
- *Extrude* the sketch to 0.25-inches thick.

Figure 4.92

Figure 4.93

170 valid sketch profiles

- Select the four vertical edges with the **Select Edges** tool and apply the **Round Edges** command with a 0.125-inch radius (**Figure 4.94**).

- Select the top face of the calculator and create a new **Sketch** called **key profiles**. Call the new Workplane **top face**.

Figure 4.94

- On the new sketch key profiles **draw** a rectangle near the lower left corner. **Constrain** the rectangle to 0.4-inches wide by 0.3-inches high (**Figure 4.95**).

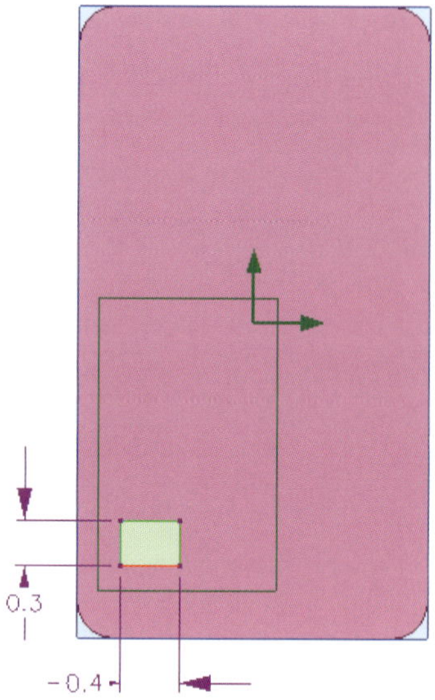

- **Constrain** the distance from the left edge of the rectangle to the left edge of the calculator to 0.225-inches (**Figure 4.96**).

Figure 4.95

- **Constrain** the distance between the bottom of the rectangle and the bottom edge of the calculator to 0.35-inches (**Figure 4.97**).

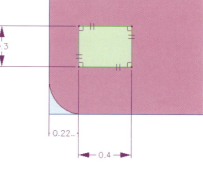

Figure 4.96

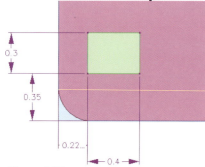

Figure 4.97

04. Sketches

valid sketch profiles   171

- Select all four lines of the *Rectangle* with the *Select Lines* tool.
- Choose the *Edit* pull-down menu and select *Duplicate*.
- In the floating dialog box enter 4 for the number in the *X-Direction* and a *Spacing* value of *0.5-inches*.
- Enter *6* for the number in the *Y-Direction* and a *Spacing* value of *0.4-inches* (Figure 4.98).
- Click on the *OK* button to close the window.
- *Extrude* the sketch to *0.04-inches* (Figure 4.99).

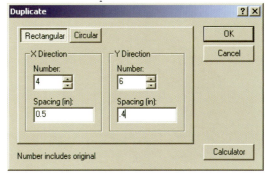

Figure 4.98

Create a window for the number display

- Create another sketch named *screen* on the top face workplane by right mouse-clicking on the *top face* workplane in the *Browser* window.
- *Draw* a rectangle so the lines on the outer edges (width) line up with the left and right edges of the keys (Figure 4.100).
- *Extrude* the sketch so you *subtract material 0.02-inches*, *below the workplane*.

Figure 4.99

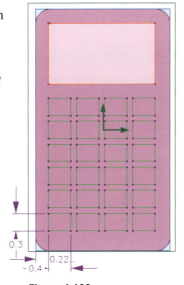

Figure 4.100

04. Sketches

- Select all the edges around the top surface and the bottom surface with the *Select Edges* tool and round them to *0.05-inch* radius (Figure 4.101).

- *Save* the file as *calculator1.des*.

The layout was planned so that the keys were centered on the calculator face.

Figure 4.101

Duplicate Command - Circular

A second choice for duplicating sketch lines is to copy them in an arc or circle. Choose the *Circular* tab near the top of the *Duplicate* dialog box (Figure 4.102) and enter the number of figures you want to end up with. Note the message near the bottom of the dialog box that states "Number includes original." For example, if you wish to

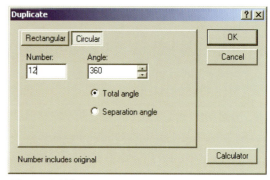

Figure 4.102

duplicate a shape to later extrude into "bumps" for a clock face entering a value of 12 includes your original shape in that number. The center of the circle around which the shapes are spaced is the sketch *Origin*. The 12 shapes are evenly spaced around the entire 360 degrees of the clock face from the *Origin* axis. The distance shapes will be from the *Origin* will depend on the location of the original sketch shape you are duplicating.

04. Sketches

valid sketch profiles 173

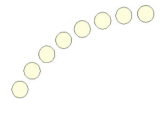

You can duplicate sketch shapes or lines a number of times in an arc. **Figure 4.103** shows eight circles duplicated in an arc of 60 degrees. The **Circular Duplicate** default is 360 degrees, so you will need to change to the number of degrees of the arc you want.

Figure 4.103

Note that you can also choose something called **Separation angle**, instead of Total angle. This option would be appropriate if you wanted to duplicate a shape a number of times with a specific angle between them. For example, in **Figure 4.104** a total of 4 sketch figures have been created with a **Separation angle** of 30 degrees. The construction line was used to accurately place the original sketch.

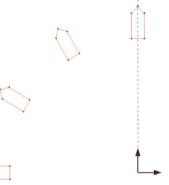

Figure 4.104

Exercise 4.9 Duplicate Assignment Two: Clock Face Project

In this exercise you will create a clock face with bumps for numbers.

- Begin a **New Design**.
- Make sure the **Units** are in **millimeters**. (**Tools** pull-down menu > *Options* > *Units* > *millimeters*)
- **Draw** a circle 170mm in diameter with the center point on the **Origin**.
- **Draw** a second circle concentric with the first, **10mm** in diameter (**Figure 4.105**). Use keyboard shortcut **Shift+T** to change the view to **Trimetric**.
- **Extrude** the circle sketch **6mm** above the workplane. This is the clock face.

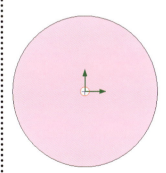

Figure 4.105

04. Sketches

- Select the top surface with the **Select Faces** tool and place a **New Sketch** there called **hour marks**.
- Use keyboard shortcut **Shift+W** to look directly at the new sketch.
- **Draw** a vertical construction line beginning at the **Origin** and ending just short of the larger circle.
- **Draw** a small circle **20mm** in diameter near the top edge of the clock face on the construction line (Figure 4.106). This will be the 12 o'clock position on the clock. You will use the **Duplicate** command to make the remaining hour marks so that they are evenly spaced around the clock face.
- With the circle selected (red) go to the **Edit** pull-down menu at the top of the screen and select **Duplicate** from the list.
- Click on the **Circular** tab in the **Duplicate** floating window.
- Enter **12** for the **Number**. Make sure the other options selected are: **Angle** is 360 degrees, and **Total angle** (Figure 4.107).
- Click **OK** to close the window.
- **Extrude** the circles **2mm** high.
- **Save** the file as **clock1.des** (Figure 4.108).

Figure 4.106

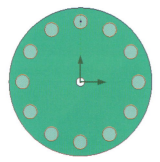

Figure 4.107

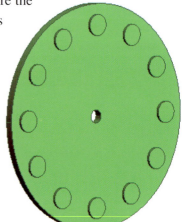

Figure 4.108

The **Duplicate** command is not a 3D feature, so it does not appear in the Browser and therefore cannot be re-defined. If you want to change sketch objects created with the ***Duplicate*** command, you will have to delete the sketch objects and apply the ***Duplicate*** command again.

Mirror Command

Sometimes it is easier to draw one-half of a complicated design and use the ***Mirror*** command to generate the other half so the figure comes out ***symmetrical***. With this command the sketch lines are not simply copied, they are also turned around. Figure 4.109 shows a

Figure 4.109

selected shape and a vertical construction line. In Figure 4.110 you see the result of the ***Mirror*** command applied to the shape using the vertical construction line as an axis.

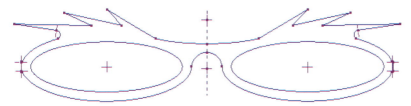

Figure 4.110

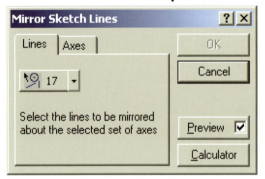

Figure 4.111

The dialog box for the *Mirror* command is shown is Figure 4.111. The box appears with the *Lines* tab selected. In this case 17 lines have been selected and will be mirrored. This is the number of lines in the sketch in Figure 4.109, above. While in this mode the *Select Lines* tool on the *Design* Toolbar menu is still active, so you can select additional lines if required.

You can use either a regular sketch line or a construction line as an axis. Construction lines appear as a dashed line. The advantage of construction lines is they are not a regular part of a sketch, so they do not cause error messages when *Extrude* and other features are applied.

Exercise 4.10 Mirror Project Assignment: Butterfly Candy Mold

In this exercise you will use the mirror command but you will also get practice using the Spline drawing tool.

Create the Mold Block

- Start a *New Design* file.
- Make sure the *Units* are in *millimeters* (*Tools pull-down menu > Options > Units*).
- Use the keyboard shortcut *Shift+W* to look down on the active workplane.
- Using the *Rectangle* drawing tool, and starting at the origin point, *draw* a rectangle *100mm* wide by *70mm* high, up and to the right (Figure 4.112).

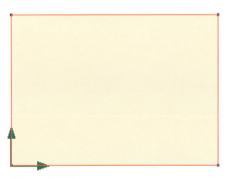

Figure 4.112

- ***Extrude*** the rectangle sketch to ***15mm***.
- ***Save*** the file as ***butterflymold.des***.
- Using the ***Select Faces*** tool, select the top surface of the block.
- Put a new sketch/workplane on the top surface of the block and name it ***mold sketch*** (Right mouse-click and choose ***New Sketch*** from the list).

Create the center axis for the Mirror command on the Mold Sketch

- Using the ***Straight Line*** tool, move the cursor along the bottom line of the rectangle and you will notice a very small black square that slides along the pre-highlighted line. As you approach the mid-point of the line a larger black square will appear and the cursor will "snap to" the line at that mid-point. ***Draw*** a vertical line from the mid-point of the bottom rectangle line, holding down the Shift key as you draw.
- While the vertical line is selected, right mouse-click and select ***Toggle Construction*** to turn the line into a construction line (**Figure 4.113**).
- While the construction line is still selected (red) go to the ***Constraints*** pull-down menu and select ***Toggle Fixed***. The line will not move or change shape.

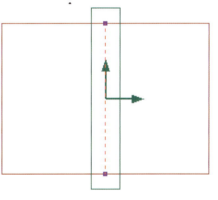

Figure 4.113

Create half of the butterfly shape with the Spline tool

- Make sure that the construction line center axis is not selected. ***Zoom*** in so the block fills the screen.
- Using the ***Spline*** tool, move the cursor over the construction line axis to ***Snap to Grid*** (0,15) (it will say ***On Line*** as you are moving the cursor on the axis line).

- **Draw** a diagonal line down and to the right to cursor readout 5, 60 (the read-out will probably have a number to several decimal places, but just try to get close) (**Figure 4.114**). Release the mouse button and click once away from the line to deselect it. If you do not deselect the line and continue drawing, the line will curve.

- Move the cursor back to the end of the diagonal line until you see the line pre-highlight and the small black square on the end. Click and drag up and to the right to cursor readout (30, 36°) (**Figure 4.115**), which means that you have a 30mm

Figure 4.114

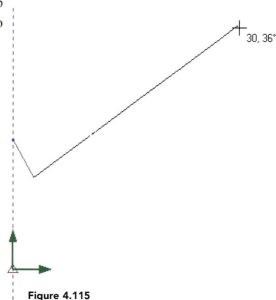

Figure 4.115

long line at an angle of 36 degrees. Release the mouse button without moving the mouse and click again, dragging down and to the left (**Figure 4.116**).

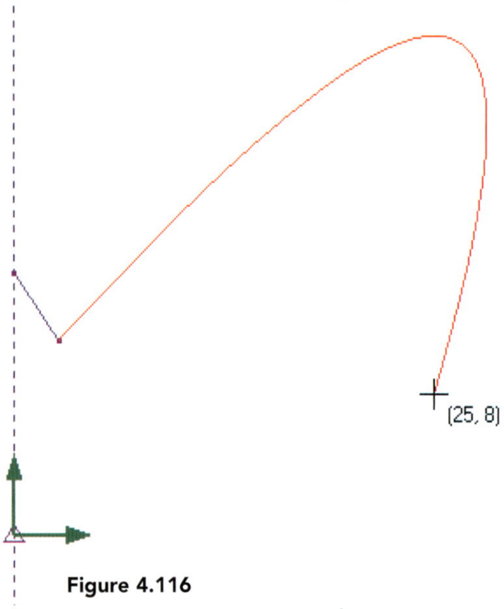

Figure 4.116

- Drag the drawing tool to cursor readout (25, 8) and release. Again, click once away from the line to deselect the line. This will make a sharp angle at this intersection.

- Move the cursor back to the end of the line until you see the attraction point (black square), click and drag down to cursor readout (8, -80°) as in **Figure 4.117**. Release the mouse button without moving the mouse, click again and drag the drawing tool to cursor readout (10, -6.5) (**Figure 4.118**).

- While the line is selected, go to the **Constraints** pull-down menu and choose **Toggle Fixed** from the list. This will prevent this line from moving.

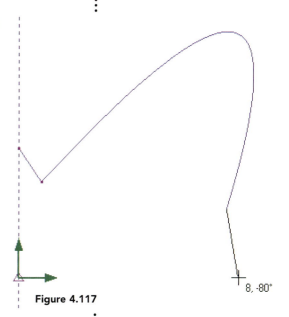

Figure 4.117

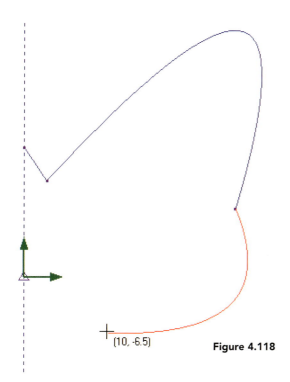

Figure 4.118

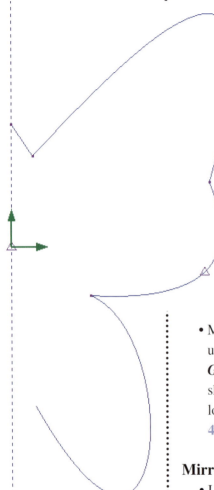

- Click once away from the line to deselect it.
- Move the cursor back to the end of the line until you see the attraction point, click and drag down and to the right to cursor readout (9, -50°). Release the mouse button without moving the mouse, click again and drag the drawing tool to cursor readout (16, -29), release the mouse button without moving the mouse and click again and drag the drawing tool to cursor readout (3, -20), release the mouse button and click once to the side to deselect the line (**Figure 4.119**).
- Move the cursor back to the end of the line until you see the attraction point, click and drag to the axis construction line.
- Move the cursor along the line until you are at location **Snap to Grid** (On Line) (0, -30). The sketch you have drawn should look reasonably close to **Figure 4.120**.

Mirror the sketch lines

- Using the **Select Line** tool, and holding down the Shift key, select all the lines you have drawn with the **Spline** tool (not the construction axis line).

Figure 4.119

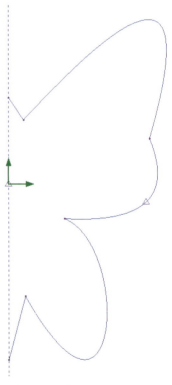

Figure 4.120

- Go to the *Line* pull-down menu and choose *Mirror* from the list. When the *Mirror Sketch Lines* dialog box appears you should see the number *5* for the number of Lines selected (*Figure 4.121*).

- Click on the *Axes* tab. Move the cursor over the construction axis line until it pre-highlights. Click on the construction line to select it. If it does not turn red, click on it once more. If the *Properties* dialog box appears, just click *OK* to close it.

- Move the cursor back over the *Mirror Sketch Lines* dialog box to make it reappear. You should see a 1 in the *Axes* tab. Click on the *OK* button to close the dialog box. Your sketch should now look like the one in *Figure 4.122*.

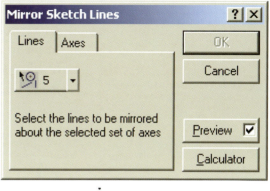

Figure 4.121

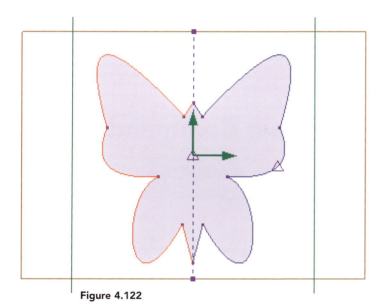

Figure 4.122

- **Extrude** the mold sketch with these options: **Subtract** material; **Below workplane**; Distance of **10mm**; and a **Taper angle** of **3** (degrees). The taper angle is useful for getting the chocolate out of the mold when it cools. Figure 4.123 shows what the butterfly mold should look like.

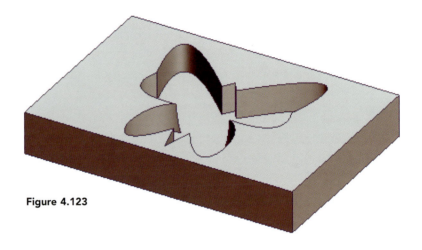

Figure 4.123

- **Save** your work.

Offset Chain Command

The **Offset Chain** command allows lines to be created parallel to original sketch lines. If the original lines are straight, the copies are parallel to the original lines. If the original lines are arcs or circles, then the copies are concentric to and proportionally larger or smaller than the original lines to keep them parallel. Figure 4.124 shows the **Offset Chain** command used to create offset lines for part of a sketch. The selected (red) lines have been created with the command. Notice that both the length of straight lines has changed and the radius of the

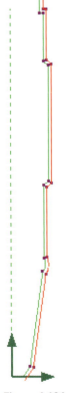

Figure 4.124

arc line has changed. But, as you can see, all new lines created are parallel to the original sketch lines.

The ***Offset Chain*** command is found in the ***Line*** pull-down menu. The dialog box for this command allows you to enter the offset distance directly and tells you how many individual line segments have been selected. It also provides you with the option to create offset lines on both sides of the lines you have selected. As with many Pro/DESKTOP® commands and features, you can use the mouse to click and drag the yellow box to create an offset if you are not concerned about exact distances at the time.

Exercise 4.11 Using the Offset Chain Command

In this exercise you will create a series of lines with the ***Straight Line*** tool and the ***Arc/Fillet*** tool. Then you will use the ***Offset Chain*** command to make parallel lines.

- Start a ***New Design*** file.
- Make sure the ***Units*** are in ***inches*** (***Tools*** pull-down menu > ***Options*** > ***Units*** > ***inches***).
- Use the keyboard shortcut ***Shift+W*** to look directly down on the initial sketch.
- With the ***Straight Line*** tool, draw a 2-inch line vertical above the origin point.
- From the top of the vertical line, draw a 2-inch horizontal line to the right.
- Beginning from the right end of the horizontal line, draw a 1-inch vertical line. Your sketch should now look like the one in **Figure 4.125**.

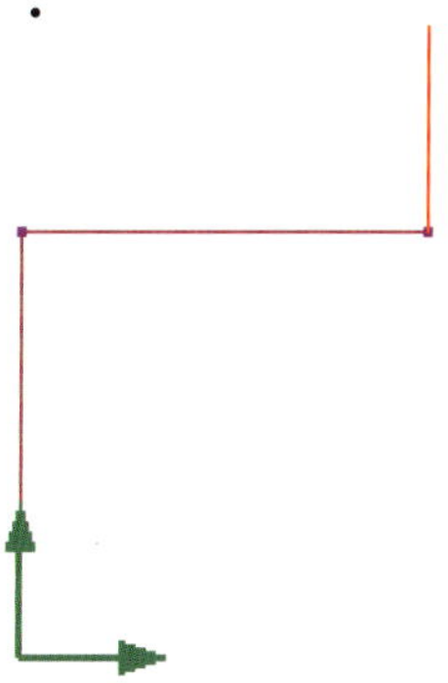

Figure 4.125

184 offset chain command

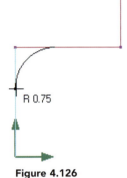

Figure 4.126

Figure 4.127

- Select the first vertical line and go to the **Constraints** pull-down menu and choose **Toggle Fixed** from the list. This will prevent the line from moving later.

- Using the **Arc/Fillet** tool, create a 0.75-inch radius arc where the first two lines meet. As you create the arc move the cursor over one of the intersecting lines. This will help you create the arc to the correct size (**Figure 4.126**).

- Using the **Arc/Fillet** tool again, create a 0.5-inch radius arc where the second and third lines meet (**Figure 4.127**).

- Holding down the **Shift** key, use the **Line Select** tool to select all the line segments you have created. There should be five line segments (three straight lines and two arcs).

- Move the cursor to the **Line** pull-down menu and select **Offset Chain** from the list.

- In the **Offset Sketch Lines** dialog box that appears, note that the number 5 appears in the small box, indicating that 5 lines are selected.

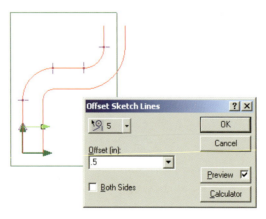

Figure 4.128

- Type in the number **0.5** in the **Offset (in):** window of the **Offset Sketch Lines** dialog box (**Figure 4.128**). Make sure there is a check mark in the **Preview** window. The new offset lines should appear.

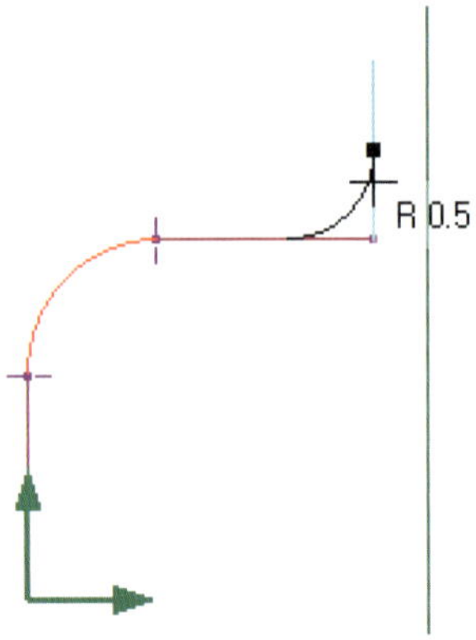

- Click **OK** in the dialog box. Your finished sketch should look like Figure 4.129.
- Save your work as *offset-1.des*

Note how the lines that were created by the **Offset Chain** command are parallel to but slightly different than the lines you created. The two arcs are different – the inside arc is smaller and the outside arc is larger – so the lines will be parallel to the lines you created.

Add Text Outline

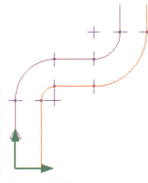

Figure 4.129

In Pro/DESKTOP® you can add text or symbols to an object, as you did in the Toy Block in **Exercise 2-2**. Almost any figure in a True Type font can be placed on a sketch and Extruded or Projected. The True Type fonts on your computer will determine what fonts you have available in Pro/DESKTOP. A wide variety of fonts and interesting dingbats can be downloaded for free on the web, so your choices are many. Figure 4.130 shows a model of a student idea for a new product that is a combination GPS and television with a company logo and text embossed on the front. The logo is a True Type font that was found on the web. The use of text outlines helps give the model a realistic appearance.

Figure 4.130

186 add text outline

04. Sketches

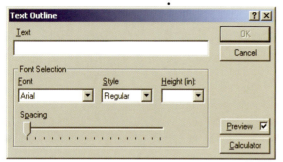

Figure 4.131

The ***Text Outline*** command is in the ***Line*** pull-down menu. When you select this command a dialog box appears (Figure 4.131) that allows you to choose a font, a style (regular, bold or italic) and a letter height. There is also a control for letter spacing.

Pro/DESKTOP® creates outlines of font letters, so the result is usually some fairly complicated shapes. On many computers these shapes will slow things down a bit, so be patient.

Exercise 4.12 Using the Add Text Outline Command

In this exercise you will create the numbers on the face of a clock.

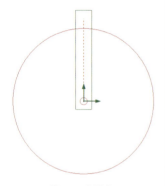

Figure 4.132

- Open the existing Pro/DESKTOP design file named ***newsketch-1.des*** that you created as one of the first exercises in this chapter.

- Select the front face of the 3D object with the ***Select Face*** tool.

- Place a ***New Sketch*** named ***spacing*** on the selected face. Name the workplane ***clockface***.

- ***Draw*** a vertical construction line from the ***Origin*** up past the edge of the 3D object (Figure 4.132).

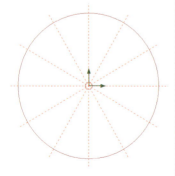

Figure 4.133

- Select the ***Duplicate*** command in the ***Edit*** pull-down menu. Click on the ***Circular*** tab and enter ***12*** for the ***Number*** and ***360*** for the ***Angle***. Click ***OK***. These construction lines will help you locate the numbers on the clock face (Figure 4.133).

- Use the ***Save As*** command to save your work as ***clocktext.des***.

- Create a ***New Sketch*** named ***numbers*** on the workplane ***clockface***.

- Go to the *Line* pull-down menu and choose *Text Outline* from the list.

- In the *Text Outline* dialog box enter the number *12* in the *Text* window, choose a font you wish to use, and in the *Height* window enter *0.75*, for three-quarters inch. You will see the number 12 in red (it is selected) somewhere on the clock face (*Figure 4.134*). You may need to change the *Height* value if the number appears too small or too large. You cannot move the number into position until you click *OK* in the dialog box to close it.

- While the number is still selected (red) move the cursor over it until you see the cross-hair arrows. If all lines are not selected the number will distort. If that happens use the *Undo* command and try again. Move the number into position at the top of the clock face (*Figure 4.135*).

- When the number 12 is in position, *Create* the rest of the hour numbers in *Text Outline*. You may notice your computer slowing down a bit. Also, you may have to click on the *Update* button (the green traffic light at the top of the screen) each time you close the *Text Outline* dialog box to avoid an error message.

- When you have created all the hour numbers on the clock face *Extrude* the sketches *0.1*-inch. Your clock face should look like *Figure 4.136*.

- *Save* your work.

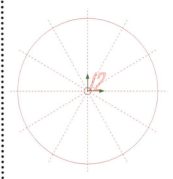

Figure 4.134

Figure 4.135

Figure 4.136

04. Sketches

Summary

In this chapter you have learned about the important role that Workplanes and sketches play in creating 3D objects. Sketches reside on Workplanes and Workplanes can be created almost any place you need them. Workplanes can be created offset from another existing workplane, at an angle to an edge of a solid, at an angle to a sketch line, or on the face of a solid. There are also other ways that Workplanes can be created.

Sketch lines are created with the six Pro/DESKTOP® drawing tools located on the Design Toolbar: Straight line tool, Circle tool, Rectangle tool, Ellipse tool, Arc or Fillet tool, and the Spline tool. Using these drawing tools almost any shape can be drawn.

When developing profiles that will be Extruded or used for other Pro/DESKTOP features, sketches must be valid. Valid sketches form a continuous outline of the shape with no stray lines or crossed lines in the sketch. Pro/DESKTOP defaults to a sketch-filled mode that shows you that a sketch is valid by filling it with color.

Pro/DESKTOP allows you to duplicate sketch lines to make sketch development easier and more accurate. Lines can be cut and pasted, duplicated in a x-y matrix or in a circular pattern around an axis. Sketch lines can also be Mirrored and Offset Chains can be created.

Text and other font symbols can be used to make raised or indented letters on solids. The Text Outline command can be used to give a design a more realistic appearance. True Type fonts are used by Pro/DESKTOP with this command.

04. Sketches

test your knowledge   189

Test Your Knowledge

Project 4.1 Model a Calculator

Locate a calculator. With a ruler, measure the calculator and make a quick drawing of it on paper. Show the overall length, width and thickness, number of keys, size of keys, spacing between keys (remember, the horizontal and vertical spacing between keys may be different) and the size of the screen. Submit this worksheet with your assignment.

design brief Develop a Pro/DESKTOP design that resembles your calculator as closely as possible. Include text outlines to place a company name with slightly raised letters on the calculator. Render it in the album with an interesting background. Save your file as **calculator2.des**.

Project 4.2 Logo Clock Face

design brief Design and develop a model of a clock face that uses numbers for the hour marks and has a company logo.

Specifications

- The clock face should be 10-inches in diameter.
- Someone standing 25-feet away should be able to read the clock face.
- A raised logo of some kind should appear on the clock face. Search the web for free specialty fonts for the logo.

test your knowledge 190

04. Sketches

Project 4.3 Model MP3 Player

Find pictures of five real MP3 players in catalogs or online. Look closely at each player to see what controls they have for song selection, stop/start, skip, volume, etc. Make a list of the controls you want to include in the model you will make with Pro/DESKTOP®. Also note the approximate size and shape of each player.

Make a short list of the things you like about each player. Make another list of the things you do not like about each player.

Sketch a new player design on paper including the location of each control. Try to make your design incorporate the things you like about the players you have seen.

design brief Develop a Pro/DESKTOP design based on your sketch. Save the file as **mp3-1.des**.

Specifications
- The player should fit in your hand.
- A small screen and controls for stop/start, skip, select, volume up/down, and back are required.
- A raised logo or company name should be placed on the front of the player.

Project 4.4 Skateboard Truck

design brief Develop a Pro/DESKTOP model of the skateboard truck pictured in Figure 4.28 earlier in this chapter. The overall dimensions of the base are 3" x 5".

Specifications
- The thickness of the base is 3/16-inches.
- The angle of the support is 22.5 degrees.
- The diameter of the support is 1.5-inches.
- You determine the other dimensions.

The elements of design (line, shape, form, space, color, texture) are organized using the Principles of Design. There are several ways to organize these principles, but we will look at only one way in this text. You may want to look into other organizing principles by searching the web.

The principles of design provide guidelines for using the elements. The principles you will use include Balance, Contrast, Repetition, Alignment and Proximity. Here is an overview of these principles:

Balance – The term used to describe the equal "weight" of design elements, such as the number and placement of windows on the front of a house on each side of an imaginary line drawn through the center of the home.

Balanced

Unbalanced

Contrast – Unlike elements create contrast, such as two different colors, sizes, shapes or text font styles.

Repetition – The repeated use of the same design element, such as a certain shape or form in a design.

Alignment – Positioning elements to line up on a horizontal or vertical line, such as the top of a camera view finder lining up with the top of the camera lens.

Camera parts aligned

Proximity – The physical distance between elements, such as a photograph near its caption.

05

project
profile
feature

194 introduction

05. Project Profile Feature

In this chapter you will learn how to:

- Create valid sketches to project
- Use the Project Profile Feature to create 3D objects
- Use the Project Profile Feature to remove material

Introduction

The Project Profile Feature is one of the most used Pro/DESKTOP® features. It allows you to make holes and create interesting shapes and forms. The holes in the aluminum motorcycle wheel in **Figure 5.1** were created with the Project Profile feature. While this feature is similar to the Extrude Profile Feature, there are important differences. To understand the differences, it will help to review the Extrude Profile feature first.

Figure 5.1

The Extrude Profile Feature uses a 2D profile sketch to create a 3D solid, or remove material from a solid. Most importantly for our purpose here, is the fact that you must specify a distance for the extrusion.

05. Project Profile Feature

introduction 195

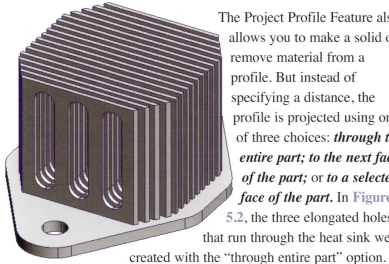

The Project Profile Feature also allows you to make a solid or remove material from a profile. But instead of specifying a distance, the profile is projected using one of three choices: ***through the entire part; to the next face of the part;*** or ***to a selected face of the part.*** In Figure 5.2, the three elongated holes that run through the heat sink were created with the "through entire part" option.

Figure 5.2

Here is one example of the appropriate use of these two features: If you need a hole that is 1-inch deep in a solid, you would use the ***Extrude Profile feature with the subtract material*** option. If you need a hole that goes all the way through the solid, you would use the ***Project Profile feature with the subtract material*** option. In Figure 5.3, the rectangular depression was created with the Extrude Profile feature. The four round holes go all the way through the part and were made with the Project Profile feature. Two sketches were used on a workplane created on the top of the block: one for the rectangle and one for the four circles.

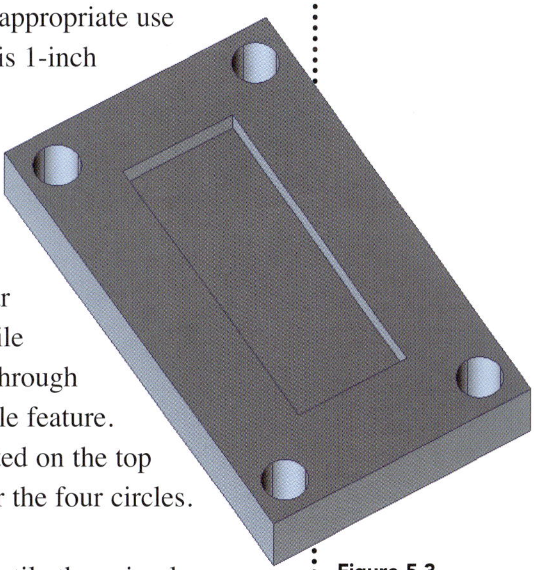

The Project Profile feature is much more versatile than simply a way to make a hole through an object. In Figure 5.4a you see a cube solid. In Figure 5.4b notice the workplane and wavy-line sketch on

Figure 5.3

05. *Project Profile Feature*

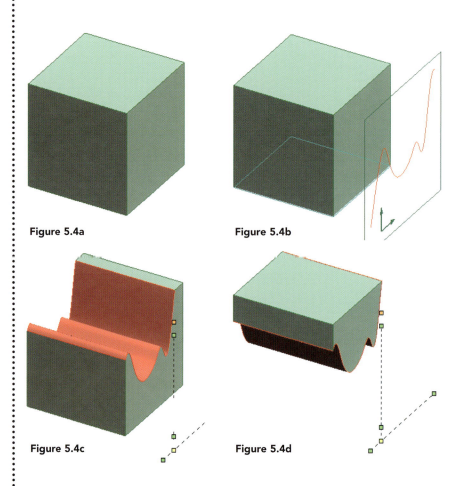

Figure 5.4a

Figure 5.4b

Figure 5.4c

Figure 5.4d

the right side of the cube. In **Figure 5.4c** the material above the wavy line has been removed with the Project Profile feature. It is also possible to remove the material below the line instead of above the line by clicking on the "Other Side" option in the Project Profile dialog box (**Figure 5.4d**).

In this chapter, the steps in the exercises will be in abbreviated form because it is assumed that you have become sufficiently familiar with the more common Pro/DESKTOP® commands and shortcuts. If you have trouble following along, you can refer to exercises in previous chapters for more detailed instruction.

Projecting a Profile Between Objects

The Project Profile feature can also be used to Add material, similar to the Extrude Profile feature. For example, imagine you would like to design a set of fitness weights, like barbells. Barbells are often cast from metal as a one-piece part. The majority of the weight lies on the two ends, and a handle connects them. In Figure 5.5, the handle between the two weights was projected from one weight to another. The model is in Transparent mode and the handle is selected.

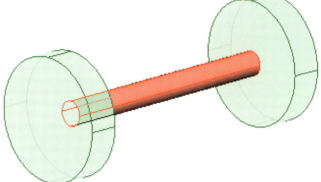

Figure 5.5

Sketches

Sketches for the Project Profile feature are in many ways similar to those you would use for the Extrude Profile feature. But the kind of sketch required depends on what you want to do with the sketch. A line – straight, curved, or wavy – can be used to subtract material from a solid object above the line or below the line, as described in the Introduction above, but it cannot be used to add material. A closed shape can be used to subtract material from a solid, but to add material the sketch must intersect the solid completely and not miss the solid by even a little bit.

Figure 5.6

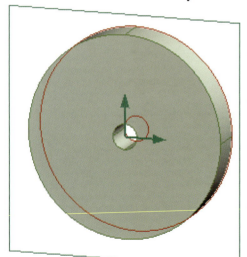

Figure 5.7

05. Project Profile Feature

Exercise 5.1 Cart Wheel

In this exercise you will use the Project Profile feature in the way it is used most often: to create holes and to remove material all the way through a part. You will first create a wheel with the Extrude Profile feature and then use the Project Profile feature to make it light weight and give it some detail.

- Start a *New Design*.
- Use *inches* for the Units.
- Create a *New Sketch* named *wheel profile* on the *frontal workplane*.
- *Save* the file as *wheel-1.des*.
- Change the view with *Shift+W*.
- Using the *Circle tool*, draw an 8-inch diameter circle on the active sketch.
- *Draw* a second circle, *1-inch in diameter*, concentric with the first circle.
- *Extrude* this sketch to *1.5 inches*. The solid should now look like Figure 5.6.
- Create a *New Sketch* on the front face of the wheel (Figure 5.7). Name the sketch *indent*.
- *Draw* a 6-inch diameter circle concentric with the wheel sketch.
- *Extrude*, subtracting material, *0.85-inches* to create a depression in the wheel (Figure 5.8).

Figure 5.8

- **Round** the inside edge of the wheel depression *0.375-inch radius* (Figure 5.9).
- **Round** the outside edges of the wheel depression *0.25-inch* (Figure 5.10).
- Select the face of the wheel at the bottom of the depression you just created (Figure 5.11).
- Create a **New Sketch** (and workplane) named **hole details** on this face.
- **Draw** a vertical **Construction line** from the Origin point to the edge of the wheel.
- **Draw** a *0.7 diameter circle* on the construction line *2.2-inches* above the Origin (Figure 5.12).
- Use the **Duplicate** command (**Edit > Duplicate > Circular**) to make 12 circles around the center axis of the wheel (Figure 5.13).

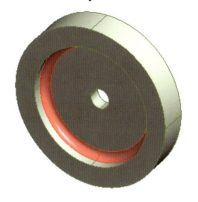

Figure 5.9

Figure 5.10

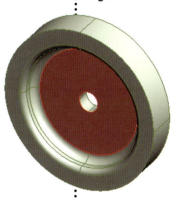

Figure 5.11

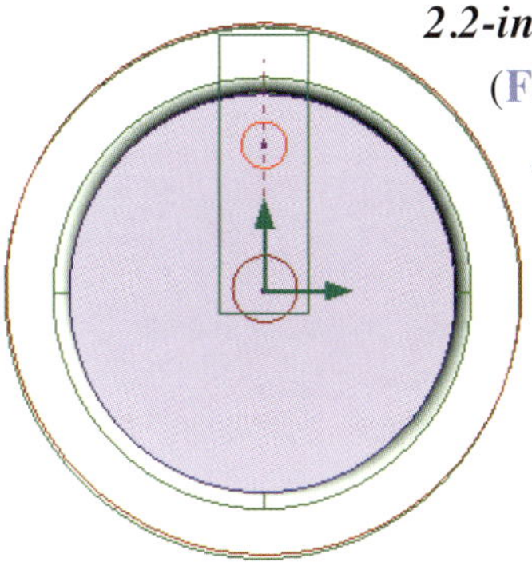

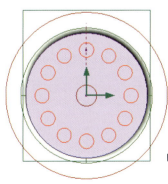

Figure 5.12

Figure 5.13

05. Project Profile Feature

- Use the ***Project Profile*** feature to subtract material from the circle sketches (**Figure 5.14**).
  - ***Round*** the front edges of the holes to a radius of 0.1-inch (**Figure 5.15**).
  - ***Save*** your work.

Figure 5.14

Exercise 5.2

In this exercise you will create a wheel similar to the one in exercise 5.1, but you will work in millimeters and develop a more interesting hole pattern.

Figure 5.15

- Start a ***New Design***.
- Use ***millimeters*** for the Units.
- Create a ***New Sketch*** named ***wheel profile*** on the ***frontal workplane***.
- ***Save*** the file as ***wheel-2.des***.
- Using the ***Circle tool***, draw a 200mm diameter circle on the active sketch.
- ***Draw*** a second circle, 20mm in diameter, concentric with the first circle.
- ***Extrude*** this sketch to 50mm. The solid should now look like **Figure 5.16**.
- ***Round*** the outside edges of the wheel with a 5mm radius (**Figure 5.17**).
- Create a ***New Sketch*** named ***recess1*** on the face of the wheel.

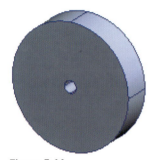

Figure 5.16

Figure 5.17

- **Draw** a 160mm diameter circle concentric with the wheel (**Figure 5.18**).
- **Extrude**, subtracting material, 10mm to create a depression in the wheel.
- Turn the wheel around and place a **New Sketch** on the other side named **recess2**.
- **Draw** a 160mm diameter circle on this side of the wheel.
- **Extrude**, subtracting material, 10mm to create a depression in the wheel.
- Select the face of the wheel at the bottom of the depression you just created and place a **New Sketch** named **hole details**.
- **Draw** a vertical **Construction line** from the Origin point to the edge of the wheel.
- **Draw** a 140mm circle (**Figure 5.19**).
- **Draw** a second circle 40mm in diameter (**Figure 5.20**).
- From the Origin point, **draw** a straight line up and to the right past the outside edge of the wheel at a 70-degree angle (**Figure 5.21**).

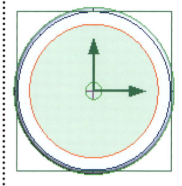

Figure 5.18

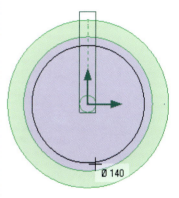

Figure 5.19

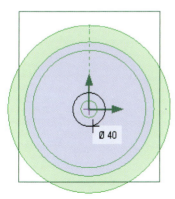

Figure 5.20

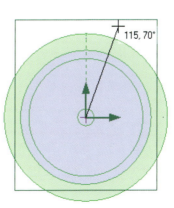

Figure 5.21

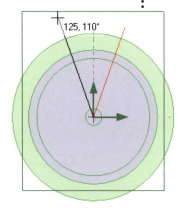

Figure 5.22

- ***Draw*** a second angled line up and to the left at a 110-degree angle (**Figure 5.22**).

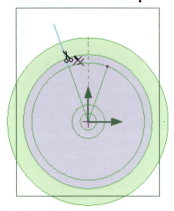

Figure 5.23

- ***Delete*** the extra line segment of both angle lines (**Figure 5.23**).

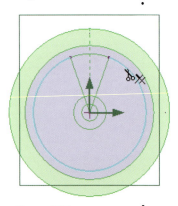

Figure 5.24

- ***Delete*** the part of the 140mm circle that falls outside the two angled lines (**Figure 5.24**).

- **Delete** the part of the 40mm circle that falls outside the two angled lines (**Figure 5.25**).

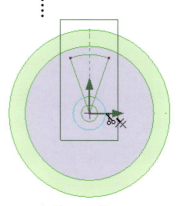

Figure 5.25

- **Delete** the bottom of both angled lines, from the Origin to the arc of the 40mm circle (**Figure 5.26**).

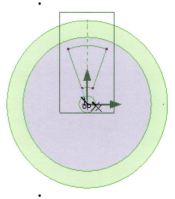

Figure 5.26

- The sketch should now look like the selected lines in **Figure 5.27**.

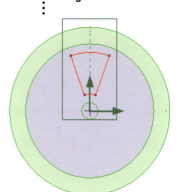

Figure 5.27

05. Project Profile Feature

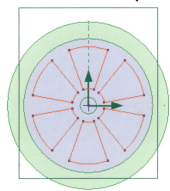

Figure 5.28

- Use the **Duplicate** command (click on **Circular** tab) to create 6 sketches around the Origin axis (Figure 5.28). Remember, the sketch lines you want to duplicate must be selected.
  - **Project Profile**, subtracting material below workplane to make the wheel detail holes (Figure 5.29).
  - **Save** your work.

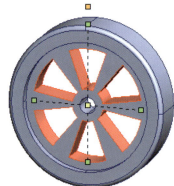

Figure 5.29

Pro/DESKTOP® allows you to use the Project Profile feature to contour solids and make shapes that are otherwise difficult to produce. In the next exercise you will use only lines, instead of closed sketches, to remove material.

Exercise 5.3 Nerdy Sunglasses

In this project you will create a wrap-around style sunglasses frame like the ones in Figure 5.30. You will use the **Mirror** command, the **Extrude Profile** feature and the **Project Profile** feature. Instead of using a closed profile shape, you will draw a curved line for the sketch that the Project Profile Feature will use to remove material from the solid.

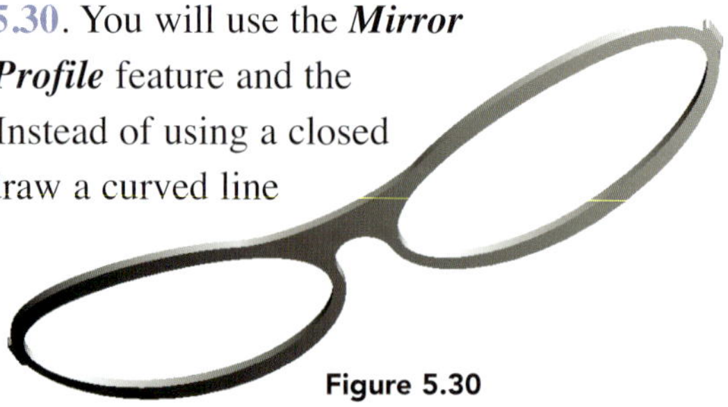

Figure 5.30

- Start a *New Design*.
- Use *millimeters* for the Units.
- Create a *New Sketch* named *frame lens profile* on the *lateral* workplane.
- Change the view with *Shift+W*.
- *Save* the file as *sunglasses.des*.

Create one-half of the frame lens profile – It is easier to make something symmetrical if you draw one side and use the *Mirror* command to make the other side. In the following steps you will draw the right side of the sunglasses frame.

Create the Center Axis Line

- *Zoom in* to *Grid Size 1mm* so that the origin point is on the left side of the Design Window. Use the mouse wheel or *Shift+Z* keyboard command to zoom.
- Draw a 40mm *Construction line* through the origin point, beginning 20mm below the origin point (Figure 5.31). This line will be the axis for the Mirror command you will use later.
- Fix the construction line with *Toggle Fixed*.

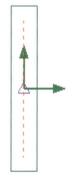

Figure 5.31

Sketch for the right side of the sunglasses

- Using the *Ellipse tool* move the cursor "cross-hairs" to the right of the Origin to location (*35,0*) and make the ellipse 56x24 (mm), as indicated on the cursor "read-out" (Figure 5.32).
- *Fix* the ellipse with *Toggle Fixed* command (*Line* pull-down menu).

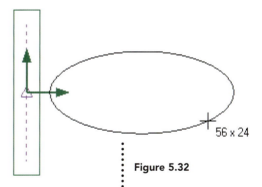

Figure 5.32

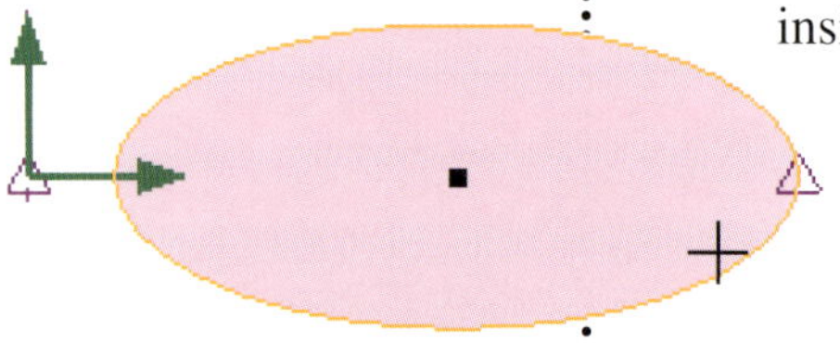

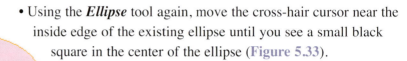

Figure 5.33

- Using the ***Ellipse*** tool again, move the cross-hair cursor near the inside edge of the existing ellipse until you see a small black square in the center of the ellipse (**Figure 5.33**).

- Then, click and hold and drag the cursor until you get an ellipse 60 x 30mm. You now have two concentric ellipses and the sketch should fill between them (**Figure 5.34**).

- Using the ***Circle tool***, begin at the origin point and draw a circle **10mm in diameter** (**Figure 5.35**).

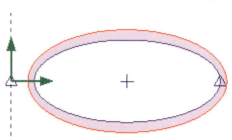

Figure 5.34

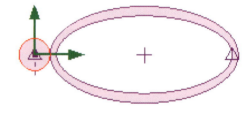

Figure 5.35

- With both the circle and the outer ellipse selected, go to the ***Constraints*** pull-down menu and choose ***Tangent*** from the list (**Figure 5.36**). This will ensure that the circle will touch the ellipse without overlapping. The small line crossing where the two ellipses meet indicates that there is a tangent constraint at that point.

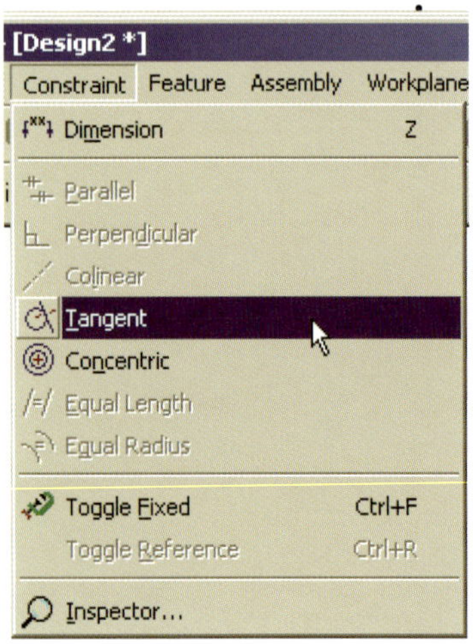

Figure 5.36

- **Delete** the segment of the circle beneath where the circle touches the ellipse. Also **delete** the half circle to the left of the axis line (**Figure 5.37**). The arc that is left will form the lower part of the sunglasses frame that fits over the nose.

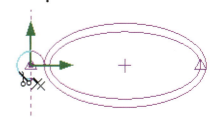

Figure 5.37

- To complete the upper part of the sunglasses frame, use the **Ellipse tool** to draw an ellipse starting at the Snap to Grid location (0,14). Drag the ellipse drawing cursor until the cursor "read-out" is (38,7), as shown in **Figure 5.38**.

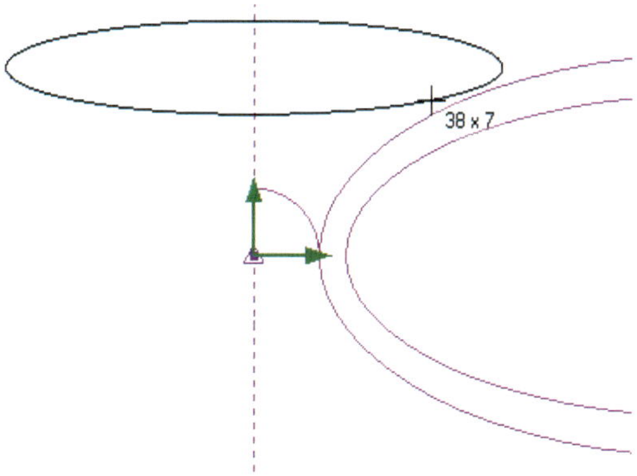

Figure 5.38

- Select both the new ellipse you have just drawn in the previous step and the outer ellipse of the sunglasses frame (they should both be red).

- Go to the **Constraints** pull-down menu and choose **Tangent** from the list. The small tangent indicator line appears across the intersection of the two ellipses (**Figure 5.39**).

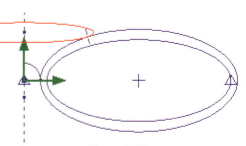

Figure 5.39

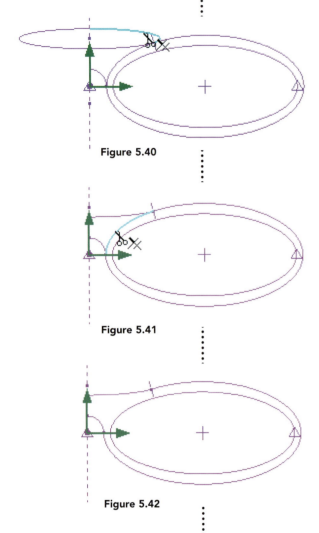

Figure 5.40

Figure 5.41

Figure 5.42

- **Delete** the upper-right segment of the ellipse (Figure 5.40) and the half ellipse to the left of the axis line. The arc that is left will form the upper part of the sunglasses frame that fits over the nose.

- **Delete** the short arc (line) segment between the tangent you created with the ellipse and the tangent you created with the circle earlier (Figure 5.41). The sketch should now look like that in Figure 5.42.

- **Zoom in** on the right side of the sunglasses frame.

- Starting at the Snap to Grid position (64,3) **draw a rectangle 1.4 x 5mm**. Use the cursor "readout" to get the rectangle dimension (Figure 5.43). If you have trouble getting the right numbers, try zooming in a bit more.

- **Delete** the extra lines so the sunglasses frame has a bump out of the right side (Figure 5.44).

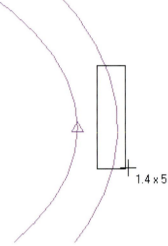

Figure 5.43

- With the *Arc or Fillet tool*, round the two sharp corners of the rectangle bump (Figure 5.45). Make the radius as close to 0.05mm as you can, or you can use the *Sketch Dimension tool* to constrain it to exactly 0.05mm radius. You will need to zoom way in to do this.

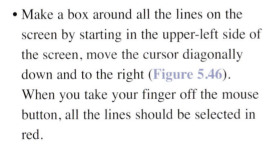

Figure 5.44

Mirror the Sunglasses Sketch

It is easier to select all the lines in the sketch and then de-select the axis then it is to try to select all the sketch lines we want to mirror individually. So this is what you will do.

- Choose the *Select Lines tool* on the Design Toolbar on the right side of the screen.

- Make a box around all the lines on the screen by starting in the upper-left side of the screen, move the cursor diagonally down and to the right (Figure 5.46). When you take your finger off the mouse button, all the lines should be selected in red.

- To de-select the axis line, hold down on the *Shift* key and move the cursor over the axis line until you see "cross hairs" and click. All the lines of the sketch, except the axis line, should still be selected. If they are not, click off to the side of the sketch and try the procedure again.

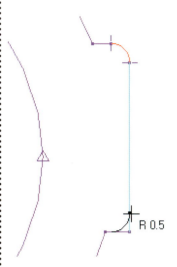

Figure 5.45

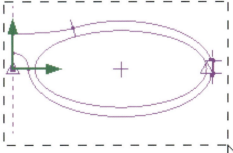

Figure 5.46

05. Project Profile Feature

- Go to the *Line* pull-down menu and select *Mirror* from the list. The *Mirror* dialog box appears and should indicate that there are 10 lines selected (Figure 5.47).

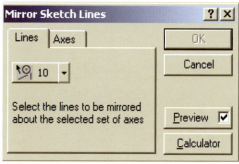

Figure 5.47

- Click on the *Axes* tab in the dialog box and then use the cursor to select the axis construction line you created in the sketch. You should see the 10 lines of the sunglasses sketch mirror on the left side of the axis and begin to look like sunglasses (Figure 5.48).

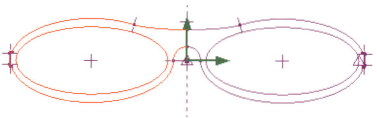

Figure 5.48

Extrude the Sunglasses Profile
- Change the view with *Shift+T*.
- *Extrude* the profile sketch to *20mm* (above the workplane and add material). The solid should look like Figure 5.49.

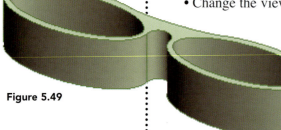

Figure 5.49

05. Project Profile Feature

- Create a *New Sketch* named *upper profile* on *frontal* workplane. You may need to zoom out to see all the workplanes (*Shift+H*) (Figure 5.50).

Create a profile to remove material

- Change the view with *Shift+W*.

- Using the *Straight Line tool*, start to the left of the solid at the (*–70,0*) Snap to Grid position and draw to the right to the (*70,0*) position (a 140mm long line as shown in Figure 5.51).

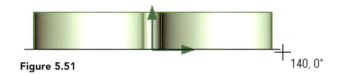

Figure 5.51

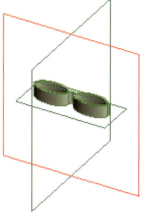

Figure 5.50

- Using the *Arc or Fillet tool* select the line and drag it up until you get an arc radius of about *150mm* (Figure 5.52). If you have difficulty dragging a radius, click off to the side to deselect the line, select it again with the *Arc or Fillet* tool, and grab it on either side of the center of the line. Sometimes you will not be able to drag an arc from the center of a line.

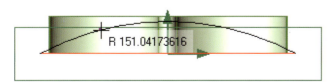

Figure 5.52

Remove material above the arc with the Project Profile Feature

- Use the **Project Profile** feature to remove material from the solid. Use the options **Subtract material**, **Symmetrical about workplane** (the workplane is running through the middle of the solid), and **Thru entire part**. Also, notice that the orange arrow at the center of the arc is pointing down. That will subtract material below the line, but we want to subtract material above the line. Click on the **Other Side** button and you will see the arrow change to point up (**Figure 5.53**).

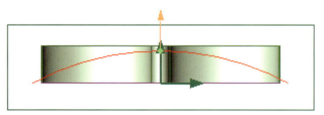

Figure 5.53

- Click **OK** or use the keyboard Return key to close the dialog box.
- The solid now has a rounded shape on the top (**Figure 5.54**).

Figure 5.54

- Create a **New Sketch** named **lower profile** on the **frontal workplane**.
- Change the view with **Shift+W**.
- Select the upper arc line with the **Select Lines** tool.
- Go to the **Line** pull-down menu and choose **Offset Chain**.

- Enter a value of 3.5mm in the *Offset Sketch Lines* dialog box (**Figure 5.55**).

Remove material below the arc with the Project Profile Feature

- Use the *Project Profile* feature to remove material from the solid. Use the options *Subtract material, Symmetrical about workplane* (the workplane is running through the middle of the solid), and *Thru entire part*. Notice that the orange arrow at the center of the arc is pointing down. That is the correct way to remove material below the arc, so do not change it this time (**Figure 5.56**).

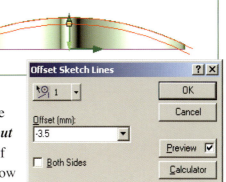

Figure 5.55

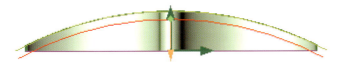

Figure 5.56

- Click *OK* or use the keyboard Return key to close the dialog box.
- Now the frame looks like sunglasses (**Figure 5.57**).

Figure 5.57

The sunglasses frame assignment is a good example of the power of the Project Profile Feature. With this feature, you can now create all kinds of interesting forms on 3D solids.

Exercise 5.4 Extension Activity
Sunglasses Earpieces
- Round the edges of the sunglass frame.
- Design simple, straight earpieces for the sunglasses. Figure out a way to attach the ear pieces to the frame.
- Design more elaborate right and left earpieces.

Summary

The Project Profile feature can be used to both subtract and add material to a design. The chief difference between this feature and the Extrude Profile feature is that fact that a distance measurement is not used with the Project Profile feature. Instead, the profile is projected to a selected surface, to the next surface, or all the way through the model.

Material can be subtracted using both closed, valid sketches and single lines. To add material with the Project Profile feature a valid sketch is necessary or the Thin Option must be used.

Test Your Knowledge

Project 5.1 Model a Shoe

design brief Using the Extrude and Project Profile features, design and model a sandal. Base your design on an existing sandal design, such as Teva™ or other popular brand.

Specifications

- Identify a standard shoe size and model to that size.
- Take measurements from an actual sandal if possible.
- Try and replicate surface and sole contours and details as closely as possible.
- Render finished model in the Album using rubber material as sole.
- Do not model fabric straps.

Project 5.2 Egg Slicer

design brief Model the egg slicer base pictured in **Figure 5.58**.

Specifications

- The egg slicer is injection molded, except for the cutting wires and their metal frame. There is a pronounced "draft" to the plastic base that would make it easy to get it out of the mold after injection. The base is shelled to a wall thickness of 0.1-inches.
- The overall dimensions of the base are 4.5" x 3.25" and 0.45" thick, although the base angles down to about 0.25" at the outside.
- The bump in the middle for the egg is about 0.75" high and 2.5" square, although all the sides are just a bit curved.
- The recess for the egg is curved and the slits for the wire cutter go all the way through the bump, except for a solid piece that runs the width of the recess to hold the material between the slits in place.
- The slits for the cutting wires are 0.07-inches wide. There are 10 cutting wires.

Figure 5.58 Egg slicer base

06

revolve profile feature

06. Revolve Profile Feature

In this chapter you will learn how to:

- Create valid sketches to revolve a profile
- Create an axis line for the revolve
- Use the Thin option in a revolve
- Add and subtract material in a revolve
- Use the Intersect Material option in a revolve

Introduction

The Revolve Profile Feature allows you to create solids or remove material from a solid by revolving a profile around an axis. A donut-like solid can be constructed by revolving a circle around an axis. In **Figure 6.1** you can see the circle profile and the axis. The profile was revolved around 270-degrees, three-quarters of the way around a full circle.

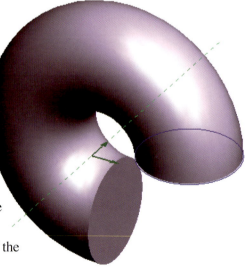

Figure 6.1

06. Revolve Profile Feature

introduction   **219**

Depending on what kind of profile you intend to revolve, Pro/DESKTOP® may require two separate sketches on the same workplane: an axis sketch and a profile sketch. Some revolves, however, can be made by using only one sketch. More about this will be explained in a little while.

Many products, and parts of products, are manufactured on lathes. Lathes are machines that spin material and shapes created by a stationary cutter that moves into the spinning material. **Figure 6.2** shows a lathe in the process of creating a staircase spindle. Wood, plastic and metals are typical materials that can be shaped by a lathe.

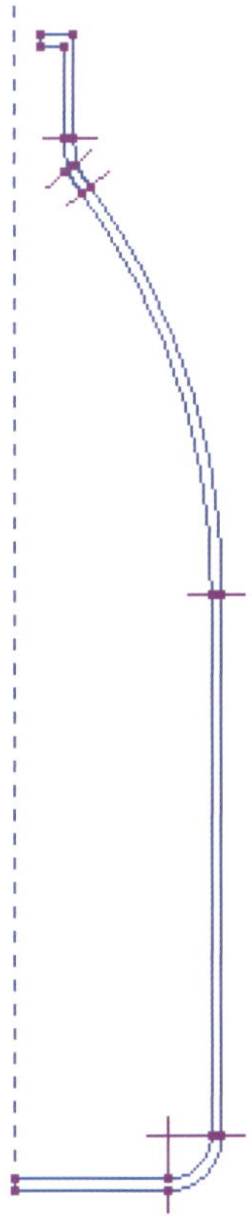

There are a number of industrial processes that can be used to produce components that look like they were created on a lathe, such as injection molding and casting. But to make the mold for these parts, the original prototype was probably made on a lathe.

Each sketch holds information about how the revolved solid will be constructed. **Figure 6.3** shows the profile for a bottle, with the axis on the left as a construction line. In **Figure 6.4** the profile has been revolved 180 degrees (half way around the axis). **Figure 6.5** shows the completed bottle.

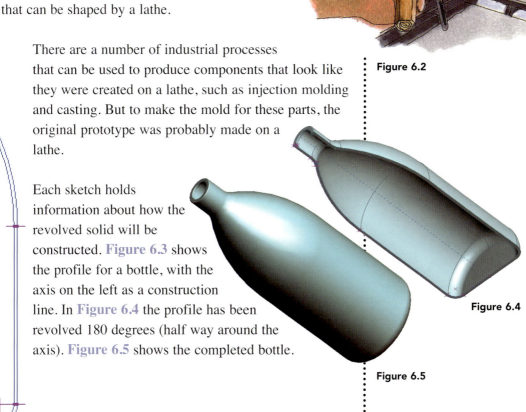

Figure 6.2

Figure 6.4

Figure 6.5

Figure 6.3

The Axis

The axis for the revolve feature is always a straight line. The line may be a regular sketch line or a construction line. The axis line may reside on its own sketch, or in some cases, it may be a straight line on the profile sketch itself. **Figure 6.6** shows a sketch profile of a pin to be revolved around the straight line that is the left side of the sketch. This is the only sketch used to create the pin.

If you want to develop a revolved solid that has a hole in the center, such as a wheel, you will need two sketches. The distance between the axis (on one sketch) and the wheel profile (on the other sketch) will be the radius of the hole in the center.

Figure 6.6

Figure 6.7

Figure 6.7 shows the profile and axis for a simple wheel.

Figure 6.8 shows what the wheel looks like in Trimetric view when it has been revolved, and you can still see the sketch.

Figure 6.8

The direction of the axis line will determine the orientation of the solid you create with the Revolve Profile feature. If, for example, you are designing a bottle, you should select either the frontal or lateral workplane to contain the axis and profile sketches. Draw the axis so that the bottle will be created standing up, as if it were sitting on a table. The bottle created above actually looks like Figure 6.9 when the keyboard shortcut **Shift+T** is used to change the view to Trimetric.

The Profile

All objects that use the Revolve Profile feature require a profile. Solid objects require a valid, closed profile, just like the Extrude feature. In Figure 6.10 the profile for a piston for a gasoline engine is illustrated. Notice that the profile touches the axis line only on the top. When the profile is revolved the top of the piston is solid but the rest of the piston is hollow (Figure 6.11). The hole was created with a circle profile on another sketch. In reality, pistons are usually constructed with more material around the side hole for strength.

Figure 6.9

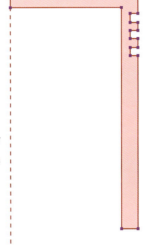

Figure 6.10

Figure 6.11

Some objects that you want to create by the Revolve Profile feature have a thin shell, such as a bottle, lamp base, etc. To create objects such as these, you can draw the outer profile and then use the Offset Chain command to develop a parallel profile. You may have to close the sketch by drawing in short lines at each end of the shape. You may also use the **Thin Option**, discussed later in this chapter.

Exercise 6.1
Model a Simple Ballpoint Pen

- Start a *New Design*.
- Use *millimeters* for the Units.
- *Save* the file as *ballpoint-1.des*
- Create a *New Sketch* named *pen profile* on the *frontal* workplane.
- *Shift+W* to look down at the active sketch.
- *Draw* a vertical line 132-mm long from the Origin up to act as the axis for the Revolve.
- *Draw* a second line, 4.5mm to the right and parallel the axis line (Figure 6.12). This line will form the outer shell of the pen.
- *Draw* a horizontal line from the Origin to the second line (Figure 6.13).
- *Zoom in* on the Origin and the horizontal line.
- Using the *Straight Line tool*, move the cursor along the horizontal line until you see the Snap to Grid numbers (0, 1.7). From this point, *Draw* a diagonal line up at **about** an 80-

Figure 6.12

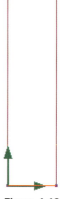

Figure 6.13

degree angle until it meets the right vertical line (**Figure 6.14**). An exact angle is not necessary.

- **Delete** the vertical and bottom horizontal lines to the right of the diagonal line. **Figure 6.15**).

- **Zoom in** to the top portion of the sketch.

- **Draw** a horizontal line 4.8mm long from the top of the axis, past the second vertical line (**Figure 6.16**).

- **Draw** a vertical line down 5mm from the end of the horizontal line just drawn (**Figure 6.17**).

- **Draw** a short horizontal line to join the outer shell vertical line.

Figure 6.16

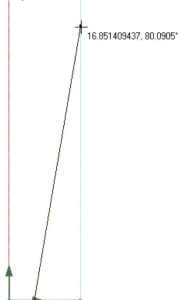

Figure 6.14

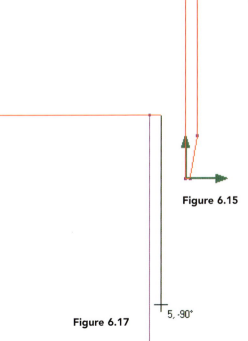

Figure 6.15

Figure 6.17

06. Revolve Profile Feature

Figure 6.18

- ***Delete*** the short outer shell line that runs from the horizontal line to the top line. The Sketch should fill (Figure 6.18).
- With the ***Select Lines tool***, select the axis line. Although you can do this after you have opened the Revolve Profile dialog box, it is sometimes easier to do it before you apply the feature.
- Go to the Feature pull-down menu (or the icon in the bottom toolbar) and choose the ***Revolve Profile*** feature. If the axis is still selected and the 360 degrees is entered in the Angle window, click OK. The Pen model should look like Figure 6.19.
- ***Save*** your work.

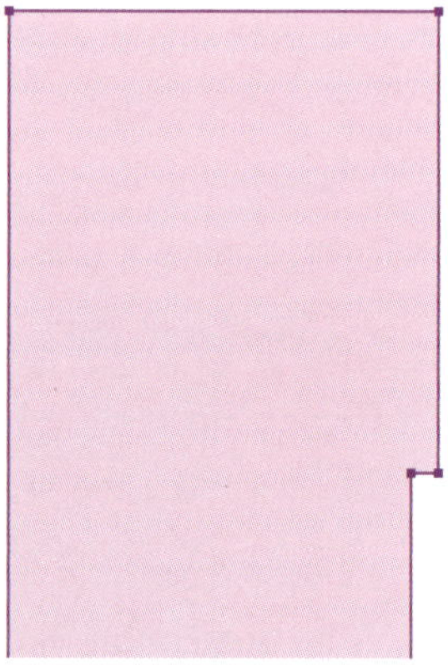

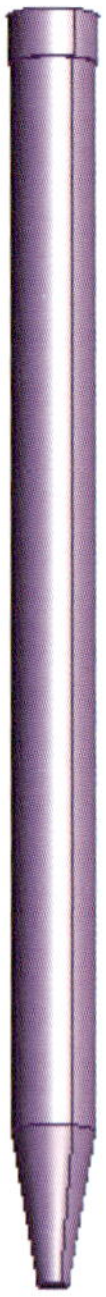

Figure 6.19

Details

Many ballpoint pens have a clip to secure it in a pocket. You will make the clip next.

- Add a ***New Sketch*** named ***clip base*** to the frontal workplane.
- ***Zoom in*** on the top of the pen and ***Draw*** a rectangle.
- Note the Snap to Grid numbers and start a rectangle at (-2.5, 131). Click and ***Draw*** down and to the right and create a rectangle 5 x 4-mm (Figure 6.20).
- ***Extrude*** the rectangle 8mm (Figure 6.21).

Figure 6.20

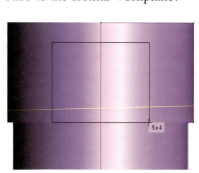

- **Select** the underside of the extrusion with the Select Faces tool. You may need to rotate the pen to select the face (**Figure 6.22**). Put a **New Sketch** named **clip** on this face.
- **Shift+W** and **Shift+A** so you can draw the next sketch accurately.
- **Draw** a 5 x 2.5mm sketch starting at one of the outside corners of the clip base (**Figure 6.23**). You may need to zoom way in to draw it accurately.

Figure 6.21

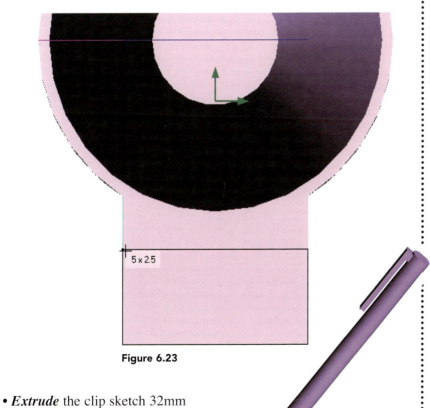

Figure 6.23

Figure 6.22

- **Extrude** the clip sketch 32mm (**Figure 6.24**).

Figure 6.24

Figure 6.25

- **Round** the bottom edge of the clip 2mm (**Figure 6.25**).
- **Round** the top edge of the clip 3mm.
- **Round** the side edges of the clip 1mm (**Figure 6.26**).
- **Select** the top of the pen.
- **Draw** a 4.2mm diameter circle centered on the Origin point (**Figure 6.27**).

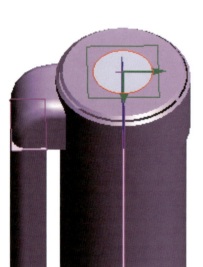

Figure 6.26

Figure 6.27

- **Extrude** the circle sketch 8mm with a 2-degree taper.
- The pen should look like **Figure 6.28**.
- **Save** your work.

Figure 6.28

Exercise 6.2 Energy Drink Bottle

- Start a *New Design*.
- Use *inches* for the Units.
- Create a *New Sketch* named **bottle profile** on the *frontal* workplane.
- *Save* the file as **drinkbottle.des**.
- *Shift+W* to look down at the active sketch.
- *Draw* an 8.5-inch vertical line (hold down shift) up from the Origin point. This will be the axis line for the bottle.
- *Draw* a horizontal line 2-inches to the right from the Origin, at the bottom of the first line.
- At the top of the first vertical line, *Draw* a horizontal line 0.5-inches to the right.
- From the end of the last line, *Draw* a line straight down 2-inches (*Figure 6.29*). These last two lines at the top will form the profile for the neck of the bottle.
- *Draw* a vertical line 2.25-inches to the right of the axis line. It does not touch any other lines but runs most of the distance from the bottom of the sketch to the 2-inch long line that hangs from the top line. Look at *Figure 6.30* to see what the line should look like.
- Using the *Ellipse tool*, start an ellipse on the axis line 2.2-inches above the Origin (*Figure 6.31*). *Draw* the ellipse down and to the right until the cursor reads 2.8 x 7.6. These numbers represent the minor and major diameters of the ellipse.

Figure 6.29

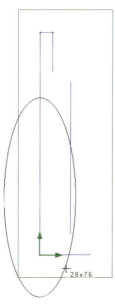

Figure 6.31

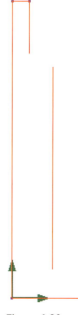

Figure 6.30

228 the profile

06. Revolve Profile Feature

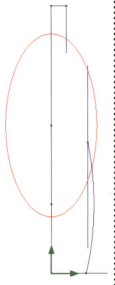

Figure 6.33

Figure 6.32

- **Delete** the part of the ellipse that is on the left side of the axis. This will keep the sketch from getting too cluttered.

- Also, **Delete** the part of the ellipse that runs between the axis line and the vertical line to the right (**Figure 6.32**).

- **Draw** a second ellipse starting on the axis line 4.7-inches above the Origin. Draw the ellipse up and to the left until the cursor reads 3 x 6 (**Figure 6.33**).

- **Delete** the part of the ellipse that is on the left side of the axis.

- **Delete** the part of the ellipse that runs between the axis and the vertical neck line (**Figure 6.34**).

- **Delete** the bottom of the ellipse that runs between the axis and the offset vertical line (**Figure 6.35**).

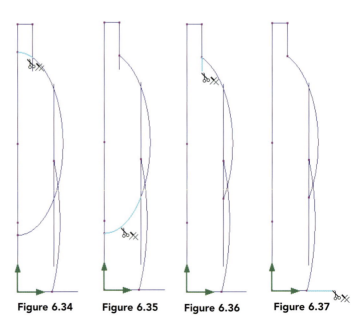

Figure 6.34   Figure 6.35   Figure 6.36   Figure 6.37

06. Revolve Profile Feature

the profile   229

- ***Delete*** the short line that hangs down from the neck profile (**Figure 6.36**).
- ***Delete*** the portion of the bottom line that overhangs off to the right of the first ellipse (**Figure 6.37**).
- Using the ***Straight Line tool***, and watching the Snap to Grid numbers, move the cursor along the offset vertical line to a position 6-inches above the Origin. ***Draw*** a line at about 45-degrees up and to the right that goes past all the other lines (**Figure 6.38**).
- ***Zoom in*** on the area of the sketch where you just drew the angled line. ***Delete*** all the necessary lines to leave the profile you see in **Figure 6.39**.
- Using the ***Straight Line tool***, and watching the Snap to Grid numbers, move the cursor along the offset vertical line to a position 2.2-inches above the Origin. ***Draw*** a line at about a –45-degrees below and to the right that goes past all the other lines (**Figure 6.40**).

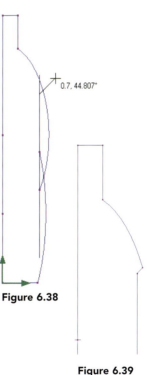

Figure 6.38

Figure 6.39

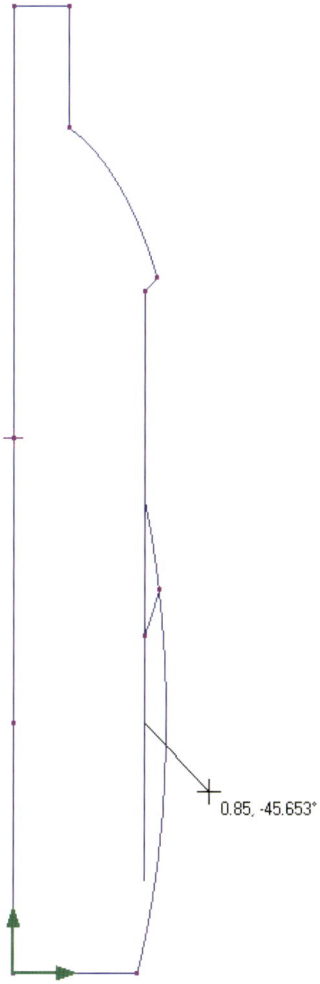

Figure 6.40

Figure 6.41

- **Delete** all the lines necessary to leave the profile you see in Figure 6.41. The sketch should fill with a color. If it does not fill, look carefully for lines you might have missed that need deleting.

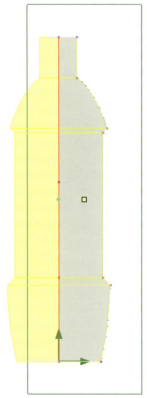

Figure 6.42

With the **Select Lines tool**, select the axis line (Figure 6.42).

- Go to the **Features** pull-down menu and choose **Revolve Profile** from the list. If the axis line is still selected, you should see the full form of the bottle in light yellow. The number of degrees should read 360 for a full revolve. Click on the OK button. If your sketch filled, the revolve should be successful.

- With the **Select Faces tool**, select the very top of the bottle (Figure 6.43).

Figure 6.43

- To make the bottle hollow, right mouse-click (shortcut) and select **Shell Solids** from the floating menu. Enter a value of **0.06** for the Offset in inches. Click **OK** to close the dialog box. The completed bottle should look like Figure 6.44.

Advanced Exercise 6.3
Aluminum Motorcycle Wheel

In this exercise you will create a model of a forged aluminum motorcycle wheel, similar to wheels that are popular on show and racing motorcycles. This time, however, you will only be given minimum instructions and a few views of the modeling process. Your task is to use the information provided to develop a similar 3D model. It does not need to be exact, but try to come as close to the finished design as possible (Figure 6.45).

Figure 6.44

- Start a *New Design*.
- *Save* the file as *mc-wheel.des*
- Use construction lines to help in your sketch development. First make a horizontal axis line through the Origin point.
- On a *New Sketch* (you need a second sketch for the Revolve feature in this case) draw the wheel profile. The wheel should be 18-inches in diameter to accommodate a standard size tire.
- You can use the *Mirror* command to create a symmetrical profile, so first draw one-half of the profile on one side of a construction line (Figure 6.46).

Figure 6.45

Figure 6.46

06. Revolve Profile Feature

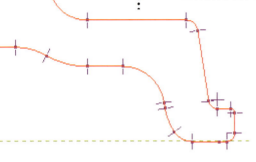

Figure 6.47

- **Figure 6.47** shows a close-up of the half profile used for the wheel. Yours should be similar.
- *Mirror* the half profile (**Figure 6.48**).
- *Revolve* the full profile (**Figure 6.49**).

Figure 6.49

- Create a *New Sketch/Workplane* on the front face of the wheel (**Figure 6.50**).
- *Draw* a cut-out sketch, *Duplicate* it around the Origin axis, and *Project* it through the wheel to create the cut-outs (**Figure 6.51**).

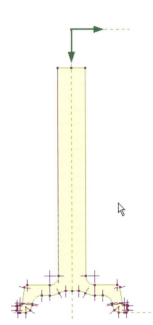

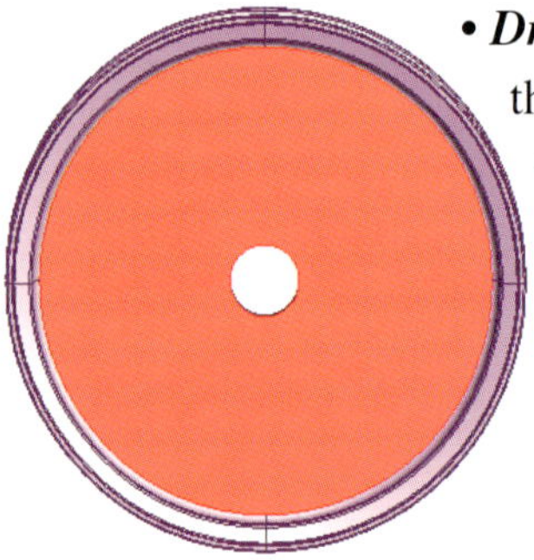

Figure 6.48

Figure 6.50

Figure 6.51

- *Draw* cut-out details between the first holes on the same sketch, *Duplicate* around the Origin axis and *Update* to Project the new detail cut-outs (Figure 6.52).
- *Save* your work.

Figure 6.52

Advanced Exercise 6.4 Triumph Valve

In this next project you will develop a model to more precise specifications without step-by-step instructions. The model is an intake valve from a Triumph Bonneville 750cc engine. The specifications are shown in Figure 6.53. The finished valve is shown in Figure 6.54.

- Start a *New Design*.
- Use *millimeters* for the Units.
- Save the file as *intakevalve.des*.
- Create a *New Sketch* on the *frontal* workplane so the valve will have the appropriate orientation.
- Begin with a vertical line from the *Origin* as the axis.
- Remember to draw only one-half of the profile so it can be revolved around the axis.
- *Save* your work.

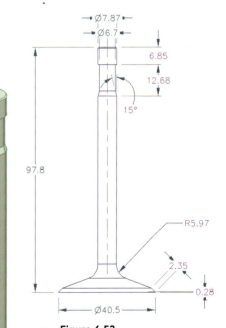

Figure 6.53

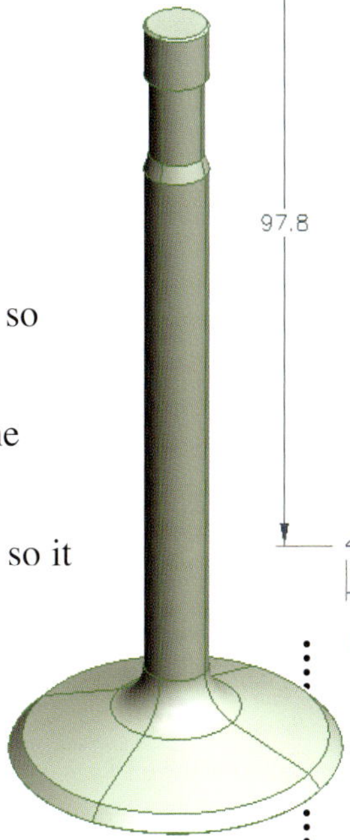

Figure 6.54

The Thin Option

Like the Extrude Profile Feature, Revolve Profile allows you to use the ***Thin*** option when constructing a solid. For creating objects that have exactly the same profile inside and out, the Thin option is a very handy command.

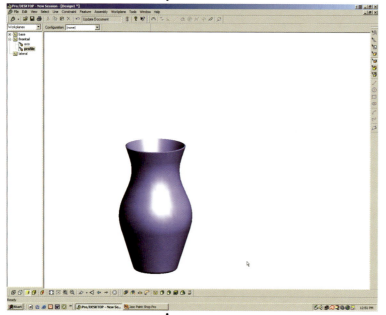

Figure 6.55

At the beginning of this chapter you saw several examples of bottles created with the ***Revolve Profile*** feature. The sketches for the bottles were shown with closed profiles, sometimes generated with the ***Offset Chain*** command. But sometimes there is an easier way to create objects such as these.

You encountered the ***Thin Option*** earlier in this text when it was introduced as an option in the ***Extrude Profile*** feature. At that time you learned that it was not always necessary to draw a valid profile to extrude. The ***Thin Option*** could be used if your sketch was a single continuous line and you defined a distance on one or both sides of that line.

You have a similar choice with the ***Revolve Profile*** feature. You can simply draw a series of connected lines and revolve them around an axis. This will require a separate axis sketch. If you forget to check the ***Thin Option*** box in the ***Revolve Profile*** dialog box, you will get an error message. Figure 6.55 shows a rather strange looking bottle that was developed using the *Spline* tool and revolved with the *Thin Option*.

Intersect Material Option

The ***Revolve Profile*** dialog box has an option similar to that in the ***Extrude Profile Feature***. It will help you create solids (or remove material from a solid) that would be difficult or impossible to accomplish with the other feature commands, although you will probably not use it very often. The ***Intersect Material*** option, can be used in conjunction with another ***Revolve*** or with an ***Extrude***. The ***Revolve*** must intersect a previous Revolve or Extrude. Figure 6.56 shows the result of using the Intersect Material option. Figure 6.57 shows the result of the two revolves done normally, without the ***Intersect Material*** option selected.

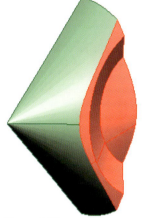

Figure 6.56

Summary

In this chapter you have learned about the ***Revolve Profile*** feature and some of the ways it can be used to create and modify solids. The ***Revolve Profile*** feature produces the kind of objects that can be made on a lathe. These objects are symmetrical and all contours and lines are equidistance from a central axis. Examples of such objects are many flashlights and lamps.

Sketches for revolves can be drawn on a single sketch if one line is straight and acts as an axis. If you want to end up with a revolved figure that has a hole in its center, you will need two sketches on the same workplane: one for the axis and one for the profile.

Figure 6.57

design link
the golden rectangle

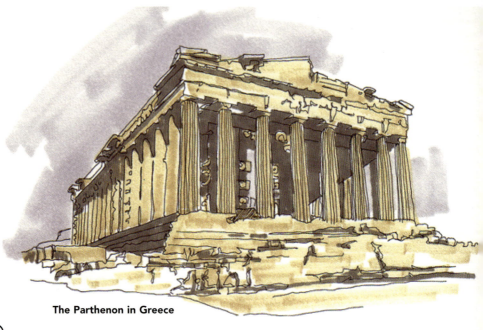

The Parthenon in Greece

While not really an engineering principle, the **Golden Rectangle** is certainly a design principle that has been around for thousands of years. Early Greeks described the Golden Rectangle as the perfect proportion and they designed many of their buildings with it. During the Renaissance many artists, such as Leonardo Di Vinci, used the Golden Rectangle proportions to layout their paintings. There are several web sites devoted to the Golden Rectangle in art and architecture. It is not uncommon today to find products designed around the Golden Rectangle proportions.

The proportions of the Golden Rectangle are 1 to 1.62. In other words, if the width of a rectangle is 1 foot long (12 inches), the depth is 1.62 feet long (or 19.44 inches long, found by multiplying 12 inches times 1.62). The 1.62 figure has actually been rounded from a more accurate figure of 1.618034, which is a little too awkward to use.

design example

Goal: Lay out the width and depth of a jewelry box to the proportions of the Golden Rectangle. The box must be 7 inches from the front to the back (depth). How wide should it be?

the golden rectangle

design link

Solution: Find the width by multiplying 7 inches (the depth) by 1.62. The answer is 11.34 inches. This figure may be entered into your Pro/DESKTOP® constraints.

If you are actually making the jewelry box, however, 11.34 inches is a little difficult to find on a ruler. But, we can get close enough. We know that 3/8 inch is equal to the decimal 0.375 inch and 5/16 inch is equal to 0.3125 inch. So, lay out the width of the box with a ruler by making your mark between the 11 5/16 and 11 3/8 lines on the ruler. You can use the same method to find the Golden Rectangle proportions when using millimeters.

When you are designing something, see if using the proportions of the Golden Rectangle will help you to get a pleasing shape for your project.

07

assemblies

07. Assemblies

In this chapter you will learn how to:

- Use the Fix Components assembly command
- Use the Center Axes assembly command
- Use the Mate assembly command
- Use the Align assembly command
- Use the Offset assembly command
- Use the Orient assembly command
- Use a combination of assembly commands to assemble several products

Introduction

An important part of learning Pro/DESKTOP® is learning how to assemble two or more components together in one file. Most of the products we buy are made from many separate parts. A car has thousands of separate parts that must each be designed, manufactured and assembled.

The parts designed in CAD can be prototyped or produced by computer-controlled machines, so most things you design need to have separate files for each component. Even a simple ball-point pen has up to a dozen parts, each of which is produced and then put together before the pen can work as a useful writing tool.

07. Assemblies

introduction 241

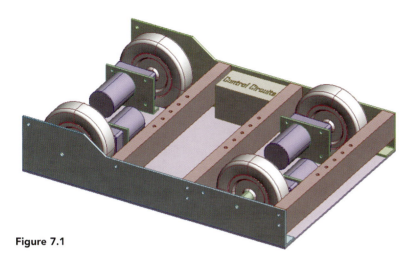

Figure 7.1

Assemblies allow you to do a number of things. With assemblies, you can create an animation of the movement of one or more parts, or you can produce drawings in the Engineering Drawing Interface so that you will have plans to hand-make each component of a product.

Assemblies allow you to find out if the separate parts you create really do fit together as you intend. With the *Tools* pull-down menu, you can find out if there is clearance or interference between two parts that you want to fit together. Checking the fit of parts is also very important when these parts are intended to move. Assemblies allow designers and engineers to see if moving parts hit other components or move the way they should. The parts in the robot platform in Figure 7.1 were developed in CAD and assembled. Even the motors, which would be purchased, were carefully modeled to see if everything would fit.

You can open assembly files in the Album Interface and render them for presentation. Many new products that appear in catalogs are CAD renderings that are so realistic they are mistaken for the real thing. Because of the "lead time" for catalog publishing, the images that are going to appear in a catalog must be submitted to the publisher several months before the catalog is mailed. Designing in CAD allows a company to use the same file information to produce the product as well as create catalog and technical manual images.

Assembling parts is creative work. With most files there are a number of ways that can be used to assemble the components. You have a choice of which parts you assemble first as well as which commands you will use. Also, you will probably have a choice of which surfaces and features you will use on each part for the assembly.

In other words, you have a lot of choices, so it is difficult to give you all the rules you need to put together all the different parts you will create. What you will need to do is recognize which surfaces and features seem appropriate and try them. The more assemblies you do the better at assembly you will become. In this chapter you will model and assemble a number of different products, starting from the simple to the more complex. This will give you the practice and experience you will need to assemble products of your own design.

Experienced CAD designers keep assembly in mind when creating components. They may use an arc or a flat surface or some other feature that will make it easy to assemble parts later. They also develop the files in an appropriate orientation in each file. For example, if you design a flashlight by extruding a cylinder shape, you would want to create many of the the sketches on the frontal or lateral workplanes so the flashlight is oriented horizontally. Then the lens, reflector, and other components would also be modeled in the same orientation (Figure 7.2). This makes it much easier to assemble all the parts.

Figure 7.2

Using Assembly Constraints

There are two primary ways to access assembly constraints once you have two faces or edges selected on two components: (1) **Select** a constraint from the **Assembly** pull-down menu at the top of the screen (Figure 7.3), and (2) right mouse-click and select a constraint from the floating menu (Figure 7.4). The second method is quicker because it involves less movement of the mouse around the screen. With both methods, you need to select two faces or edges before trying to select the assembly command. If the assembly constraint you want is not appropriate for the surfaces or edges you have selected, then the command will be "grayed out" and not "clickable" on the menu (such as the **Center Axes** command in Figure 7.4).

Figure 7.3

Figure 7.4

Constraints in the Browser Window

To view or change the constraints you have applied, go to the Browser window on the left side of the screen and choose **Components** from the pull-down menu (Figure 7.5). The parts you have brought in to your assembly file now appear as a list in the Browser. Select a component and a folder of Constraints appears at the bottom of the Browser window. If you have applied constraints, a "+" sign appears to the left of the folder. Click on the plus sign so you can see the constraints used on each part.

Figure 7.5

07. Assemblies

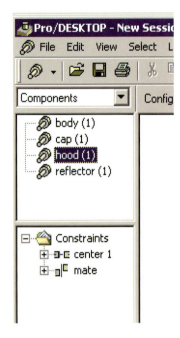

Figure 7.6

Figure 7.7
Select Parts Tool

If you are going to use the **Components** Browser window often, you may want to reposition the constraints folder to make it more convenient to use. Drag the gray bar above the constraints folder up to the center of the screen (**Figure 7.6**).

Deleting or Suppressing Assembly Constraints

There may be times when you want to apply one of the following constraints to a component and later suppress or delete this constraint so you can move the part. To remove any assembly constraint, go to the **Components Browser** window and click on the plus sign so you can see the constraints used on each part. Right mouse-click on a constraint and choose **Delete** from the floating menu.

Assembly Constraints

There are six major assembly constraints. Each constraint is intended to hold two parts together in some mathematical relationship. Remember, underneath all the nice icons and lines, CAD programs are really just math programs. So, assemblies are mathematically driven as well.

Fix Components

The **Fix Components** constraint is used when you want to keep a part from sliding around on the screen. This is important when you want one part to stay put and the others to move into position against it or into it.

To use the Fix Components constraint use the **Select Parts Tool** on the Design Toolbar (**Figure 7.7**). As you move the cursor you will see the edges of the part pre-highlight in blue. When the part pre-highlights click and release. The component will change red and the pre-highlighted lines will change to orange. The cursor will change from an arrow to an arrow with a box (**Figure 7.8**). Once the part is selected you can either use the ***Assembly*** pull-down menu or ***right mouse-click*** and select ***Fix Components*** from the floating menu.

Center Axes

The first assembly constraint is the ***center axes***. This constraint is commonly used when two components have circles, cylinders, round holes or arcs. The center axes command can also be used on straight edges of objects to make the edges line up (colinear).

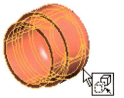

Figure 7.8

First, let us review a few terms and concepts that will help you when you use the center axes command.

- A ***circle*** has a center point called an axis (axes is plural, meaning more than one axis).
- ***Arcs*** are parts of a circle. An arc may be only a very small part of a circle.
- A ***full circle has 360 degrees***; a half circle is an arc that has 180 degrees; etc.
- When a circle is extruded into a cylinder, the center point of the circle becomes a ***center axis*** line, stretching the length of the cylinder (the same holds true for a round hole through a material).
- When two circles share the same axis it is said that the circles are ***concentric***.
- When two lines share the same axis it is said that the two lines are ***colinear***.
- The ***radius*** of a circle is the distance from the center of the circle to the edge of the circle. It is one half the diameter.
- The ***diameter*** of a circle is the distance from one edge of the circle to the opposite edge. It is twice the radius.

07. Assemblies

In Pro/DESKTOP®, when you use the **Center Axes** command on two circles or arcs, they become concentric. In other words, the two circles (or arcs) share the same center point. Figure 7.9 shows two cylindrical objects that do not share the same center axis.

Figure 7.10 shows the two objects that now share the same center axis.

There are two ways you can use the center axes constraint on circles, arcs and cylinders: you can select edges or select faces (surfaces). Figure 7.11 shows two components that have been selected using the **Select Edges Tool**. Figure 7.12 shows the same two components that have been selected using the **Select Faces Tool**. Both techniques will cause the same results when the Center Axes constraint is used. However, there are some parts configurations when only the Select Edges tool will give you the Center Axes constraint in the Assembly menu.

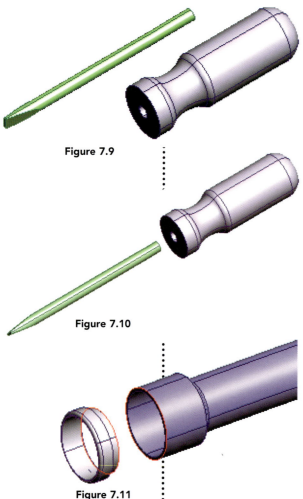

Figure 7.9

Figure 7.10

Figure 7.11

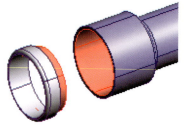

Figure 7.12

07. Assemblies

introduction   247

Mate

The *Mate* constraint is used to force two surfaces to face each other. Figure 7.13 shows two bookends before the vertical faces are mated. Figure 7.14 shows the same bookends now mated. Notice that while the two faces are together the front and bottom surfaces do not line up. You will need to use other assembly constraints if you want to make the bookends line up perfectly. The *Mate* constraint only forces the two surfaces to face each other.

Figure 7.13

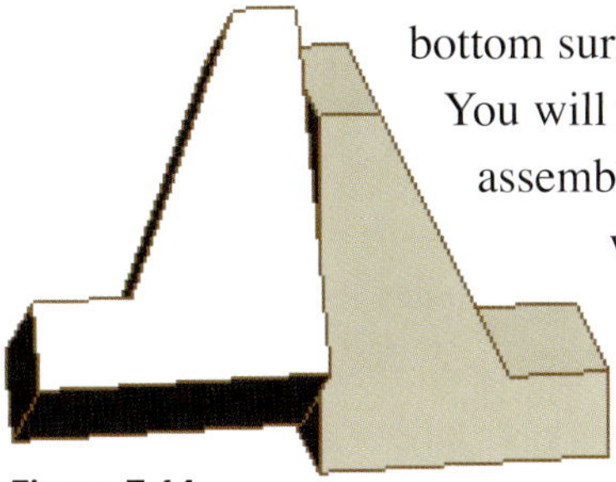

Figure 7.14

In order to use the *Mate* constraint you must select two surfaces using the *Select Faces Tool*. Then use the *Assembly* pull-down menu or right mouse-click and select *Mate* from the floating menu.

Align

The *Align* constraint is used when you want the faces of two objects to line up. Figure 7.15 shows a row of CDs (compact disks) sitting on a shelf. The front of the CDs are not aligned. In Figure 7.16 the front of all the CDs are aligned. Can you think of other places where you see things aligned and unaligned in your everyday routine? Books on a shelf; the fronts of houses along the street; etc. How about the text on this page? The left edge of text is aligned. What about the right edge?

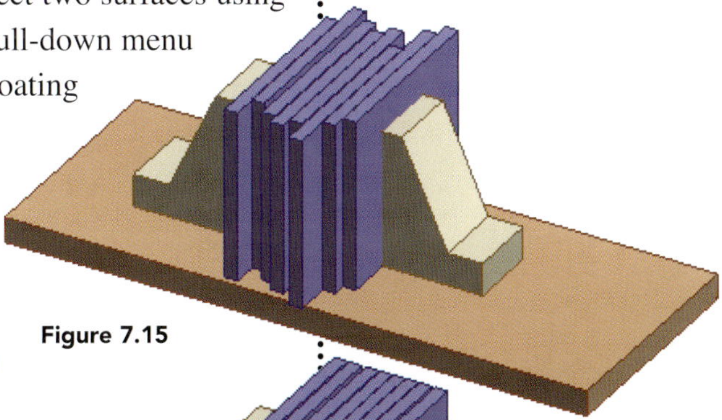

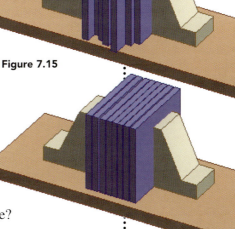

Figure 7.15

Figure 7.16

To use the ***Align*** constraint, select two faces, one on each of the two parts you want to constrain. **Figure 7.17** shows two faces selected on Lego™ block parts before the ***Align*** constraint has been used. **Figure 7.18** shows the parts after they have been aligned. Of course real Lego blocks automatically align because of how they are designed with the circle bump on the top of one that fits into the recess in the block above.

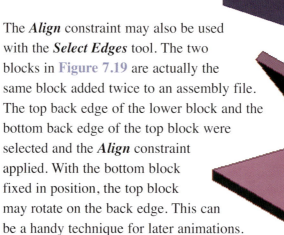

Figure 7.17

Figure 7.18

The ***Align*** constraint may also be used with the ***Select Edges*** tool. The two blocks in **Figure 7.19** are actually the same block added twice to an assembly file. The top back edge of the lower block and the bottom back edge of the top block were selected and the ***Align*** constraint applied. With the bottom block fixed in position, the top block may rotate on the back edge. This can be a handy technique for later animations.

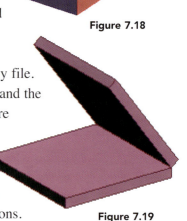

Figure 7.19

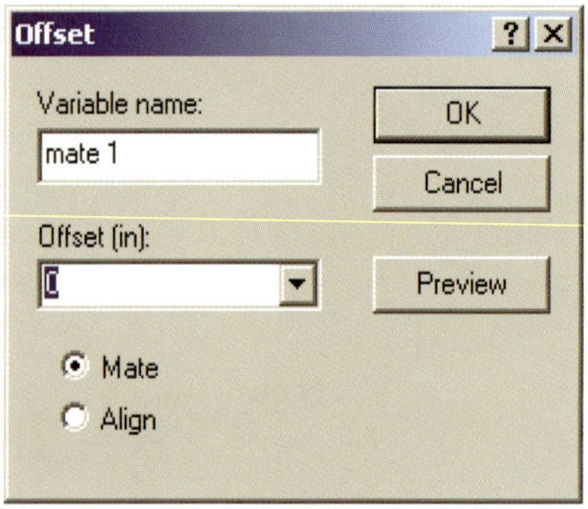

Offset

The offset constraint is very useful in assembly. When you use this constraint a dialog box appears and allows you to choose either an ***Offset Mate*** or an ***Offset Align*** (**Figure 7.20**). An offset Mate of zero distance is the same as a simple Mate constraint. An offset Align of zero distance is the same as a simple Align constraint.

Figure 7.20

07. Assemblies

introduction 249

To use the ***Offset*** constraint, select two faces, one on each of the two parts you want to constrain. Use the ***Assembly*** pull-down menu or right mouse-click and choose ***Offset*** from the floating menu. Choose either ***Mate*** or ***Align*** and type in a distance.

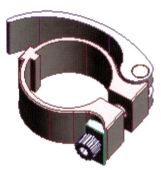

Figure 7.21

The ***Offset*** constraint is very useful for animations. The value of the Offset can be changed to create the effect of parts flying in to an assembly, or parts flying away creating a disassembly. In Figure 7.21 you see a scooter neck clamp ring that has been assembled with Offset Align and Offset Mate constraints. All offsets were set to zero. In Figure 7.22 you see what happens when the value for the offsets have been changed to some positive value (either 0.5-inches or 1-inches). To create the "exploded view" is simply a matter of changing the offset value.

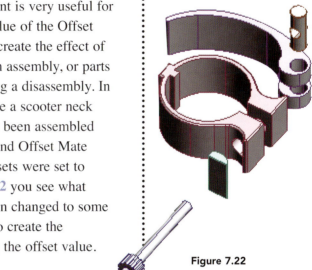

Figure 7.22

Orient

The ***Orient*** constraint allows you to constrain the angle between two surfaces or two edges on two separate objects. You will use this constraint when you want to change the position of one of the parts in an assembly. You will also use this constraint when you intend to create the movement of one part in relation to another in a animation. Since the Orient constraint works with angles, you will enter a number of degrees of arc in the Orient Constraint dialog box (Figure 7.23).

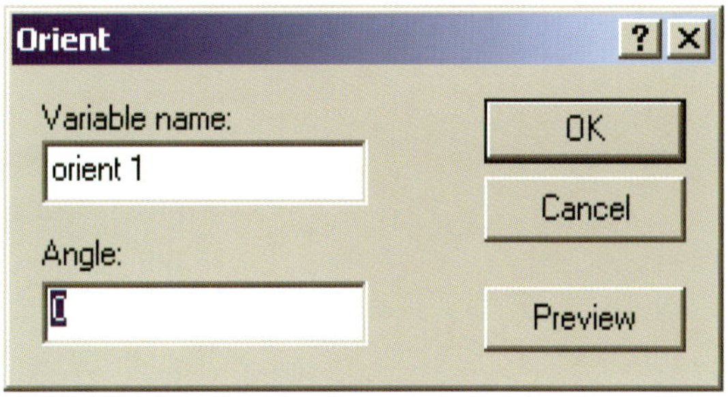

Figure 7.23

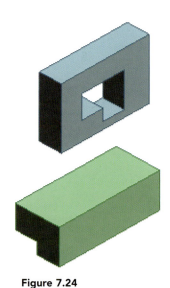

Figure 7.24

It is usually a good idea to use a **Fix Component** constraint on one of the objects before using the Orient constraint. This will force one of the parts to change position while the other remains fixed.

In Figure 7.24 two components that obviously need to fit together are added to an assembly file. The problem is that they have different orientations. The solution to this problem is to change the position of one so that it is facing the other. First, the block with the hole was fixed in place, then two faces were selected and an Orient constraint with 180-degree angle was applied (Figure 7.25).

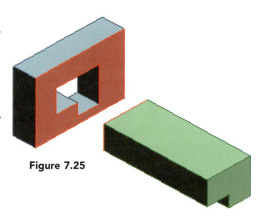

Figure 7.25

Sometimes, you will want to change the position of a component with the Orient constraint, and once it has changed positioin, **Delete** the constraint. Deleting the Orient constraint will allow you to then apply another assembly constraint.

Beginning Assemblies

Assemblies are started with a **New Design File**. If you bring components into a file that has already been used to design a part, that part cannot be moved. For example, if you tried to assemble the parts of a clock in a file that was used to create a clock face that had been modeled on the base workplane, the clock face could not be moved into an upright position. The final assembled clock would lie flat on the base workplane. Every time the file was opened, the clock face would lie flat. In other cases, key parts that you would like to move in

07. Assemblies

introduction 251

an animation will not move because you did not start with a New Design file.

If all components were assembled in a New Design File, then the clock face could be oriented vertically and all the other parts could be assembled to the clock face in that position. The finished clock would stand vertical when the file was opened.

Assembly files are dependent on the individual files of the components of the assembly. To keep track of assembly files, it is good practice to create a new folder for the project, and keep all the individual part files and the assembly file in that folder. If you move a part file after you have created an assembly, Pro/DESKTOP® will have a difficult time finding the file. The same is true if you rename a file after you have created an assembly. It is a good idea to make sure the names of the parts are correct before you create the assembly.

Exercise 7.1 Create the Parts for the Ballpoint Pen

In this project you will create the parts to a ballpoint pen by using both Extrude and Revolve features.

The ballpoint pen will be created in three parts: the barrel, the top, and the ink refill. We will leave out the spring and tip retractor. At some point you may want to reverse-engineer a ballpoint pen and create all the parts.

Part One - Pen top
- Create a ***New Folder*** named ***pen***. The parts of an assembly should be kept in a labeled folder.

07. Assemblies

- Start a *New Design*.
- Change *Units* to *millimeters*.
- Inside the folder *Save* the file as *pentop.des*.
- Create a *New Sketch* named *axis* on *frontal* workplane.
- *Shift+W* to look onto the active workplane.
- *Draw* a vertical line (holding down the Shift key) *75mm* up from the *Origin Point*. *Toggle Construction* for this line. This line will be the axis for the Revolve.
- Create a *New Sketch* named *profile* on the frontal workplane.
- *Draw* a second 75mm long vertical line parallel and 5mm to the right of the axis line (**Figure 2.26**). Make sure you start at the bottom at Snap to Grid position (5, 0). This line will form the profile of the Revolve, which will result in a 10mm diameter cylinder.

Figure 7.26

- Join the top of the axis line and the second vertical line by drawing a short horizontal line at the top.
- *Round* the upper right corner with a 1mm arc (**Figure 7.27**).
- *Revolve* the profile using the *Thin option* with a value of 0.8mm (**Figure 7.28**). The pen top should look like **Figure 7.29**.
- *Save* your work.

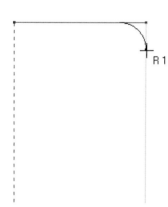

Figure 7.27

Part Two Pen Barrel

- Start a *New Design*.
- Create a *New Sketch* named *axis* on the *frontal* workplane.
- Save the file as *penbarrel.des*.

07. Assemblies

introduction   **253**

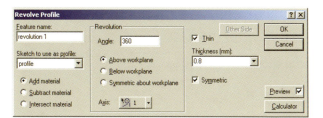

Figure 7.28

- *Shift+W* to look onto the active workplane.

- *Draw* a vertical line (holding down the Shift key) *65mm* up from the *Origin Point. Toggle Construction* for this line. This line will be the axis for the Revolve.

- Create a *New Sketch* named *profile* on the *frontal workplane*.

Figure 7.29   **Figure 7.30**

- *Draw* a second *53mm* long vertical line parallel and 5mm to the right of the axis line. Make sure you start at the bottom at Snap to Grid position (5, 0). This line will form the profile of the Revolve.

- *Zoom in* and draw a short, horizontal 0.8mm line to the left toward the axis on the top end of the line in the last step.

- *Draw* a vertical 12mm line from the end of the short line. The top of this line should align with the top of the construction line axis (**Figure 7.30**).

- *Zoom in* on the bottom of the axis and profile lines.

- Starting at the Snap to Grid position (2, 0) *Draw* a line up at a 75-degree angle past the vertical profile line (**Figure 7.31**).

- Delete the angled short line segment that hangs out past the profile line and the short vertical line that hangs below the angle line (**Figure 7.32**).

Figure 7.31

Figure 7.32

07. Assemblies

Figure 7.33

- *Revolve* the profile using the *Thin option* with a value of 0.8mm (look back at Figure 7.28).
- The pen barrel should look like Figure 7.33.
- *Save* your work.

Part Three Pen Ink Cartridge
- Start a *New Design*.
- Create a *New Sketch* named *profile* on the *frontal* workplane.
- *Save* the file as *inkcartridge.des*.
- *Shift+W* to look onto the active workplane.
- *Draw* a vertical line (holding down the Shift key) *110mm* up from the *Origin Point*. This line will be the axis for the Revolve.
- *Draw* a second *110mm* long vertical line parallel and 3mm to the right of the axis line. Make sure you start at the bottom at Snap to Grid position (3, 0). This line will form the profile of the Revolve, which will result in a 6mm diameter ink cartridge.
- *Draw* a short horizontal line to join the top of the axis line and the top of the second vertical line. *This step is not pictured.*
- *Zoom in* on the bottom of the axis and profile lines.
- Move the cursor of the *Straight Line* tool along the profile line to the *Snap to Grid* position (3, 20). *Draw* a short 0.6mm horizontal line to the left (Figure 7.34).
- On the end of this line, *Draw* a *5mm* long line straight down (Figure 7.35).
- On the end of this line, *Draw* a short *0.4mm* horizontal line to the left (Figure 7.36).
- On the end of this line, *Draw* a *6mm* line straight down (Figure 7.37).

07. Assemblies

introduction   **255**

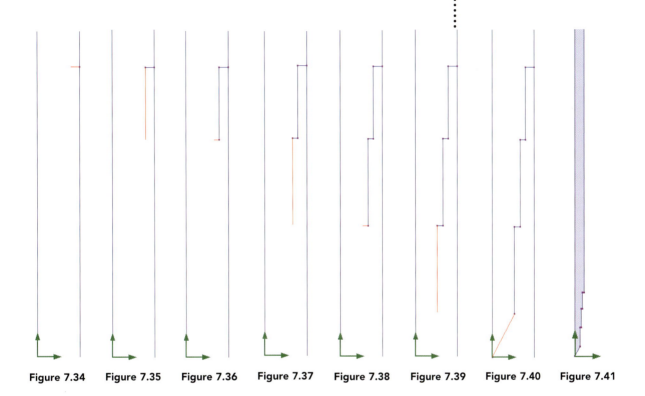

Figure 7.34   **Figure 7.35**   **Figure 7.36**   **Figure 7.37**   **Figure 7.38**   **Figure 7.39**   **Figure 7.40**   **Figure 7.41**

- On the end of this line, **Draw** a short **0.4mm** horizontal line to the left (**Figure 7.38**).
- On the end of this line, **Draw** a **6mm** line straight down (**Figure 7.39**).
- On the end of this line, **Draw** a diagonal line to the bottom end of the axis line (**Figure 7.40**).
- **Delete** the vertical line that hangs down from the intersection with the first horizontal line that you drew (**Figure 7.41**).
- Revolve the profile using the axis line as the axis. (No Thin option this time).
- The model should look like **Figure 7.42**.

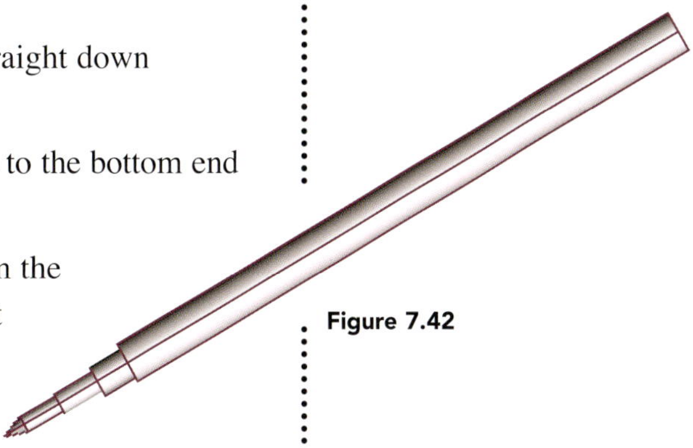

Figure 7.42

Assemble the Parts of the Ballpoint Pen

This first assembly will involve only two commands: *Center Axes* and *Mate*.

- Begin with a *New Design* file.
- *Save* file as *penassembly.des*.
- Use the *Assembly* pull-down menu and select *Add Component*.
- Find the folder *pen* and inside it the file *penbarrel.des* and select. Click *OK* (Figure 7.43).

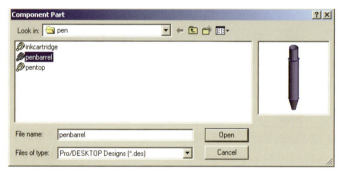

Figure 7.43

The barrel of the pen should appear in the center of the new Design File.

- Using the same method, bring in the files:
    pentop.des
    inkcartridge.des

Each time you select a file and click *OK* the file appears in the center of the Design window. You may want to use the *Select Parts Tool* and drag each component away from the center of the window to avoid congestion (Figure 7.44).

Figure 7.44

Sometimes, parts will come in the Design file in the right location and it will appear as if they are assembled. A test to see if parts are assembled correctly is to use the **Select Parts Tool** and select a part (click and release) and then click it and drag. If the part moves from its correct location, the assembly is not complete. Another check is to go to the Browser window on the left side of the screen and select **Components** from the pull-down menu. When you select a component in the Browser window, the Constraints folder at the bottom of the Browser window will have a "+" sign if constraints have been applied. If there is no plus sign to the left of the Constraints folder, then no assembly constraints have been applied.

Use the Browser Window to see Components

To double-check and see if all the part files have been brought into the assembly file, you will check in the Browser window (of course in this case there are only three files, but in more complex assemblies, you will use the Browser window often).

- Go to the Browser window and click on the pull-down menu entitled **Workplanes**.
- Select **Components** from the list.

You will see a list of the ballpoint pen parts (Figure 7.45). At the bottom of the Browser window you will also see the Constraints folder icon and the word Constraints. It is in this section of the window you will see the constraints you have made for each part. Refer to the Components Browser in the next steps.

Now that you have all the parts of the ballpoint pen you can begin to apply the assembly constraints.

Figure 7.45

Use the Fix Component Constraint

Next, you will *Fix* the barrel so it will not move. This will help make it easier for you to assembly the other components. If you do not fix one component, then parts move back and forth as you assemble them.

- Use the *Select Parts Tool* to select the *penbarrel* (click once and release).

- Right mouse-click and select *Fix Component* from the floating menu (Figure 7.46).

- Go to the Browser window and select *penbarrel*. You will now see a plus sign + at the bottom of the Browser window to the left of the Constraint folder icon.

Figure 7.46

- Click on the "+" sign. You will see the icon for a lock and key and the word *Fixed* next to it (Figure 7.47). This tells you that the Fix constraint has been applied to the barrel. You know this because you just did it – but this procedure allows you to go back and check on the constraints of any part at any time.

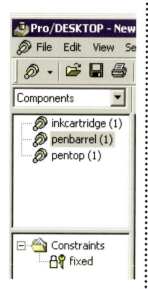

Figure 7.47

Remember, you must first select a part from the list at the top of the Browser window and then click on the "+" sign to see the constraints that have been applied to that part. You can enlarge the small bottom "constraints window" by dragging the separation bar upward.

Use the Center Axes Constraint

Both the ***penbarrel*** and the ***pentop*** are cylinder shapes, so you will use the ***Center Axes*** constraint to align them so they share the same center axis. You may want to move the two parts closer together so you can select both without zooming in or out.

Figure 7.48

- Use the ***Select Edges Tool*** and select the outer edge of the top of the ***penbarrel*** (Figure 7.48).
- Holding down the ***Shift+Key***, use the same tool to select the outer edge of the bottom of the ***pentop***.
- Right mouse-click and select ***Center Axes***. The ***penbarrel*** and the ***pentop*** will align (Figure 7.49). In this case, the ***pentop*** moved over the ***penbarrel***.

Test what happens to the freedom of movement of the two parts now that you have constrained them into sharing the same center axis.

- Use the ***Select Parts Tool*** and select the pentop (click and release).
- Click again and drag the cursor. The ***pentop*** should only move up and down along the center axis of the ***penbarrel***. You cannot move the barrel because you fixed it in place (Figure 7.50).

Next, you will constrain the ink cartridge using a slightly different technique.

- Use the ***Select Faces*** tool and select one of the outer surfaces of the ink cartridge.
- Holding down the ***Shift-Key***, use the same tool to select the outer face ***penbarrel*** shoulder (Figure 7.51).

Figure 7.50

Figure 7.49

07. Assemblies

Figure 7.51

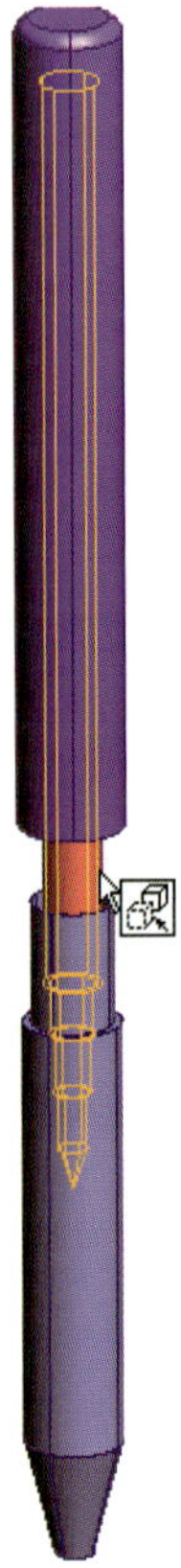

Figure 7.52

- Right mouse-click and select **Center Axes**. The **pentop** will align with the **penbarrel**. In this case, the ink cartridge has moved inside the penbarrel, so it was selected so it could been seen (Figure 7.52).

All three components now share the same axis. The ink cartridge and the pentop can be moved along this axis. The **penbarrel**, because it is Fixed, cannot move.

Next you will constrain the parts so the model looks like a finished product. But, you will use an **Offset** constraint so that later you can "explode" the assembly.

- With the **Select Faces tool**, select the top of the ink cartridge and the top rim of the penbarrel (Figure 7.53).
- Right mouse-click and select **Offset** from the floating menu. Click on the **Align** radio button and enter a value of –40mm (Figure 7.54). If you forget to check **Align** the ink cartridge will flip over.
- The **penbarrel** and **ink cartridge** components should now look like Figure 7.55.
- Drag the **pentop** part near the assembly so it will be easy to select the faces of both components.
- With the **Select Faces tool**, select the bottom rim of the pentop and the shoulder rim on the penbarrel (Figure 7.56). The view has been changed to transparency so that the faces are clear.

Figure 7.53

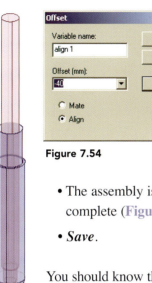

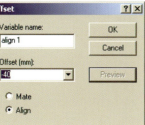

Figure 7.54

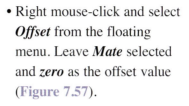

- Right mouse-click and select ***Offset*** from the floating menu. Leave ***Mate*** selected and ***zero*** as the offset value (**Figure 7.57**).

- Click ***OK*** to close the ***Offset*** dialog box.

- The assembly is now complete (**Figure 7.58**).
- ***Save***.

Figure 7.57

You should know that if you change any component file, the change will be reflected in the assembly. For example, if you go back to the ***pentop*** file and create a clip, the assembled pen will now have a clip.

- Go to the constraints browser window and select ***pentop***. Go to the bottom of the Browser window and click on the "+" next to the Constraints folder.

- Right mouse-click on the ***Offset*** constraint and select ***Redefine*** from the list.

- Change the offset from zero to ***50mm***. What happens? You may have to click on the green "update" icon at the top of the screen.

- ***Save***.

Figure 7.55

Figure 7.56

Figure 7.58

Exercise 7.2 Modify the Pen

Make several changes to make the pen more realistic.

1. Create a clip on the pentop.
2. Round the tip of the ink cartridge.
3. Put your school name embossed in the side of the pen.
4. Save the changes.

Most products are made up of a number of separate parts. Although each part is individually designed, each part must work together with the other parts to make the whole. In Pro/DESKTOP® individual components are designed and then assembled in a new file. Assemblies may be used to check relationships between parts (such as *clearance*, which is the space between the two parts) and used to create renderings and animations.

Summary

Assemblies are design files that have component parts added. It is always a good idea to begin an assembly file with a new, empty design file. This permits all parts to be moved and joined with constraints.

The assembly constraints include **Fix Component**, **Center Axes**, **Mate**, **Align**, **Offset** and **Orient**. The Offset constraint can be applied to either a Mate or Align constraint.

The Center Axes constraint forces two objects with an arc or circle feature to share a common center line axis. The Mate constraint forces the selected facing surfaces of two components to move together. The Align constraint forces two selected surfaces to share the same plane.

07. Assemblies

test your knowledge

Test Your Knowledge

Project 7.1 Develop a New Construction Kit

There are a number of construction kits on the market today, including LEGO™, K'Nex™, Fishchertechnik™, Mecanno™ and others. These kits have been carefully engineered to fit together, usually with friction. The parts make "modules" of regular size, so that the components will allow the user to create large structures.

design brief Develop five components and then use them to create a number of different configurations.

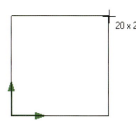

Figure 7.59

Figure 7.60

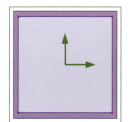

Figure 7.61

The 20x20 Block
- **New Design**
- **Save** file as **20x20.des**.
- **Draw** a 20mm x 20mm square on the **base** workplane (**Figure 7.59**).
- **Extrude** the sketch to 5mm.
- Create a **New Sketch** on the top of the block.
- **Draw** a 18mm x 18mm square centered on the block (**Figure 7.60**).
- **Extrude** the sketch to 4mm (**Figure 7.61**).
- **Shell** the block to a 1mm wall thickness with the bottom open (**Figure 7.62**).
- Select the four edges of the bottom part of the block and apply a **Chamfer** of 1mm (**Figure 7.63**). This will allow you to see the individual blocks when you assemble them.
- **Save** your work.

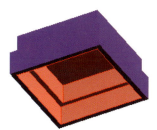

Figure 7.62

Figure 7.63

test your knowledge   **264**

07. Assemblies

Figure 7.64

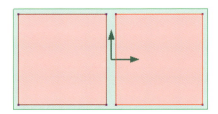

Figure 7.65

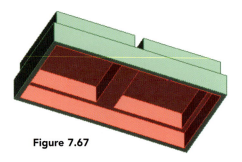

Figure 7.66

Figure 7.67

The 20x40 block

- **New Design**
- **Save** file as **20x40.des**.
- **Draw** a 20mm x 40mm rectangle on the **base** workplane (**Figure 7.64**).
- **Extrude** the sketch to 5mm.
- Create a **New Sketch** on the top of the block.
- **Draw** two 18mm x 18mm squares. Each should be 1mm from each of three sides (**Figure 7.65**).
- **Extrude** the sketch to 4mm (**Figure 7.66**).
- **Shell** the block to a 1mm wall thickness with the bottom open (**Figure 7.67**).
- Select the four edges of the bottom part of the block and apply a **Chamfer** of 1mm (**Figure 7.68**). This will allow you to see the individual blocks when you assemble them.

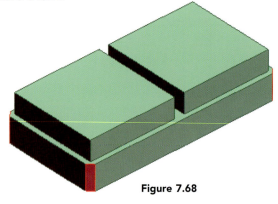

Figure 7.68

07. Assemblies

test your knowledge

265

The 20x20x20 Block

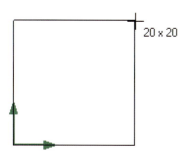

Figure 7.69

- **New Design**
- **Save** file as **20x20x20.des**.
- **Draw** a 20mm x 20mm square on the **base** workplane (**Figure 7.69**).
- **Extrude** the sketch to 20mm.
- Create a **New Sketch** on the top of the block.
- **Draw** a 18mm x 18mm square centered on the block.
- **Extrude** the sketch to 4mm (**Figure 7.70**).
- **Shell** the block to a 1mm wall thickness with the bottom open (**Figure 7.71**).
- Create a **New Sketch** on one of the side faces of the block.
- **Draw** a 4mm circle on the **Origin** point.
- **Project** the circle through the entire block to create holes on two opposite sides (**Figure 7.72**).
- Select the four edges of the bottom part of the block and apply a **Chamfer** of 1mm (**Figure 7.73**). This will allow you to see the individual blocks when you assemble them.

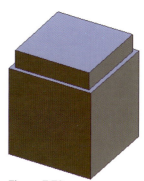

Figure 7.70

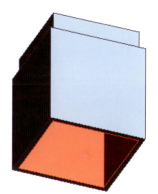

Figure 7.71

Figure 7.72

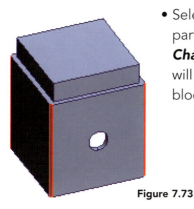

Figure 7.73

07. Assemblies

test your knowledge — **266**

The Axle
- **New Design**
- **Save** file as **axle110.des**.
- Create a **New Sketch** on the **frontal** workplane.
- **Draw** a 4mm circle.
- **Extrude** the sketch to 110mm (**Figure 7.74**).

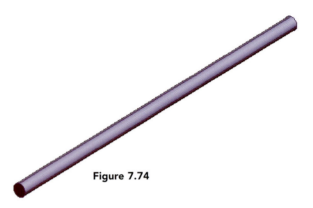

Figure 7.74

The Wheel
- **New Design**
- **Save** file as **wheel50.des**.
- Create a **New Sketch** on the **frontal** workplane.
- **Draw** a 30mm circle centered on the **Origin**.
- **Draw** a 4mm circle concentric with the first circle.
- **Extrude** the sketch to 10mm (**Figure 7.75**).

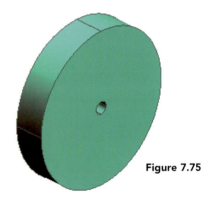

Figure 7.75

ASSEMBLE THE KIT PARTS
Align Two Blocks
Here are some hints that may help you with assembling the kit pieces. To line up two blocks next to each other you will need three constraints, one for each of the 3-Dimensions. Use the **Select Faces** tool.

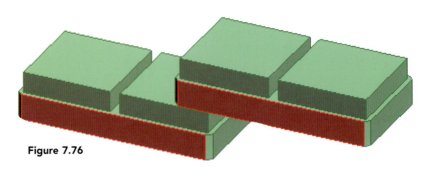

Figure 7.76

07. Assemblies

test your knowledge **267**

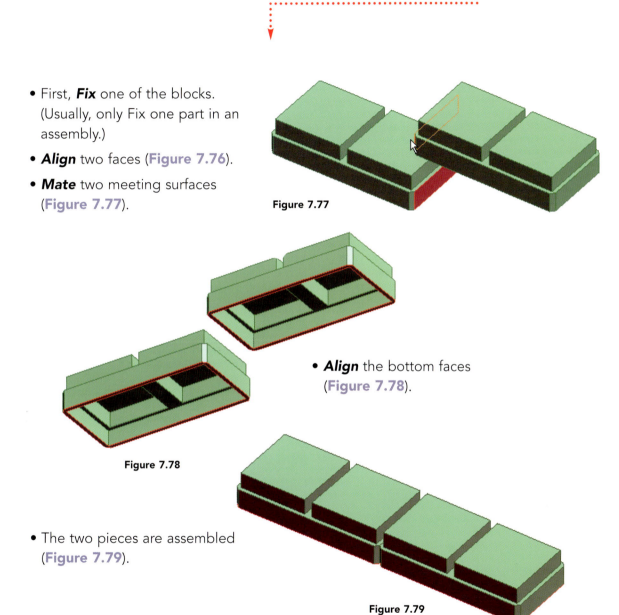

- First, **Fix** one of the blocks. (Usually, only Fix one part in an assembly.)
- **Align** two faces (**Figure 7.76**).
- **Mate** two meeting surfaces (**Figure 7.77**).

Figure 7.77

- **Align** the bottom faces (**Figure 7.78**).

Figure 7.78

- The two pieces are assembled (**Figure 7.79**).

Figure 7.79

07. *Assemblies*

test your knowledge **268**

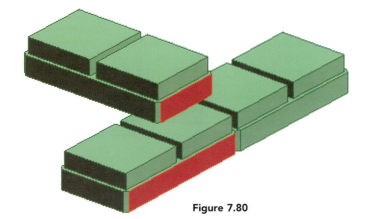

Figure 7.80

Rotating a Block into Position

You can rotate a piece by selecting two faces at right angles to each other (**Figure 7.80**). Choosing the **Align** constraint will cause the piece that is not fixed in place to rotate and align with the fixed block (**Figure 7.81**). You can also use the **Orient** constraint to rotate the block. If you use the Orient constraint, you may need to delete it to place other constraints on the block.

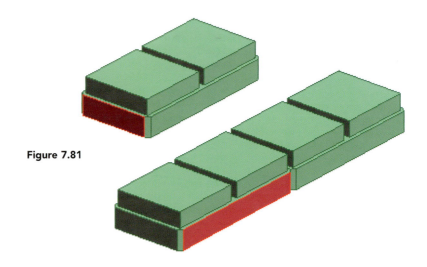

Figure 7.81

Project 7.2 The Buggy

Using the components you have developed, construct the buggy in **Figure 7.82**. **Save** the file as **kit-1.des**. Here are some additional views so you can see all the parts (**Figures 7.83** and **7.84**).

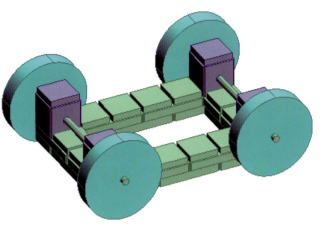

Figure 7.82

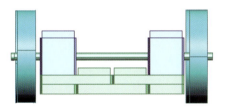

Figure 7.83

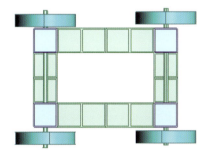

Figure 7.84

To test if you have the parts assembled correctly, use the **Select Parts** tool and select various parts and try to move them. If you cannot move them, you have assembled the buggy correctly.

Project 7.3 Three Additional Blocks

 Develop at least three additional blocks that will fit with the existing parts you have already modeled. Some suggestions are: blocks with three or four "bumps;" double-thick blocks; more interesting looking wheels of different sizes; specialty items like cams, levers, pulleys, and gears. Save the files using descriptive names.

Make something using at least 30 different components in an assembly. **Save** the file as **kit-2.des**.

07. Assemblies

test your knowledge   **270**

Project 7.4 Flashlight

design brief   Design the parts for a simple flashlight, including a barrel to hold the batteries, an end cap on the rear of the flashlight that would allow the user to change batteries, a "flared" end to hold the bulb and reflector, and the reflector and bulb. Include a lens and front cap. Assemble the flashlight parts using appropriate assembly constraints (**see Figure 7.2**).

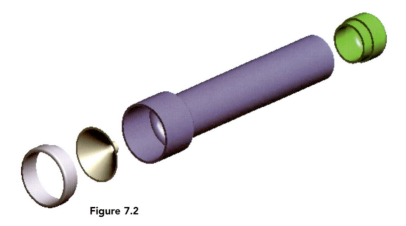

Figure 7.2

Specifications:

- Design the barrel to hold four "C" batteries.
- Make the design of the bulb similar to a "no. 40" 6-volt bulb.
- Design the reflector to be at least 2.5-inches in diameter.
- Design a front cap to hold the reflector and lens in place.
- Model a "C" battery and use four of them in the assembly.

08

sweep profile feature

08. Sweep Profile Feature

In this chapter you will learn how to:

- Create valid sketch paths for the Sweep
- Create valid sketch profiles for the Sweep
- Sweep a profile around an axis
- Sweep a profile along a helix
- Use the Pattern command

Introduction

The Sweep Feature allows you to create solids or remove material from a solid along a path. The Sweep is actually two different features, one sweeps a profile along a path and the other sweeps a profile along a helix. In **Figure 8.1** the bicycle handlebars are an example of a circle profile swept along a path. The coil spring in **Figure 8.2** is an example of a circle profile swept along a helix.

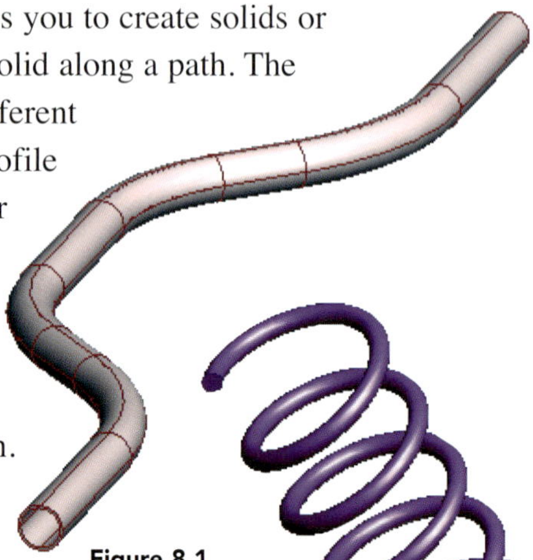

Figure 8.1

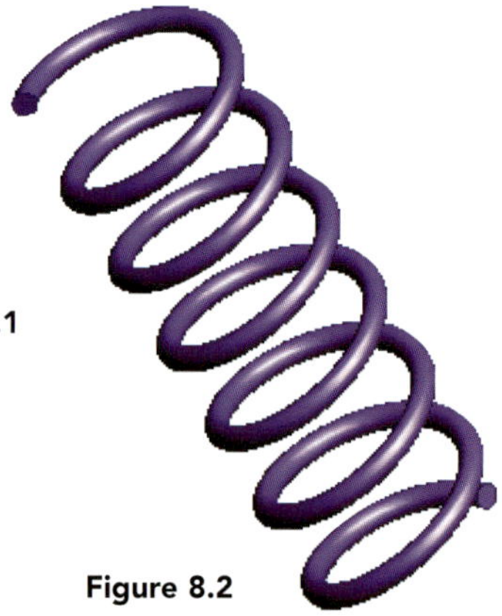

Figure 8.2

Sweep Profile Along a Path Feature

The Sweep along a Path feature requires two sketches that intersect perfectly perpendicular (90 degrees). The Sweep feature is one of the more difficult to use because of the perpendicular requirement. To help assure that the sketches are perpendicular, use two of the existing perpendicular workplanes whenever possible, such as the base and frontal, or the frontal and lateral. Starting your sketches at the Snap to Grid (0,0) origin point also helps ensure that the sketches are perpendicular.

Exercise 8.1 Sweep Profile along a Path: Paper Clip

Creating paths for the sweep feature to follow must be done accurately and carefully. For the first project, you will construct a paper clip (Figure 8.3).

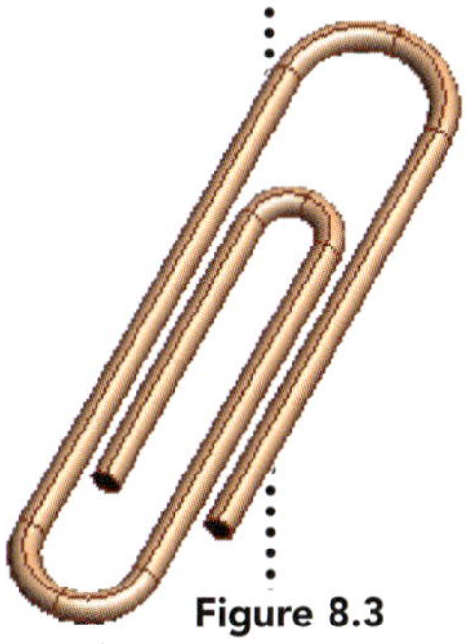

- Begin a *New Design*.
- Change *Units* to *millimeters*.
- *Save* the file as *paper clip.des*.
- Change the name of the initial sketch on the base workplane to *path*.
- *Shift+W* to look down on the active workplane.

Figure 8.3

Draw two vertical lines
- *Draw* an 18mm vertical line up from the Origin point.
- *Fix* this line with the *Toggle Fixed* constraint. This will prevent the line from moving during the next steps. Figure 8.4 shows the location of the first line with the Fixed constraint.

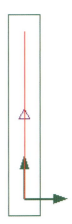

Figure 8.4

274 sweep profile along a path

08. Sweep Profile Feature

Figure 8.5

- *Draw* a vertical line to the left of the one you have just drawn. Start at the Snap to Grid (-6, 18) position and draw straight down to the (-6, -3) position. You have drawn a 21mm line, 6mm to the left and parallel to the fist line. It falls slightly below the Origin point (Figure 8.5).

Connect the two lines with a rounded top using the Arc or Fillet tool.

- Click on the *Arc or Fillet tool*.
- With the cross-hair cursor click and hold on the top end of the line on the right (Figure 8.6).
- Still holding down the mouse button, drag the cursor to the left until the arc "snaps-to" the top end of the left line (Figure 8.7). If the arc goes the wrong way, *Undo* and click on the right line first and try again.

Figure 8.6

Draw a third vertical line

- *Draw* a vertical line just to the left of the first line beginning below the origin point at the Snap to Grid position (-1.5, -3), drawing up, and ending at the (-1.5,12) position (Figure 8.8).

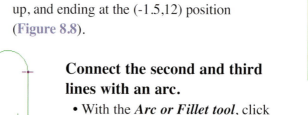

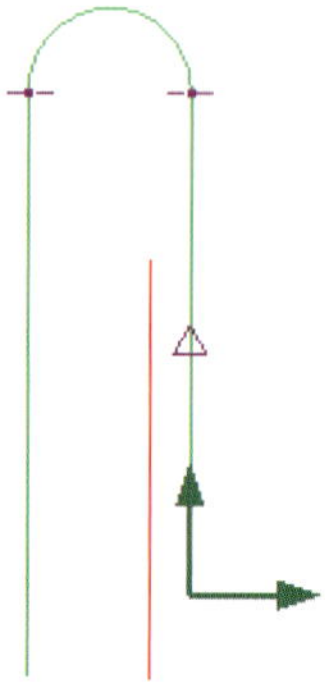

Connect the second and third lines with an arc.

- With the *Arc or Fillet tool*, click and hold on the bottom end of the line on the left and drag to the bottom of the line on right (Figure 8.9).

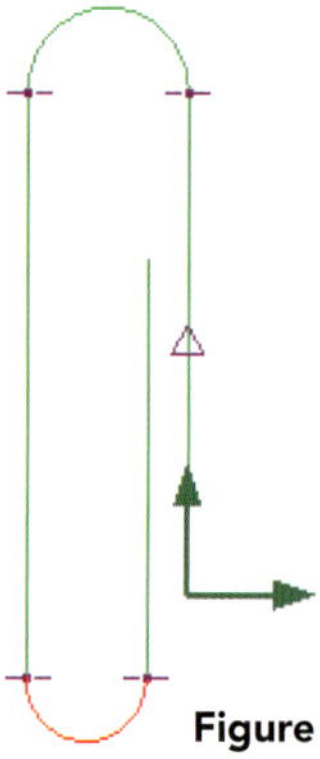

Figure 8.7

Figure 8.9

Draw a fourth vertical line

- ***Draw*** a vertical line beginning at the Snap to Grid position (-4.5, 0) and ending at the (-4.5, 12) position (**Figure 8.10**).

Connect the third and fourth lines with an arc

- With the ***Arc or Fillet tool***, click and hold on the top end of the line on the right and drag to the top of the line on the left (**Figure 8.11**).

The path for the paper clip in now complete. Next, a profile of the solid wire is needed that will follow the path. In this case, the profile of the wire is a circle 1.1mm in diameter.

The profile for the Sweep Feature must be perpendicular to the path at one point. The path was deliberately drawn in a location so that the frontal workplane will intersect the path at 90 degrees.

- Create a ***New Sketch*** named ***profile*** on the ***frontal*** workplane.

Create the profile for the sweep

- Select the ***Circle*** drawing tool. The path sketch reappears.
- ***Shift+W*** to view directly onto the active workplane.
- Centered on the Origin point, zoom in and ***draw*** a small circle.
- Constrain the Diameter of the circle to ***1.1mm*** (**Figure 8.12**). Make sure the circle is selected (red) before you dimension it. If it is not selected, you will be asked to enter a radius distance instead of a diameter distance.

Figure 8.10

Figure 8.11

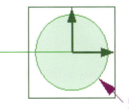

Figure 8.12

sweep profile along a path

Sweep the profile

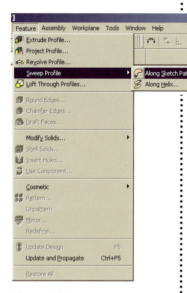

Figure 8.13

- Go to the *Features* pull-down menu and select *Sweep Profile*. When the secondary menu opens select *Along Sketch Path* (Figure 8.13).

- Make sure the sketches *profile* and *path* appear in the appropriate boxes and click *OK*. Figure 8.14 shows the paper clip design.

- *Save* your work.

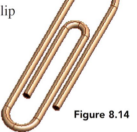

Figure 8.14

Exercise 8.2 Sweep Profile Along a Path: High-Rise Handlebars

The Sweep Profile feature has a Thin Option, similar to the other features. In this exercise, you will create handlebars for a racing BMX bike (Figure 8.15).

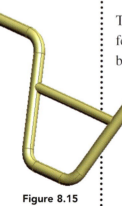

Figure 8.15

- Begin a *New Design*.
- Change *Units* to *inches*.
- *Save* the file as *handlebars.des*.
- *Shift+W* to look down on the active workplane.
- *Draw* a short *construction line* vertical from the Origin on the base workplan.
- With the *construction line* selected, go to the *Workplanes* pull-down menu and choose *New Workplane* from the list.
- Click on the *Angled* radio button if it is not already selected.
- Enter 125-degrees for the angle (Figure 8.16). Click *OK*.

sweep profile along a path

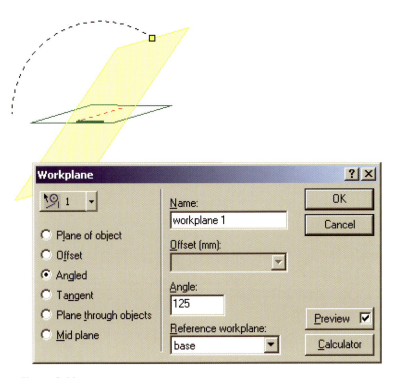

Figure 8.16

Figure 8.17

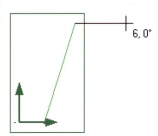

Figure 8.18

- Create a *New Sketch* named *path* on this workplane.
- *Shift+W* to look directly down on the active sketch.
- *Draw* a 3-inch horizontal line from the Origin to the right (hold Shift).
- From the right end of this line, *draw* a 12-inch line angled at 72-degrees, up and to the right (**Figure 8.17**).
- Starting at the end of the angled line, *draw* a 6-inch horizontal line to the right (**Figure 8.18**). Remember to hold the shift key when drawing the line.

08. Sweep Profile Feature

Figure 8.19

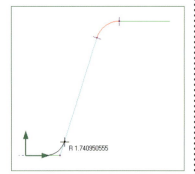

Figure 8.20

Figure 8.21

- Using the ***Arc or Fillet tool***, draw an arc between the last two lines. Make the arc close to a 2-inch radius (**Figure 8.19**). Constrain the arc radius to 2-inches.
- Use the same procedure to draw an arc between the bottom line and the angled line. Make the arc close to 1.75-inch radius (**Figure 8.20**). Constrain the arc radius to 1.75-inches.
- ***Draw*** a short vertical ***construction line*** up from the Origin (**Figure 8.21**). This line will be the axis for a ***Mirror lines*** command.
- With the ***Select Lines tool***, select all the lines except for the construction line (**Figure 8.22**).
- ***Mirror*** the sketch lines using the construction line for the axis (**Figure 8.23**).

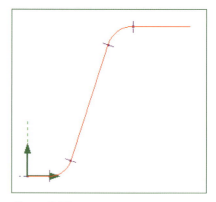

Figure 8.22

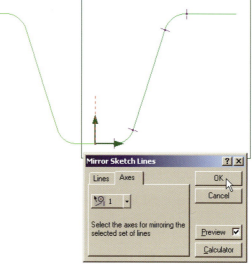

Figure 8.23

- Create a *New Sketch* named *profile* on the *frontal* workplane.
- *Shift+W*
- *Draw* a 1-inch diameter circle centered on the Origin point (*Figure 8.24*).
- Go to the *Features* pull-down menu and select *Sweep Profile*. When the secondary menu opens select *Along Sketch Path*.
- Choose the *profile* sketch for the sketch to use as profile, and the *path* sketch for the sketch to use as path. Click on the Thin option box and enter a thickness of 0.15-inches (*Figure 8.25*).

Figure 8.24

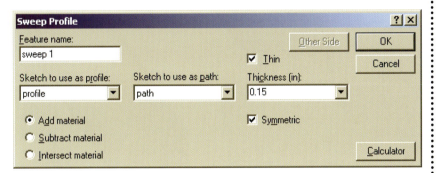

Figure 8.25

- Click *OK*.
- The handlebars model should look like *Figure 8.26*.

Many BMX bicycle handlebars have a brace to reinforce them for additional strength. To add the brace you will use the Project Profile feature.

- Create a *New Sketch* named *brace profile* on the *frontal* workplane.
- *Shift+W*

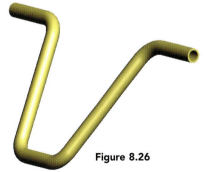

Figure 8.26

280 sweep profile along a path

- **Draw** a diagonal **construction line** up 7-inches from the Origin point. Make sure the angle is 55 degrees (**Figure 8.27**). The end of this construction line will establish the center of the cross-brace.

- **Draw** a 1-inch diameter circle using the end of the construction line as the center (**Figure 8.28** and **8.29**).

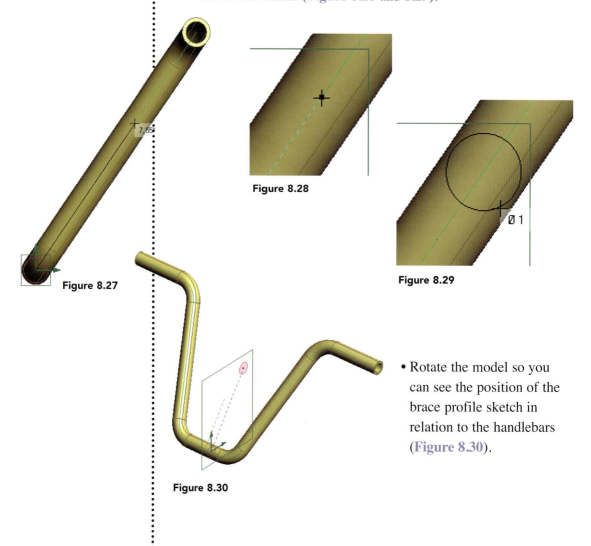

Figure 8.27

Figure 8.28

Figure 8.29

- Rotate the model so you can see the position of the brace profile sketch in relation to the handlebars (**Figure 8.30**).

Figure 8.30

08. Sweep Profile Feature

sweep profile along helix   281

- Use the ***Project Profile*** feature to project the brace profile sketch to the handlebars. Use the options ***symmetrical about workplane*** and ***thru to next face*** (Figure 8.31).

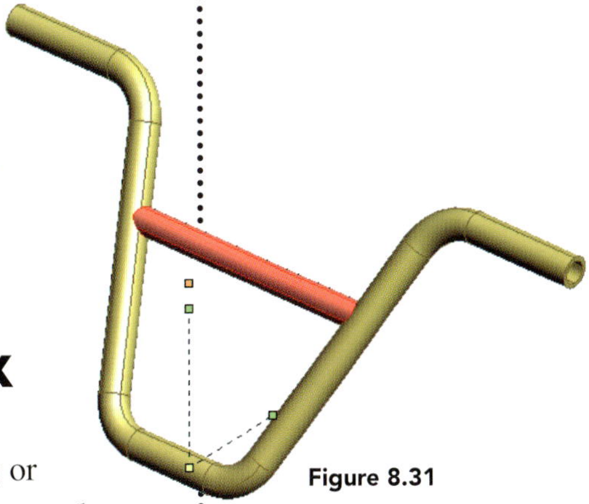

Figure 8.31

Sweep Profile Along Helix

A ***helix*** is a spiral figure, like a coil spring or curl. The threads of a screw form a spiral around a core cylinder (Figure 8.32). The stairs on a spiral staircase form a helix around the center support. Pro/DESKTOP® has a feature that allows you to easily create helical forms.

The ***Sweep Profile Along Helix*** feature is separate but related to the regular Sweep feature. There are two strategies you can use when developing a helix sweep. The first method is to use one sketch for both the axis and the profile. In this case, the axis must be a ***construction line***.

Figure 8.32

The second method is to use two sketches, one for the axis and one for the profile. In this case, the axis can be either a regular line or a construction line.

The dialog box for the ***Sweep Profile Along*** a Helix allows you to choose the sketch that contains the profile (Figure 8.33). The axis is chosen by selecting it with the ***Select Lines*** tool. Sometimes you will have to click twice on the axis to select it (it will turn red when selected).

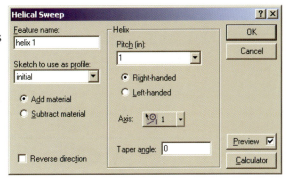

Figure 8.33

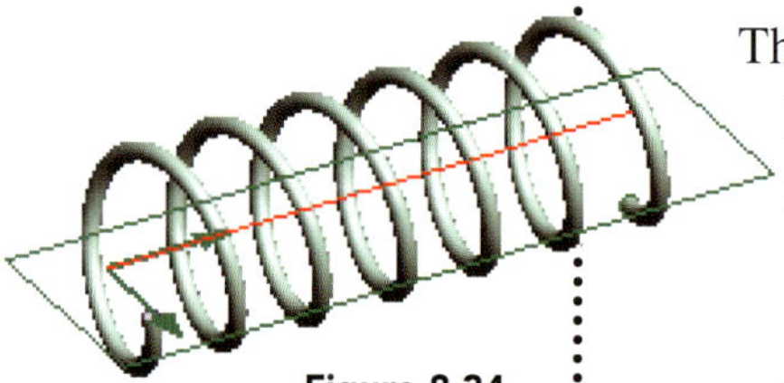

08. Sweep Profile Feature

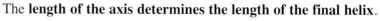

Figure 8.34

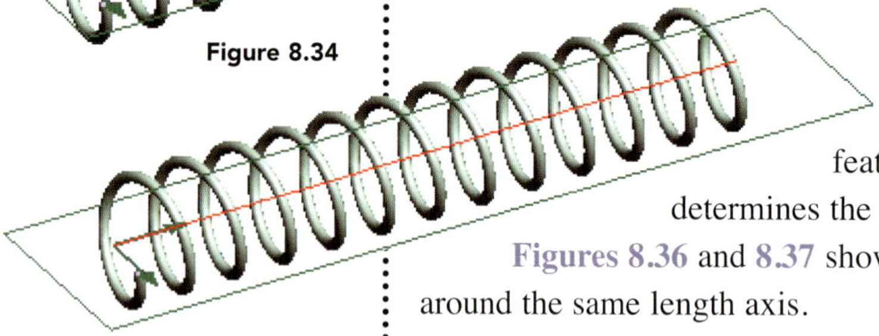

The **length of the axis determines the length of the final helix**. In the spring example shown in Figure 8.34, the axis length is 3-inches. In Figure 8.35, the axis length is 6-inches, so the spring is twice as long.

Figure 8.35

The second drawing required for the Sweep Profile Along a Helix feature is the *profile*. This sketch determines the shape that is swept around the axis. Figures 8.36 and 8.37 show two different profiles swept around the same length axis.

The distance between the axis and the profile shape will also affect the appearance of the solid developed. Figures 8.38 and 8.39 show two helical sweeps. The distance between the axis and the profile is greater on one than the other.

Figure 8.36

Figure 8.37

Figure 8.38

Figure 8.39

The helix shape created also depends upon a factor called the pitch. The concept of pitch is best described by relating it to a screw thread. The distance between the threads (actually, it is the distance between the center of adjoining threads) is the pitch. Figure 8.40 illustrates the concept of pitch. In this figure the screw has a pitch of 0.05-inches, which results in 20 threads-per-inch.

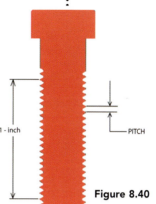

Figure 8.40

The bolt in Figure 8.41 is a Unified National Fine (UNF) thread and the bolt in Figure 8.42 is Unified National Course (UNC) thread. These are standards for thread sizes that have been developed. The UNF thread pitch is about 0.0375-inches and results in 28 threads per inch (tpi). The UNC thread pitch is 0.05-inches and results in 20 tpi. When creating a Sweep Along a Helix, you must specify a pitch. This will become clear when you create the spring in the next section.

Figure 8.41

Figure 8.42

Exercise 8.3 Sweep Profile Along Helix: Coil Spring

This exercise will guide you through a simple spring helix.

- Begin a *New Design*.
- Change *Units* to *inches*.
- *Save* the file as *spring-1.des*.
- *Shift+W* to look down on the active workplane.
- *Change* the name of the *initial* sketch to *axis*.
- *Draw* a 10-inch vertical *construction line* starting from the Origin point. This line will be the axis for the helical sweep.
- Create a *New Sketch* named *profile* on the base workplane.
- *Draw* a 0.25-inch circle, 2-inches to the right of the axis line (Figure 8.43).

Figure 8.43

Figure 8.44

Figure 8.45

- *Shift+T* to change the view to *Trimetric*.
- Go to the *Features* pull-down menu and select *Sweep Profile*. When the secondary menu opens select *Along Helix*.
- In the *Helical Sweep dialog box*, make sure that the *profile* sketch is selected in the profile window and the *axis* sketch is selected in the axis window.
- Enter the value 1-inch in the *Pitch* window.
- Click *OK*. Depending on the speed of your computer, this operation may take a few seconds or longer (Figure 8.44).

Redefine the Helix properties to change the Pitch

- Remember, once you have applied a feature you must *Redefine* to change it.
- Go to the *Browser window* and click and select *Features* from the menu.
- Right mouse-click on *helix 1* so you can redefine its properties. Choose *Redefine* from the list.
- The *Helical Sweep dialog box* reappears.
- Change the Pitch to *2-inches*. Click *OK*.
- *Update* the file (Figure 8.45).

The spring now has fewer turns of the profile because you have changed the distance between adjoining turns from 1-inch to 2-inches.

Redefine the Helix properties to change the Taper

- Right mouse-click on *helix 1* in the Browser window so you can *Redefine* its properties.
- *Change* the *pitch* back to 1-inch.

- The Taper angle is now *0 degrees* (no taper). Change the Taper to *5 degrees*.
- Click *OK* to close the dialog box.
- *Update* the file (Figure 8.46).

The spring now gets narrower toward the top.

Exercise 8.4 Sweep Profile Along Helix: Archimedes Screw

Archimedes was a Greek mathematician who lived over two thousand years ago. Today, we would also call him a technologist and designer because he thought up many very creative and practical ideas. The screw pump is thought to be one of his designs. It is constructed of a screw inside a hollow cylinder and used to move water for irrigation.

Figure 8.46

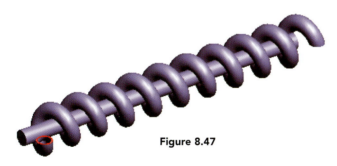

Figure 8.47

In this design you will make a modified Archimedes Screw. It will use two workplanes, although both sketches for the sweep feature will be located on the base workplane. The second workplane will be used to create the cylinder that runs down the center of the screw. The model will be developed at a one-tenth scale.

286 sweep profile along helix

08. Sweep Profile Feature

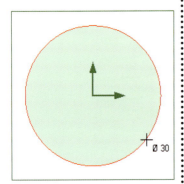

Figure 8.48

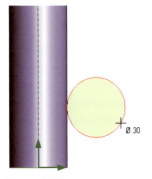

Figure 8.50

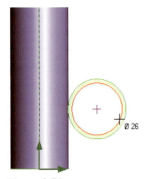

Figure 8.51

- Begin a *New Design*.
- Make sure you are working in *millimeters*.
- *Save* the file as *archimedes screw.des*.
- Change the name of the initial sketch on the base workplane to *axis*.
- *Draw* a 600mm vertical *construction* line from the Origin.
- Create a *New Sketch* named *core* on the *frontal* workplane.
- *Draw* a 30mm circle centered on the Origin of the core sketch (Figure 8.48).
- *Extrude* the circle to 600mm below the workplane (Figure 8.49).
- Create a *New Sketch* named *profile* on the *base* workplane.
- *Shift+W*

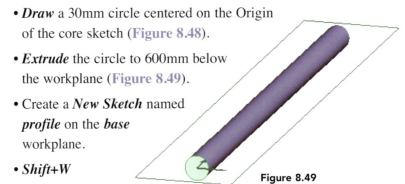

Figure 8.49

- Zoom in on the bottom portion of the core extrusion.
- *Draw* a 30mm diameter circle with the center 30mm to the right and 30mm above the Origin point (Figure 8.50).
- *Draw* a second circle 26mm in diameter, concentric with the first (Figure 8.51).
- Go to the *Features* pull-down menu and select *Sweep Profile*. When the secondary menu opens select *Along Helix*.
- In the *Helical Sweep dialog box*, make sure that the *profile* sketch is selected in the profile window and the *axis* sketch is selected in the axis window.
- Enter the value 60mm in the *Pitch* window.

- Click **OK** to close the dialog box (**Figure 8.52**).
- **Save** your work.

The Archimedes Screw works by immersing one end in water at a shallow angle. (As the screw turns, water moves along its length and gets trapped in the lower part of the screw.) Eventually, water comes out the other end. This Archimedes screw will not work if the angle of the screw is too steep.

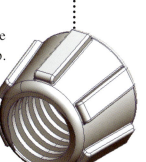

Figure 8.52

Exercise 8.5 Sweep Profile Along Helix: Acme Thread

An acme thread is one that has a flat top and bottom, like the thread you see if you unscrew the handle of a broom or mop. Acme threads are generally stronger than conventional threads and are also used as lead screws on lathes and other machine tools, as well as on propane gas tank connections. This exercise will take you through the steps of modeling the propane tank nut pictured in **Figure 8.53**.

- Begin a **New Design**.

Figure 8.53

- Change **Units** to **millimeters**.
- **Save** the file as **propanenut.des**.
- Create a **New Sketch** named **nutbody** on the **frontal** workplane.
- **Shift+W**
- **Draw** a 38mm circle centered on the Origin point.
- **Extrude** the circle sketch to 40mm with a -8 degree (minus 8) taper, below workplane (**Figure 8.54**).
- Create a **New Sketch** named **hole** on the **frontal** workplane.
- **Draw** a 28mm circle centered on the Origin point.
- **Extrude** the circle 33mm, subtract material, below workplane (**Figure 8.55**).

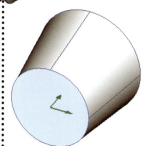

Figure 8.54

Figure 8.55

288 sweep profile along helix

Figure 8.56

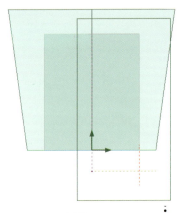

Figure 8.57

- Change the name of the *initial* sketch (on the base workplane) to *central axis*. Double-click on it to make it the active sketch (bold) in the Browser window.
- *Shift+W*.
- Beginning 6mm below the Origin point, *draw* a vertical construction line 39mm long (step not shown).
- Create a *New Sketch* named *thread profile* on the *base* workplane.
- *Draw* a horizontal *construction line* from the bottom of the central axis to the right past the edge of the nut body (**Figure 8.56**). This construction line will serve as the axis for a Mirror command for the thread profile.
- Change the view to *transparent* so you can see the extruded interior hole.
- *Draw* a second construction line down from the edge of the extruded hole past the horizontal construction line. This will identify the edge of the inside hole (**Figure 8.57**).
- *Draw* the half thread profile in **Figure 8.58**. Make sure it overlaps just to the left of the hole edge construction line in the previous step. You will need to zoom in to do this step.

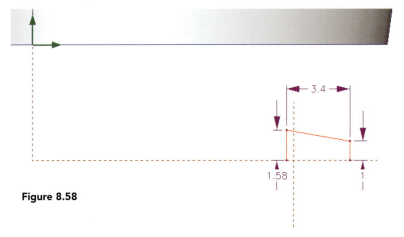

Figure 8.58

sweep profile along helix

- ***Mirror*** the three sketch lines using the horizontal construction line as the axis.
- ***Sweep*** the ***thread profile*** sketch ***around a helix*** using the ***central axis*** as the axis. Use 5.25mm as the ***pitch*** (**Figure 8.59**).

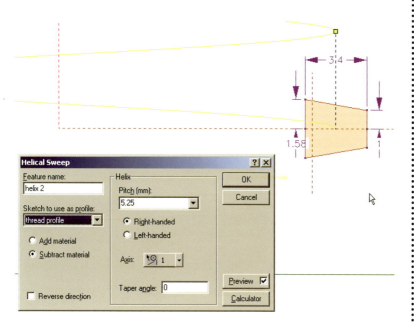

Figure 8.59

Figure 8.60

- Change the view to ***transparent*** and rotate the model to see the inside threads (**Figure 8.60**).
- ***Save*** your work.
- Create an ***Offset Workplane*** 18.5mm above the base workplane (**Figure 8.61**).

Figure 8.61

Figure 8.62

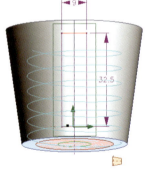

Figure 8.64

- Place a *New Sketch* named *angle axis* on the offset workplane.
- *Draw* a short *construction line* perpendicular to the central axis (Figure 8.62). This axis will make it possible to create an angled workplane.
- Select the *angle axis* construction line and go to the *Workplanes* pull-down menu. Choose *New Workplane* from the list.
- With the *Angled* radio button selected, enter a value of 8 degrees for the Angle (Figure 8.63). Click *OK*.

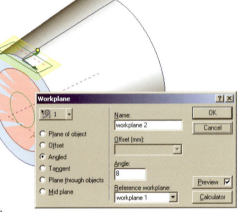

Figure 8.63

- Create a *New Sketch* named *bump* on the angled workplane.
- *Shift+W* to look directly down on the angled workplane.
- *Draw* a rectangle 9mm wide by 32.5mm long centered on the central axis when viewed from above (Figure 8.64). Center the sketch so it is equidistance from both the front and the back of the model. You can do this by eye.
- *Extrude* the rectangle to 4mm (Figure 8.65).

Figure 8.65

08. Sweep Profile Feature

sweep profile along helix

- **Round** the front and back of the extrusion to a 2mm radius (**Figure 8.66**).
- **Round** the sides of the extrusion to a 1mm radius (**Figure 8.67**).
- **Round** the edges of the extrusion where it meets the body of the model to a 0.5mm radius (**Figure 8.68**).
- **Round** the front and back of the model body to a 3mm radius (**Figure 8.69**). You may need to use a smaller valve if you get an error message.
- **Save** your work.

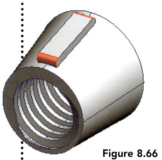

Figure 8.66

Figure 8.67

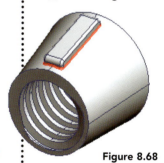

Figure 8.68

You will now group several features you have applied so that they can be treated together.

- Go to the **Browser window** and select **Features** from the pull-down menu.
- Hold down the **Shift** key and select the extrusion that created the bump, and the three Round features that you applied to round the edges of the bump.
- When you have the four features selected, right mouse-click and select **Group** from the floating menu (**Figure 8.70**). The word Group appears in the Feature menu along with a new icon.

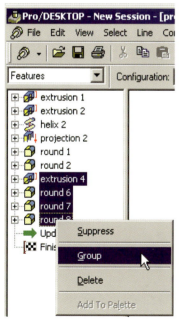

Figure 8.70

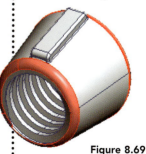

Figure 8.69

- Select the *Group* icon and right mouse-click. Choose *Pattern* from the floating menu (**Figure 8.71**).

- The dialog box for *Pattern* appears (**Figure 8.72**). You need to tell the Pattern command that you want to duplicate the group of features around the body of the model.

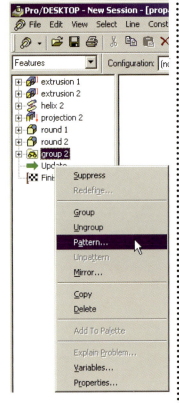

Figure 8.71

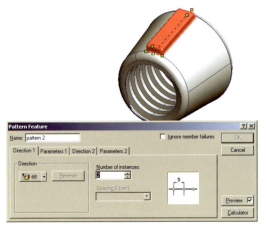

Figure 8.72

- Click on the down arrow in the Direction box and choose *Edges* from the list (**Figure 8.73**).

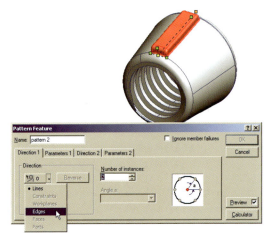

Figure 8.73

- Use the *Edge Select tool* and select the edge of the model at the Round feature just in front of the bump. Fill in 6 for the number of instances and 60 for the angle (**Figure 8.74**).

Figure 8.74

The propane tank nut should now look like **Figure 8.75**.

- *Save* your work.

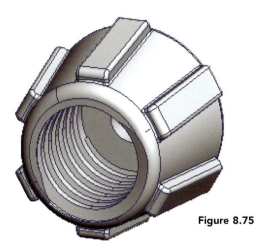

Figure 8.75

Summary

The Sweep Profile feature is actually two features: **Sweep along a path** and **Sweep along a helix**. While the **Sweep along a path** can create a solid or remove material from a solid along a wide variety of path shapes, the **Sweep along a helix** only creates "coil-spring-like" solids of different profile shapes, or removes material from a solid in a similar manner.

Sweep features require both an axis and a profile. In the case of the **Sweep along a helix**, the axis and profile can reside on the same sketch if the axis is a construction line. Also, the length of the axis will determine the length of the helix.

When using the **Sweep along a path** feature, separate sketches for the axis and the profile must be used. The profile must intersect the path at 90 degrees.

Test Your Knowledge

Project 8.1 Padlock

design brief Design and model a combination padlock using the Sweep feature for the hasp.

Specifications

- Create the padlock as one file, not an assembly.
- Develop a round combination dial with 30 possible increments with the numbers 0, 5, 10, 15, 20, and 25. The remaining increments should be small extruded lines.
- Make the hasp 5/16-inches in diameter.

Project 8.2 Bicycle Frame

design brief Design and model the parts for a bicycle frame using the Sweep feature.

Specifications

- Create one file as the frame.
- Use an actual bicycle frame as a guide for the sizes of the components.

Project 8.3 Bicycle Handlebars

design brief Design and model handlebars for the bicycle frame developed in Project 8.1.

Specifications

- Take size and shape from existing bicycle handlebars.
- Avoid trying to develop a path in more than one plane. Modify the existing bicycle handlebar design for one plane.

Project 8.4 Handlegrips

design brief Design and create a handle grip for the model *handlebars.des*.

Specifications

- The grip must be the correct size to fit snugly over the handlebar ends. If made from pliable plastic material, the inside diameter of the grip would be slightly smaller than the outside diameter of the bars. This is called an interference fit.
- The grip should be long enough to accommodate a normal sized hand, and of appropriate thickness to provide some cushion for the shock forces that travel up through the handlebars.

- One end of the grip must close off the end of the handlebar to prevent dirt from entering the tube. A small vent hole should be included so that air can escape when the grips are pushed onto the bars.
- The inside end of the grip should prevent the rider's hand from sliding in toward the center of the bars.
- Some provision for resisting hand slippage should be incorporated into the design, such as ribs or other textures.
- The grip should be assembled to the handlebars (add same grip twice) in a new, empty design file. **Save** file as **handle assembly.des**.
- Render the final assembly applying appropriate materials. **Save** the rendering as **handlebar render.alb**.

Project 8.5 Archimedes Screw Support

design brief Design and develop a scaled support for the Archimedes Screw in Exercise 8.3. The model will be used in a museum display of ancient inventions.

Specifications

- Investigate the Archimedes Screw to find pictures and descriptions that will help you in your design.
- The material of the support will be wood timber.
- The lower end of the screw will be submerged in water when in use.
- The support should hold the screw at a 20 degree angle and allow it to turn on the axis of the central core. Some provision for bearing each end (so the screw can rotate) should be incorporated in the design.
- On the upper end of the core a crank of suitable proportions for human operation should be incorporated into the design.
- The whole frame should be braced to make it sturdy.
- The support file should be saved as **arch support.des**.
- The support and the archimedes.des file should be assembled in a file named **archimedesfinished.des**.
- The final assembly file should be rendered with appropriate materials in the **Album** and saved as **archimedes rend.alb**.

09

animation

09. Animation

Introduction

Pro/DESKTOP® allows you to create animations of your designs by changing variables. You can also animate the relationship between components in an assembly. Animation is a multi-step process that involves identifying the variables, creating a number of different configurations and assigning values to the variables for each constraint. Once you have a number of configurations that you want to animate, the remaining steps are straightforward.

To understand animation in Pro/DESKTOP you must first understand the concept of variables.

Variables

Variables are constraints and characteristics of a part, or the relationship among parts in an assembly. For example, a part may be designed with an extrusion. The length of the extrusion becomes a variable. It is a variable because the exact distance of the extrusion is specified in the extrusion dialog box, whether the distance has been entered from the keyboard or the extrusion handle in the sketch has been dragged with the mouse. Also, the taper angle is a variable, even though in most cases it remains zero. Pro/DESKTOP® keeps track of variables in case you want to use them.

Pro/DESKTOP calls variables that are created when you apply a feature (such as Extrude, Project Profile, Revolve, Loft and Round Edges) **System-defined variables**. System-defined variables also include length (which includes diameter and radius because Pro/DESKTOP calls any distance dimension value *length*), angle,

---

Did you know?

Variables are constraints that can be changed.

Configurations are combinations of variables.

density, and a suppressed or unsuppressed feature. Figure 9.1 shows some of the variables for a simple cube with rounded edges.

When you dimension the length and width of a rectangle sketch, for example, both of these values become variables, usually with names such as length 1 and length 2. If you plan to use these variables later, it is a good idea to change the variable names to something you will recognize, such as ***base length*** and ***base width***.

Figure 9.1

If you draw a rectangle and do not constrain it with the ***Sketch Dimension*** tool, the program will not treat the length and width of the rectangle as variables. You must dimension these distances for them to become variables.

Mass Properties Variables

Some variables must be activated before they are available for use. All variables that relate to mass, volume, density and center of gravity are only active if you have looked at them. If you look back at Figure 9.1 you will notice that there is no "+" next to the Measurements folder. This means that no Measurements variables are active. To activate these variables, go to the ***Tools*** pull-down menu and choose ***New Measurement*** and then from the sub-menu choose ***Mass Properties*** (Figure 9.2).

Figure 9.2

The window that opens (Figure 9.3) contains information related to the physical characteristics of the solid model. Note the Center of Gravity (CG) locations for the cube. The cube is 2-inches on each side so the location of the CG is in the center of the cube. Using the 3 axes (X, Y, Z), the location of the CG is 1-inch from one edge of the

Figure 9.3

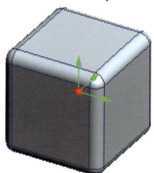

Figure 9.4

base (X), 1-inch from the other edge of the base (Y), and 1-inch above the base (Z). If you drag the dialog box away from the center of the screen, you can see the CG located as a red dot with three green arrows that represent the three axes (**Figure 9.4**).

When you click the **OK** button to close the Mass Measurements dialog box, these characteristics are now available as variables. To open the Variables window go to the **Tools** pull-down menu and choose **Variables**. A look at the rounded-edge cube variables shows that the measurement variables are now available (**Figure 9.5**).

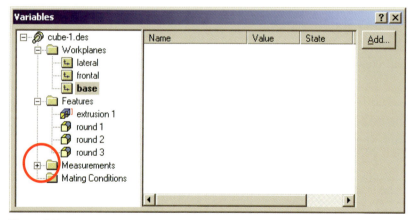

Figure 9.5

Click on the "+" sign next to Measurements in the Variables window and you will see a list of the variables that Pro/DESKTOP® tracks for the cube solid (**Figure 9.6**). Some of the most useful variables are the volume (in this case cubic inches) and surface area (square inches) of the cube. These measurements can be used to help design liquid containers, from bottles to swimming pools.

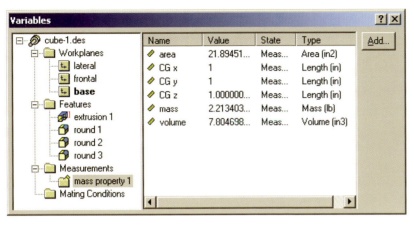

Figure 9.6

The Center of Gravity (CG) measurements may be useful in the design of tools, clothes irons or other devices that would be awkward to use if the CG point was not carefully located. Model rockets and CO_2 vehicles are unstable if the CG is not in the appropriate location.

Variables and Animations

Animations are created by changing variables. For example, changing the distance of an extrusion would result in a change in the length of the tape protruding from the tape measure in **Figure 9.7**. The Variables window in **Figure 9.8** shows the value of the ***length of tape*** to be 2-inches (top row). Notice that it is easy to spot the correct variable because the names of the extrusions have been changed. Look back at **Figure 9.1** and you will see what variables look like when they have not been changed. It is especially important to rename variables if you are planning to create animations.

Figure 9.7

09. Animation

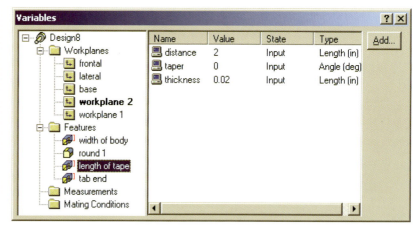

Figure 9.8

You can change a variable directly by clicking on the value in the right side of the Variables window. In **Figure 9.9** the value of the

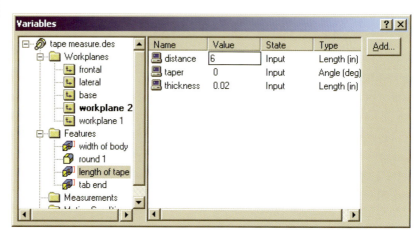

Figure 9.9

length of tape distance has been changed from 2-inches to 6-inches. The variable window is closed by clicking on the X in the upper right

corner of the window. After updating, the tape measure looks like
Figure 9.10. Although the ***length of tape*** variable has been changed
by hand, it may also be changed to create an animation.

Another simple example of a variable is the number of degrees a
profile has been revolved with the Revolve Profile feature. The bell
profile has been revolved only partially (about 30 degrees) in
Figure 9.11. In **Figure 9.12** it has been revolved a
full 360 degrees. An animation can be created that
shows the bell beginning as a narrow profile and
revolving into a 3D bell (and back again to a narrow
sliver, if you would like).

Figure 9.10

Figure 9.11

Figure 9.12

09. Animation

The next exercise will give you first-hand experience with variables and how to access them.

Exercise 9.1 Model Railroad Crossing Gate
To become familiar with variables, try this exercise

- Start a *New Design*.
- *Units = inches*.
- *Save* the file as *gate.des*.
- Create a *New Sketch* named *lever sketch* on the *frontal workplane*.
- *Draw* an 8-inch horizontal line from the Origin to the right.
- Starting 0.5-inches above the Origin, *draw* a second 8-inch line to the right but this time angle it down 2 degrees (-2°), as in **Figure 9.13**.

Figure 9.13

- *Zoom in* on the right side and draw a vertical line from the bottom line to the top line.
- *Delete* the very small line segment that hangs out to the right from the top line (**Figure 9.14**).

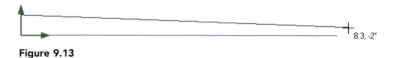

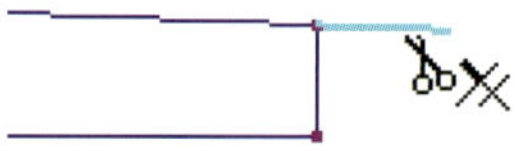

Figure 9.14

- On the left side of the sketch, complete the profile by drawing a vertical line connecting the top and bottom lines. The sketch should fill (**Figure 9.15**).

Figure 9.15

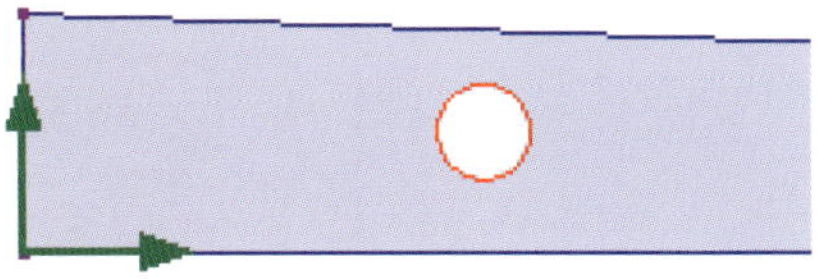

- **Draw** a small circle 0.2-inches in diameter with its center 1-inch to the right of the Origin and 0.2-inches above the bottom line (**Figure 9.16**). Use the Snap to Grid as a guide.
- **Extrude** the sketch to 0.25-inches.
- **Save** your work.

Figure 9.16

You have created a simple part with a hole near one end. Now let's look at the variables Pro/DESKTOP® has kept of your work.

- Go to the **Tools** pull-down menu at the top of the screen and select **Variables** from the menu. A floating window called Variables appears. The window has a Browser on the left side (**Figure 9.17**). On the right side the window appears empty but there are four headings: Name, Value, State and Type. Each variable will have these four characteristics.

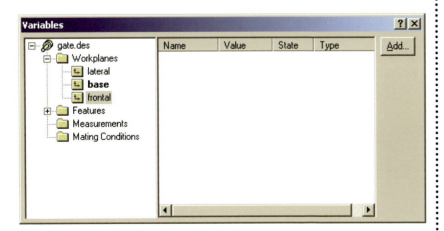

Figure 9.17

- Click on the top icon (the small shaft and pulley). Eight variables are listed in the right side of the window but only one

09. Animation

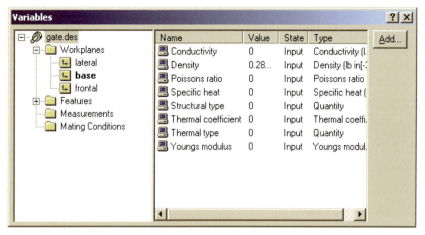

Figure 9.18

variable, ***density***, has a value (**Figure 9.18**). The reason these variables have no value is because the material properties of the model have not been set.

- Close the ***Variables*** dialog box by clicking on the ***X*** in the upper right corner.

- You can set these properties by going to the ***Assembly*** pull-down menu and choosing ***Set Material Properties*** at the bottom of the menu. A new dialog box appears.

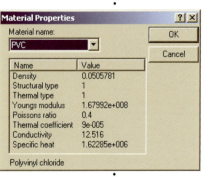

Figure 9.19

- The model railroad crossing gate will be made from plastic so choose ***PVC*** from the pull-down list (**Figure 9.19**). Although this is not a necessary step in this exercise, you should know that it is possible to specify the material characteristics of a solid model. These variables can be used in engineering calculations, but they will not help us with animation.

- ***Close*** the ***Material Properties*** dialog box.

- Open the *Variables* dialog box again (*Tools > Variables*).
- Click on the icons next to *Workplanes, base, frontal,* and *lateral*. You will get no results in the right window. This is because no variables were assigned when you created the sketch for the gate. Had you dimensioned any of the lines in the sketch, those constraints would have appeared in this section.
- Click on the icon next to *Features*. Still no results in the window.
- Now click on the "+" sign next to the Features icon. One feature was used to create the lever: an extrusion. The extrusion should appear under the Features folder.
- Click on the extrusion icon (Figure 9.20). Two variables now appear in the right window: ***distance and taper***. Note that both of these variables are ***input*** variables. Input variables are those that result from redefining or changing a feature or length measurement. ***Output variables*** are not something you can change directly. They result from the application of Design Rules, so we are not going to bother with them here.

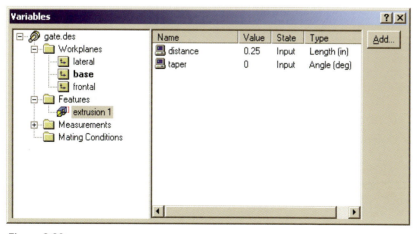

Figure 9.20

- Note that the value of *0.25* appears in the value column for extrusion distance. This is the value you entered in the Extrusion dialog box when creating the model.

Only three variables were assigned for the lever: density, extrusion distance and taper angle.

- Close the Variables window by clicking on the X in the upper right corner.
- *Shift+W*
- Use the keyboard shortcut *Z* to access the **Sketch Dimension** tool.
- Constrain the length of the sketch rectangle with the **Sketch Dimension** tool (**Figure 9.21**).

Figure 9.21

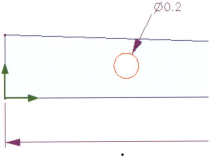

Figure 9.22

- Constrain the circle diameter by clicking once on the circle to select it and then click and drag to dimension it (**Figure 9.22**).
- Update the file and *Save*.
- Go to the *Tools* pull-down menu at the top of the screen and select **Variables** from the menu. The Variables floating window appears.
- Click on the icons next to **Workplanes, base, frontal**, and *lateral*. When you click on the frontal workplane, the variables diameter 1 and length 1 will appear in the right side of the window, along with the values and other characteristics. Because

you have constrained the length of the gate and the circle, variables for these values now appear.

- Close the Variables window.

Next you will change the names of the variables so they are more easily identified in the list.

- Using the *Select Constraints* tool, double-click on the circle constraint. A floating window called *Properties* appears.

- Change the name of the variable to *axle hole diameter* (**Figure 9.24**).

- Click *OK* to close the window.

- With the *Select Constraints* tool, double-click on the long dimension. Change the variable name to *gate length*.

- Click *OK* to close the window.

- Again, open the *Variables* dialog box. You will see the names of the variables you just entered (**Figure 9.25**). Close the dialog box.

- *Save* the file.

Figure 9.24

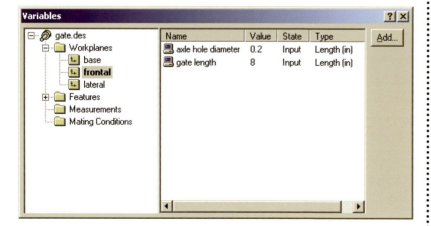

Figure 9.25

It is always a good idea to re-name variables so you can easily find them later in the variables list. This will save you a lot of time on more complex models when you are searching for a particular variable you would like to use in a configuration or animation.

Variables from Assembly Constraints

Variables also include the relationships among parts in an assembly. A proper assembly includes assembly constraints such as **Align, Mate, Offset, Center Axes**, and **Orient**. When these assembly constraints are made, you have access to them as variables in an animation. For example, if you create an offset mate of zero (instead of just a mate) the two parts will be touching. You can then change the zero value to a positive number and make the two parts fly apart.

Figure 9.26

The pneumatic cylinder in Figure 9.26 was assembled from a number of individual part files: a cylinder, end caps, bolts, nuts and a piston. During assembly, the parts were constrained with both Center Axes constraints and Offset Mate constraints. In Figure 9.27 the assembly has been "exploded" by changing the value of the Offset Mate constraints.

Figure 9.28

Another assembly variable that is handy for animation is the **Orient** constraint. Orient specifies the angle between two surfaces or edges. To animate the motion of a railroad crossing gate, you would select the underside surface of the gate and the vertical surface of the gate support and orient them to 90 degrees (Figure 9.28). Changing the orient value to 60 degrees raises the gate (Figure 9.29).

Figure 9.29

Figure 9.27

Configurations

Configurations allow you to use variables to change characteristics of your designs without losing your original work. For example, the toaster in **Figure 9.30** has two openings on the top for bread. You could create your design and save it, and then see what it would look like if it were wider (to accommodate rolls or bagels), longer, higher, had larger openings, etc. (**Figure 9.31**). For each change, or combination of changes, you could create a configuration. Each configuration would have a different value for one or more variables, such as extrusion distances, length of sketch lines, diameter or radius of arcs, and other characteristics.

Figure 9.30

To create different configurations for a model, go to the ***Tools*** pull-down menu and click on ***Configurations***. The ***Configurations*** dialog box appears (**Figure 9.32**).

Figure 9.31

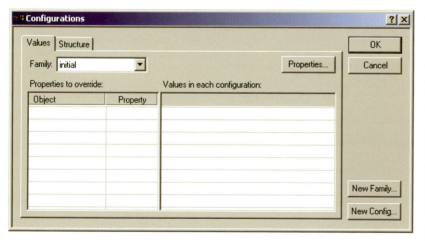

Figure 9.32

09. *Animation*

In order to create configurations you will have to change the value of a variable. Right now, no variables can be seen in the Configurations window. Note that on the left side the column is labeled "properties to override." The first thing that needs to be done is to have some property (variable) in that column. The following exercise will help you learn how to create a configuration.

Exercise 9.2 Configurations

- Start a *New Design*.
- Make sure you are working in *inches*.
- *Save* the file as *gate support.des*.
- Create a *New Sketch* called *support base* on the *base workplane*.
- *Shift+W*.
- *Draw* a rectangle *2.5 x 1.5 inches* (Figure 9.33).
- *Extrude* the sketch *0.3-inches* Change the Feature name to *base height* in the dialog box (Figure 9.34).

Figure 9.33

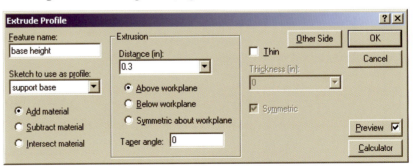

Figure 9.34

- *Round* the four edges 0.2-inch radius.
- *Round* the top edges 0.1-inch radius (Figure 9.35).

Figure 9.35

- *Select* the top face of the base and create a *New Sketch* named *post*.
- *Draw* a rectangle 1.2-inches by 0.6-inches centered on the base.
- *Constrain* the length and width of the rectangle using the *Sketch Dimension* tool (Figure 9.36). Re-name the 1.2-inch variable to *support width* and the 0.6-inch variable to *support depth*.

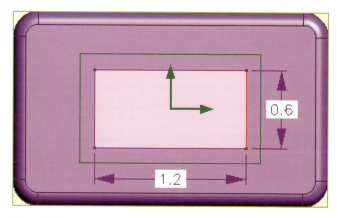

Figure 9.36

- *Extrude* the rectangle sketch to 2-inches. Change the Feature name to *support height* in the dialog box.
- *Round* the two narrow top edges to a radius of 0.4-inches.
- *Round* the sides to a radius of 0.1-inch (Figure 9.37).
- Create a *New Sketch* named *axle hole* on the side of the post.
- *Draw* a 0.2-inch diameter circle 0.6-inches above the Origin (Figure 9.38).
- *Project* the profile of the circle, subtracting material, through the support.

Figure 9.37

Figure 9.38

09. Animation

You are going to create three different configurations for the post, so you can see which one you like best.

- Go to the ***Tools*** pull-down menu and select ***Configurations*** from the list. The Configurations window appears.
- Click on the ***Properties*** button. A new floating ***Add/Remove Properties*** window appears. The variables in the left window are ***Available*** for use in ***Configurations***.
- Move the cursor over the line that divides the ***Object*** column from the ***Property*** column in the Available window. The cursor changes (**Figure 9.39**). Drag the column to the right to reveal the complete text of the variable names in the Object column. This will make it easier to find variable names.

Figure 9.39

- In the ***Available*** window (left) find ***base height/distance*** (one of the extrusions you renamed) and click on it to highlight it. Then,

Figure 9.40

click on the right arrow in the center of the dialog box. The variable ***base height/distance*** now appears on the right in the ***Selected*** window of the dialog box (**Figure 9.40**).

- Click ***OK*** to close the window.

You are now back to the ***Configurations*** window. The next step is to create the three configurations you will use to make your first animation.

- Click on the ***New Config*** button on the lower right side of the Configurations dialog box.

- A new floating dialog box appears (**Figure 9.41**). You do not need to rename the configuration, so just click ***OK***.

- Repeat the previous step to create a total of three "configs."

- Notice that the value of the extrusion distance is ***0.3*** in all three configurations (**Figure 9.42**).

- To change a value for ***config 2*** click once in the cell underneath. Change the value for ***config 2*** to ***0.5*** and ***config 3*** to ***0.7*** (these values are in inches and will change the height of the base). Leave the value for ***config 1*** at ***0.3*** (**Figure 9.43**).

Figure 9.41

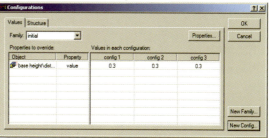

Figure 9.42

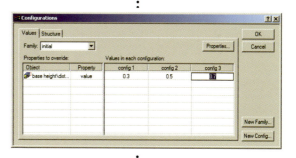

Figure 9.43

09. Animation

• Click on **OK** to close the Configurations window.

• **Save** your work.

Now you will check to see what the gate support looks like in all three configurations.

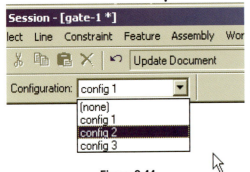

Figure 9.44

• Move the cursor to the top of the Design window and click on the Configurations pull-down menu arrow next to the word **none** (**Figure 9.44**). You will see a choice of three configurations or none. Choose **config 1** and **Update** (green traffic light) if necessary. You should see no change because you left the value of base height as 0.3-inches in this configuration (**Figure 9.45**).

Figure 9.45

• Choose **config 2** and **Update** the file. You should see the gate support base become thicker and look like **Figure 9.46**. This configuration had a value of 0.5-inches for the base height extrusion.

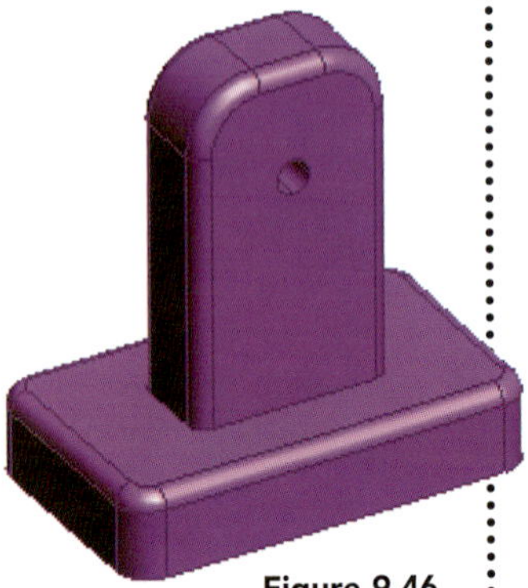

• Choose **config 3** and **Update** the file. The gate support should now look like **Figure 9.47**.

Figure 9.46

Figure 9.47

Note that the hole seems to have moved lower. Actually, it has remained in the same location relative to the base workplane and it is the post that has extended higher. If you want the hole to remain the same distance from the top of the support, you will need to constraint that distance on the ***axle hole*** sketch.

- Go back to the ***axle hole*** sketch, and dimension the distance from the center of the hole to the top of the post (**Figure 9.48**). This will keep the hole located the same distance from the top of the post in all configurations.

Also, note that the post extrusion remains the same height. This is because the profile was drawn on a sketch created on the top face of the base. Since the base was raised, that sketch was too.

When creating new configurations, you will discover that many variables are affected by other variables, as in the case of the hole above. It may take you a few tries to get all the variables and constraints right to create the configurations you want.

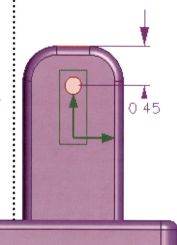

Figure 9.48

You are now ready to create an animation. The animation is simple, as it will just cause the base to grow thicker. Because you have constrained the pin to stay 0.5-inches from the top of the post, it will move as the post grows.

Create an Animation

Creating an animation once the configurations have been set is really easy. First, you will set the "look" of the animation and then go through the steps to create it.

- Click on the ***Select Faces*** tool on the Design Toolbar on the right side of the screen. This will make any sketch lines disappear (**Figure 9.49**). You can also change the view to enhanced, shaded, transparent or wireframe if you would like. For best viewing, however, you will probably want to choose either the enhanced

Figure 9.49

or shaded view. Remember, you can change the color of an object by selecting it with the **Select Parts** tool, a right mouse-click and by choosing **Set Component Color** from the menu (**Figure 9.50**). If you want to set the background color for an animation go to the **Tools** pull-down menu and choose **Options** at the bottom of the menu. You can create a solid color or gradient on the **Appearance** tab.

- Next, go to the **Tools** pull-down menu and select **Animation** from the list.
- A new **Design Animation** floating window will appear.
- Click on the boxes next to *config 1* and *config 3* so a check mark appears in both. If you have many configurations you can use only the ones you want by checking them.

Figure 9.50

Now you will enter the time duration for the animation. Time accumulates, in other words, if you begin at zero for the first configuration and enter 2 seconds for the last configuration. Then, the animation takes 2 seconds. If you have three configurations you might want to enter zero for the first, 1 second for the next configuration and 2 seconds for the third. The number you enter for the time is when, during the animation, you want that configuration to occur. The more seconds between configurations, the slower the animation.

- Click in the cell under **Time** (seconds) next to *config 1* and enter a zero (*0*).
- Click in the cell in the row underneath the zero (next to *config 3*) and enter a *2* (you may have to click twice before you can enter a value).
- Click on the row below once to enter the value (**Figure 9.51**).

09. Animation

create an animation   319

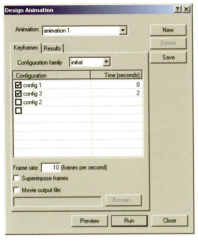

Figure 9.51

- Drag the ***Design Animation*** window out of the way so you can see the post. Use the blue stripe at the top of the window to drag the window.

- Click on the ***Run*** button. The animation may take some time to build.

You may want the animation of the gate support to show the base growing and then returning to the original thickness. In that case, you need to tell the animation to move from ***config 1***, to ***config 3***, and then back to ***config 1*** again.

Figure 9.52

- Click on the empty box at the bottom of the Configuration list. A pull-down menu of all configurations appears. Choose ***config 1*** from the list (**Figure 9.52**).

- Enter new times for the animation, starting at ***0*** for ***config 1***, ***1 second*** for ***config 2***, and ***2 seconds*** for returning to ***config1*** (**Figure 9.53**).

Run the animation again, dragging the dialog box out of the way.

Create an AVI Movie of the Animation

Pro/DESKTOP® enables you to create an AVI movie of your animation. This permits your animation to be saved and viewed by anyone with Windows Media Player. Here are the steps:

- With the ***Animation*** window open, check the boxes next to ***config 1*** and ***config 3*** (if they are not already checked) and enter the times as you did in the previous steps.

Figure 9.53

09. Animation

- Click in the small square window next to *Movie output file*. A check mark appears in the box.
- Click on the *Browse* button to give the AVI file a name and place it on the desktop, hard drive or removable drive. Name the file *test1*.

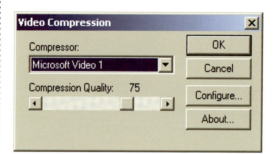

Figure 9.54

- Click on the *Run* button. A floating *Video Compression* window appears (**Figure 9.54**). Leave the defaults as they are and click *OK* to close the window.

- The animation will run and create a file called *test1.avi*.

- Find the *test1.avi* file and double-click on it to view it in Windows Media Player (**Figure 9.55**).

You have animated one variable within a design file. You can animate more than one variable at a time by using the steps you have just completed, including identifying the variables and making configurations that incorporate these variables.

Figure 9.55

Animating Assemblies

Animating assemblies is very much like animating single design files. You need to first create configurations using variables. But there are important differences. In this next exercise, you will assemble the model railroad gate and gate support. Then, create configurations that change the angle of the gate. Finally, you will create an animation of the gate opening and closing.

Exercise 9.3 Assemble the railroad crossing gate

To learn about animating assemblies, you will first need to create an assembly. You will use the *gate.des* and *gate support.des* files. Even if you feel comfortable with assemblies, follow the steps below so you will have the proper variables to animate.

- Start a *New Design*.
- *Save* the file as *gate assembly.des*.
- Using the *Assembly* pull-down menu select *Add Component* at the top of the list.
- Find the files you created previously and double-click on *gate support.des* (it may appear as gate without the *.des*).
- While it is selected, move the *gate support* to the right.
- Fix the position of the *gate support* with the *Fix Component* constraint.
- Again, using the *Assembly* pull-down menu select *Add Component* and choose the file *gate.des* (Figure 9.56).

Figure 9.56

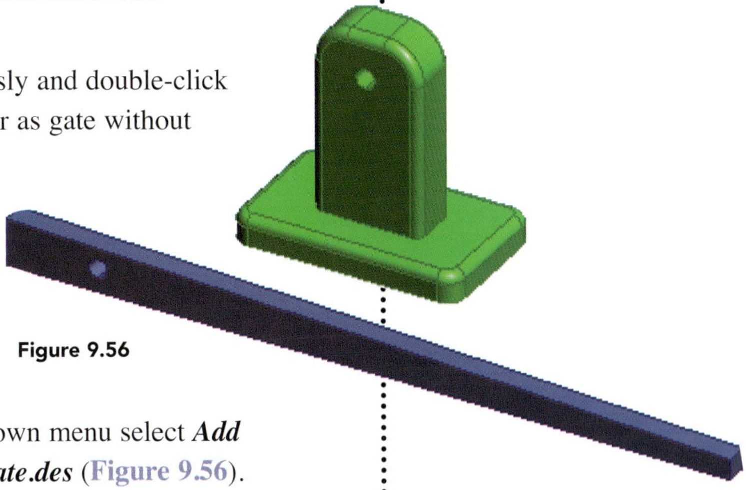

- Using the ***Select Edges*** tool, select the edge of the hole in the ***gate*** and shift-click the edge of the hole on the ***gate support*** (**Figure 9.57**).

- Right mouse-click and select ***Center Axes*** from the floating menu.

- Using the ***Select Faces*** tool, select the two facing surfaces of the ***gate*** and the ***gate support*** and apply a ***Mate*** constraint.

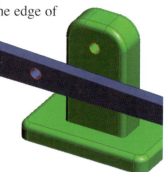

Figure 9.57

- Your assembled railroad crossing gate should look like the one in **Figure 9.58**.

- ***Save*** your work.

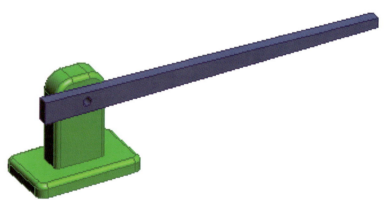

Figure 9.58

To animate the crossing gate you will need to create one more assembly constraint:

- Using the *Select Face*s tool, select the surface on the underside of the gate and the top surface of the support base (**Figure 9.59**).
- Right mouse-click and select *Orient* from the list. A floating Orient window appears.
- The angle value will probably be 180. Pro/DESKTOP® will enter the current angle of the two selected faces.
- Change the *Variable name* to *gate angle*. This will make it easier to pick out this variable from the list when you create configurations (**Figure 9.60**).
- *Save* your work.

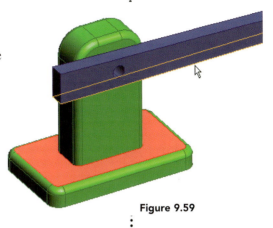

Figure 9.59

Figure 9.60

You could have used other faces to create the Orient constraint, such as the bottom of the lever and the front face of the gate support (**Figure 9.61**). If you selected these two surfaces, then the original Orient angle would be 90 degrees, with the gate in a horizontal position. Often, you have several alternatives to choose from when creating orient assembly constraints.

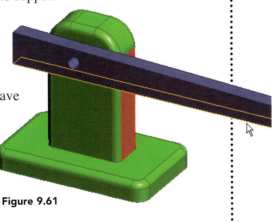

Figure 9.61

You are now ready to create configurations for the animation.

- Go to the *Tools* pull-down menu and select *Configurations*.
- Click on the *Properties* button to access the *Add/Remove Properties* window.
- In the list on the left side of the window, select *gate angle\angle* (Figure 9.62).
- Click on the right arrow to put it in the *Selected* list.
- Click *OK* to close the *Add/Remove Properties* window.
- Create two configurations by clicking the *New Config* button twice (you need to click *OK* in the window that appears each time).
- Leave 180 for the value in *config 1* but change the angle value of *config 2* to *230* (Figure 9.63).
- Click on the *OK* button to close the *Configurations* window.
- Test the configurations by using the *Configurations* button on the top toolbar. Click on the word (*none*) in the small window and you will see *config 1* and *config 2*. Choose each and see what happens to the gate (Figure 9.64).

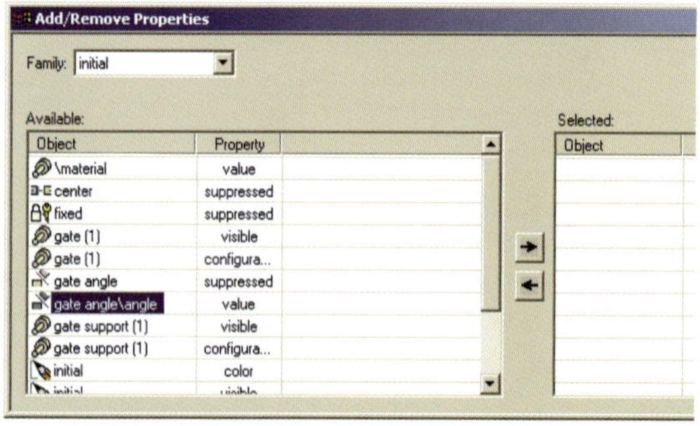

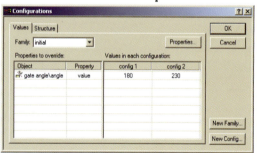

Figure 9.62

Figure 9.63

Figure 9.64

Animate the Gate

Make sure that (*none*) is selected in the pull-down *Configurations* menu above the Design window before you start.

- Go to the *Tools* pull-down menu and select *Animation* from the list.
- Click on the boxes next to *config 1* and *config 2* to check them.
- Enter a time of *0* for *config 1* and *3* for *config 2* in the *Time* column. The animation will take 3 seconds to complete.

This time, you will make the animation go through a complete cycle of down/up/down by using the first and the second configurations, and then the first one again to bring the gate back to the starting point.

- Click on third box under *config 2*. You will get a pull-down list with both configs. Choose *config 1*.
- Put a check in the box next to this new *config 1*.
- Enter a time of *6* next to this third config. (**Figure 9.65**).
- Click on *Run* and watch what happens.
- You can make another AVI movie of this animation. Use the same steps as you did before but give this animation the name *gate action.avi*.

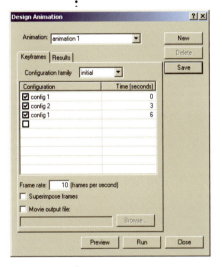

Figure 9.65

Summary

In this chapter you were introduced to variables and configurations. Variables are really the constraints applied and characteristics of a component or the relationship among components in an assembly. Some variables must be activated before they can be used. Activation is usually done by simply viewing the variables, as in the case of mass properties.

The key to successful animation lies in using constraints (variables), such as dimensions, and the assembly constraints of mate, align, center axes, offset and orient. These constraints can then be changed to create an animation. It is important to re-name constraints so you can identify later the ones you want to animate.

A designed part or assembly, with all its constraints, forms one configuration. By changing one or more of these constraints another configuration of the part is created. An example of one configuration is the measuring tape in **Figure 9.7**. This configuration specified the tape length as 2-inches. A second configuration of the same measuring tape can be made where the tape length is 6-inches (**Figure 9.10**). Animations are created when a part or an assembly moves between the configurations you have developed, in this case, the tape "grows" in length from 2-inches to 6-inches. Animations fill in the gaps between the two configurations with a series of intermediate steps. The more time specified between configurations in the Design Animation dialog box, the more slowly the animation takes place.

Test Your Knowledge

Project 9.1 Animate the file penassembly.des

Exercise 7.1 in Chapter 7 was the development of parts of a pen and then the assembly of those parts. Besides the Center Axes constraint, one Offset Align and one Offset Mate constraints were used.

design brief Create an animation that will cause the parts of the pen to "explode" apart and then come back together. Make the components return to their assembled position more slowly than they "explode."

Project 9.2 Create a flip-phone and animate

A major cellular network provider would like to advertise a new cell phone to potential customers in a TV ad. The ad would showcase an animation of their new phone opening and closing.

design brief Design and model a contemporary looking flip-phone and animate it.

Specifications:
- Flip-phone should be about the same size as current cell phones.
- Flip-phone should have a display and all the keys necessary to dial and use the phone.
- Animation should be in a *.avi* format.
- Make the model in at least two files and assemble.

10

design evolution, animation & style projects

10. Design Evolution, Animation & Style Projects

In this chapter you will learn how to:

- Apply what you have learned in the creation of more complex products and assemblies
- Develop assemblies rapidly and go back and add details to individual components later
- Create products in a particular design style

The following projects are intended for students who have become familiar with the basic features of Extrude, Project, Revolve, and Sweep, as well as Round Edges and Chamfer Edges. Minimal directions are provided that assume skills in drawing sketches and using the drawing tools, and creating New Workplanes and Sketches.

Project 10.1 Design Evolution: Table Lamp

Many designs evolve as the designer works out how different parts go together and interact with each other. Designs that involve moving parts often require the designer to develop a rough plan and then work out the relationships among the parts with models. When these relationships have been established, the details of the overall design can be worked out and the project completed.

This project will be developed first as rough components, and then assembled into a working product. After you have completed the assembly, you will go back and detail the individual parts to make them more attractive and to use materials efficiently.

10. Design Evolution, Animation & Style Projects

projects 331

In this project you will develop the lamp pictured in Figure 10.1. First, you will need to create the individual parts and then assemble them in a new file. After assembly, you can create animations of the moving lamp parts, similar to the Pixar™ lamp animation you may have seen in the movies.

Desk Lamp Base

- Start a *New Design*.
- On the initial sketch on the base workplane, *draw* a 6.5-inch square. Start at the origin and draw the square up and to the right (Figure 10.2).
- Save the file as *lampbase.des*.
- *Extrude* the sketch to 1.375-inches.

Figure 10.1

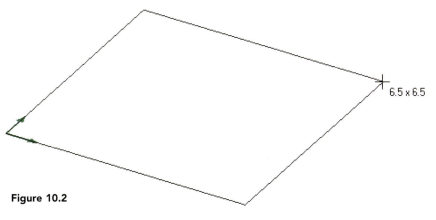

Figure 10.2

- Create a *New Offset Workplane* in the center of the lamp base, 3.25-inches to the right of the origin. Name the new workplane: *center* (Figure 10.3). You will use this workplane later.
- Create a *New Workplane* and sketch on top of the extrusion.

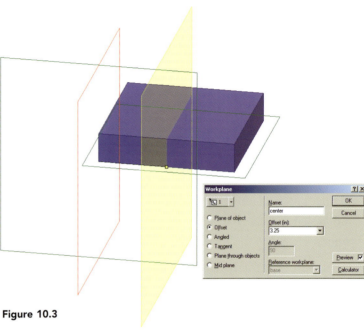

Figure 10.3

Name the new workplane: *top* and the sketch: *support*.

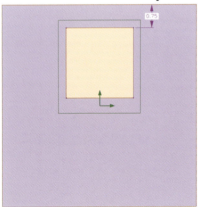

Figure 10.4

- On the sketch *support*, *draw* a 2.25-inch square. Locate the square 0.75-inches from the back of the base and in the center (**Figure 10.4**).

- *Extrude* the sketch support to 1.6-inches.

- On the top of the support create a new workplane and sketch. Name the new workplane *top of support* and the sketch *post*.

- In the center of the support, *draw* a .05-inch circle (**Figure 10.5**).

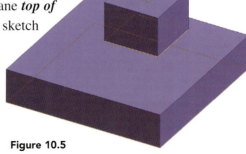

Figure 10.5

- **Extrude** the circle to 1.25-inches.
- Create a new sketch on the workplane *center* you made earlier. Name the new sketch: ***post pivot***.
- On the ***post pivot*** sketch ***draw*** a circle 0.75-inches in diameter with the center on top of the post (hint: the circle is 90 degrees to the post).
- **Extrude** the circle 0.75-inches using the "Symmetrical about workplane" option.
- Create a new sketch called: ***pivot hole*** on the workplane: ***center***.
- ***Draw*** a 0.3-inch diameter circle concentric with the previous circle (**Figure 10.6**.

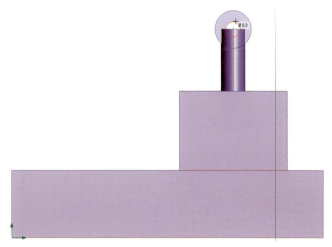

Figure 10.6

- **Project** the profile of the 0.3-inch circle to make the hole in the pivot, using the "Symmetrical about workplane" and "subtract material" options (**Figure 10.7**).
- **Save** your work.

Figure 10.7

Figure 10.8

Lower Arms

- Start a *New Design*.
- On the base workplane, *draw* a 0.4-inch diameter circle with the origin point as the center.
- *Extrude* the circle to 9.25-inches.
- *Save* the file as *lowerarm.des*.
- On the *lateral* workplane create a new sketch called *lower pivot*.
- In the center of the lower end of the first extrusion *draw* a circle 0.75-inches in diameter.
- *Extrude* the circle 0.75-inches using the "Symmetrical about workplane" option (Figure 10.8).
- Create a new sketch called: *bottom pivot hole* on the *lateral* workplane.
- *Draw* a 0.3-inch diameter circle concentric with the previous circle.
- *Project* the profile of the 0.3-inch circle to make the hole in the pivot, using the "Symmetrical about workplane" and subtract material options (Figure 10.9).
- *Save* your work.
- On the *lateral* workplane create another new sketch called *upper pivot*.
- In the center of the top end of the lower arm *draw* a circle 0.75-inches in diameter.
- *Extrude* the circles 0.75-inches using the "Symmetrical about workplane" option.

Figure 10.9

- Create a new sketch called: *top pivot hole* on the *lateral* workplane.
- *Draw* a 0.3-inch diameter circle concentric with the previous circle.
- *Project* the profile of the 0.3-inch circle to make the hole in the pivot, using the "Symmetrical about workplane" option (**Figure 10.10**).
- *Save* your work.

Upper Arm

- Start a *New Design*.
- On the *frontal* workplane, create a new sketch called *rod profile*.
- *Draw* a 0.4-inch diameter circle with the origin point as the center.
- *Extrude* the circle to 6-inches.
- *Save* the file as *upperarm.des*.
- On the *lateral* workplane create a new sketch called *lower pivot*.
- In the center of the one end of the first extrusion *draw* a circle 0.75-inches in diameter.
- *Extrude* the circle 0.75-inches using the "Symmetrical about workplane" option.
- Create a new sketch called: *bottom pivot hole* on the *lateral* workplane.
- *Draw* a 0.3-inch diameter circle concentric with the previous circle.
- *Project* the profile of the 0.3-inch circle to make the hole in the pivot, using the "Symmetrical about workplane" and "subtract material" options (**Figure 10.11**).

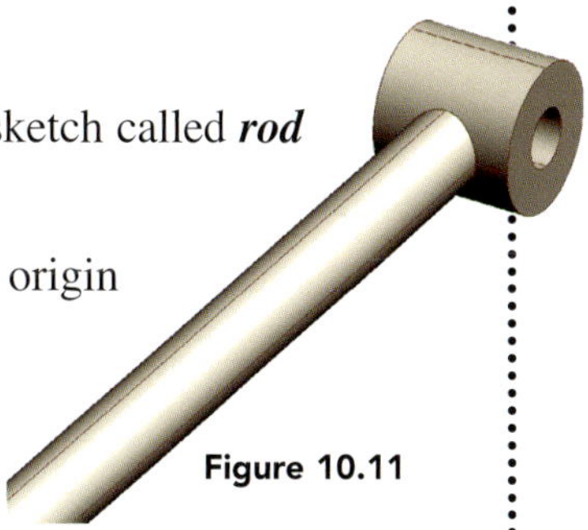

Figure 10.11

Figure 10.10
Finished lower arm

- *Save* your work.
- Create a *New Workplane* and sketch on the other end of the rod, using the face of the end. Name the New Sketch: *lamp end*.
- Concentric with the rod, *draw* a circle 0.75-inch diameter on the new sketch.
- *Draw* a concentric circle 0.3-inches in diameter on the same sketch (Figure 10.12).
- *Extrude* the circles 1-inch (Figure 10.13).
- *Save* your work.

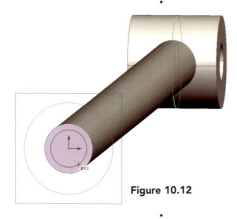

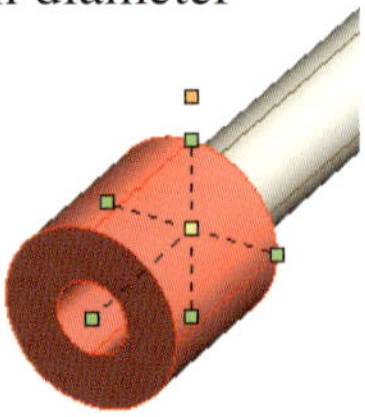

Figure 10.12

Figure 10.13

Lamp Head

- Start a *New Design*.
- On the *base* workplane, *draw* a 2.5-inch diameter circle with the origin point as the center.
- *Extrude* the circle to 2.4-inches.
- Round the top edge of the cylinder with a 0.5-inch radius (Figure 10.14).
- *Save* the file as *lamp head*.
- Create a new sketch called *recess* on the *base* workplane.

Figure 10.14

10. Design Evolution, Animation & Style Projects

Figure 10.15

Figure 10.16

- **Draw** a circle 2.2-inches in diameter on the new sketch, centered on the origin.
- **Extrude** the sketch, above the workplane and subtract material, 0.25-inch. This will create a recess for the shade to be assembled to the lamp head (Figure 10.15).
- Create a new sketch called: **pin** on the **frontal** workplane.
- **Draw** a 0.3-inch diameter circle in the center of the lamp head, just under the lower edge of the round (Figure 10.16).
- **Extrude** the circle to create a pin that sticks out about 0.75-inches beyond the outside of the lamp head. This pin will be used to attach the lamp head to the upper rod (Figure 10.17).
- **Save** your work.

Lamp Shade

- Start a **New Design**.
- On the **base** workplane, draw a circle 2.2-inches in diameter
- **Extrude** the circle 4.25-inches **below the workplane**, with a tapered angle of 32 degrees so it becomes a cone-shaped shade (Figure 10.18). If you enter the values in the dialog box you will have to put a minus sign in front of the 32.

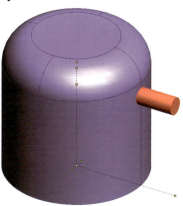

Figure 10.17

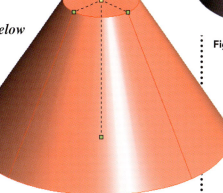

Figure 10.18

10. Design Evolution, Animation & Style Projects

- Select both the top and bottom face of the cone and **Shell** it with an offset of 0.1-inches (**Figure 10.19**).
- Select the top surface of the narrow end of the cone (**Figure 10.20**) and create a **New Workplane** called: **top** and **New Sketch** called: **mount**.

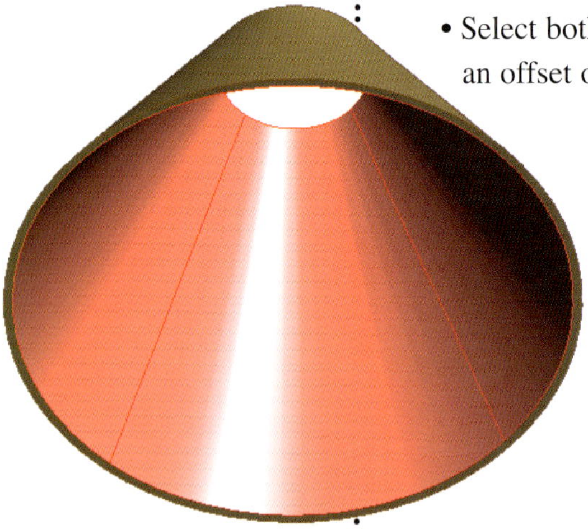

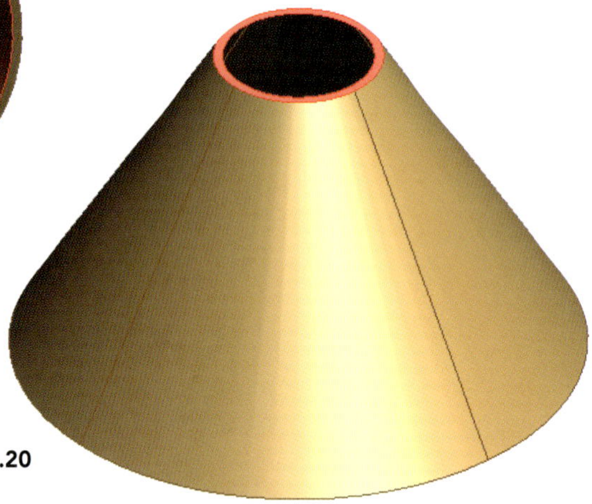

Figure 10.19

Figure 10.20

- **Draw** a circle concentric with and the same diameter as the outside of the cone.
- **Draw** another circle the same as the inside diameter of the cone and concentric with the first.
- **Extrude** the sketch to 0.3-inches. This is the lip of the shade that will go into the lamp head (**Figure 10.21**).
- **Save** your work as **lampshade.des**.

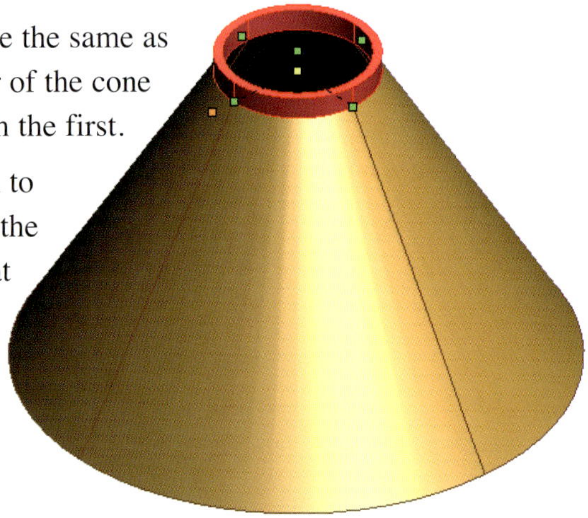

Figure 10.21

Assemble the Lamp

- Start a *New Design*.
- Bring in the lamp parts you have created using the *Add Component* command in the *Assembly* pull-down menu. Bring in the lamp base, the upper arm, the lamp head, the lamp shade and two lower arms (**Figure 10.22**).

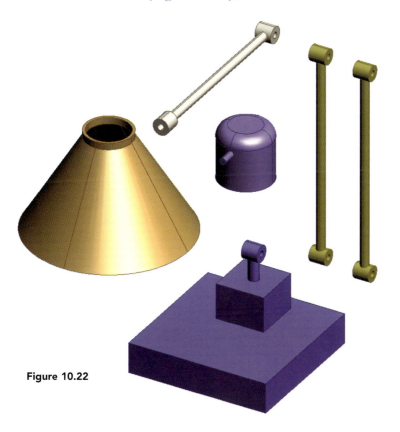

Figure 10.22

- *Save* the file as ***lampassembly.des***.
- *Fix* the lamp base so it will not move.

- Assemble two *lower arms*, one on each side of the *post pivot*, which is the horizontal cylinder with the hole in it on the lamp base (Figure 10.23). Use both *Center Axes* and *Mate* constraints.

- Assemble the *upper arm* between the two top ends of the lower rods (Figure 10.24). Use both the *center axes* and *mate* constraints on these as well.

- Assemble the *lamp head* to the *upper rod*. First, *Center Axes* the lamp head pin and hole in the rod. Second, select the end of the pin on the lamp head and the face on the end of the upper rod with the *Select Faces tool* (Figure 10.25), then apply an *Offset Mate*. Experiment with the offset distance to get the appropriate position. If you use the Orient constraint to turn around one of the parts, do not forget to delete that constraint before you try to add new constraints.

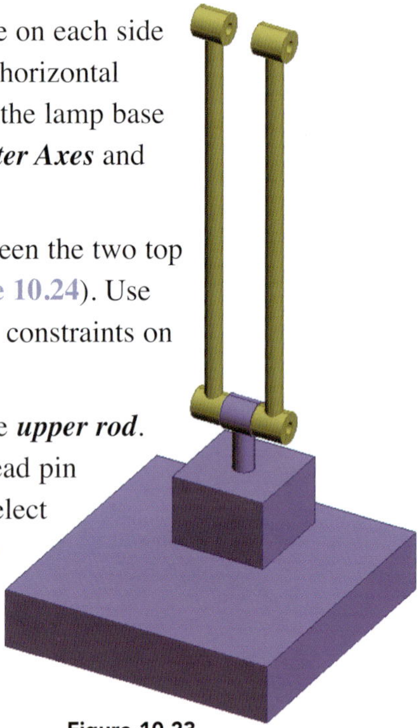

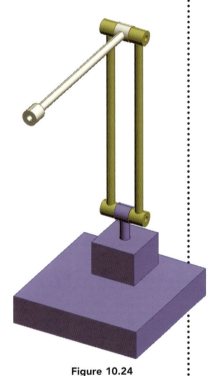

Figure 10.24

Figure 10.23

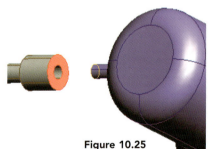

Figure 10.25

- Assemble the *lamp shade* to the *lamp head*. Use both *Center Axes* and *Mate* constraints (**Figure 10.26**).
- *Save* your work.

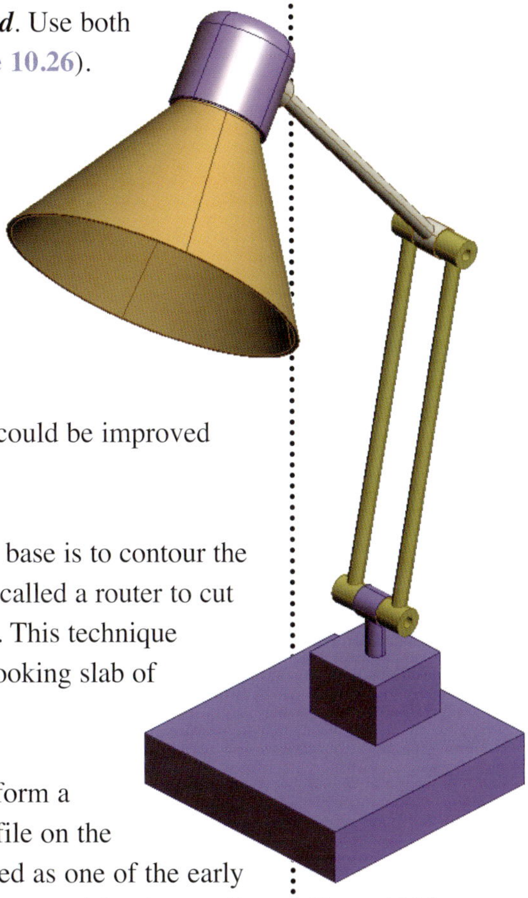

Try out the movement

With the lamp base fixed in place the arms should move and provide a good idea how the mechanism of the lamp will function.

Improve the Design

The lamp base looks heavy and unattractive. It could be improved considerably.

One way to improve the appearance of the lamp base is to contour the side of the lamp base. Cabinetmakers use a tool called a router to cut patterns into the edges of wood in a similar way. This technique narrows the appearance of an otherwise heavy-looking slab of material.

In Pro/DESKTOP®, the *Sweep Feature* can perform a similar function to the router. A new sketch profile on the workplane called *center*, a workplane you created as one of the early steps in the development of the lamp base, will be used for the profile of the Sweep. The square sketch used to extrude the bottom portion of the lamp base will be used as the path of the Sweep.

Figure 10.26

- Open the file *lamp base.des*.
- Identify the workplane *center* and create a new sketch on it called *sweep profile*.
- Zoom in on the workplane where it intersects the back edge of the lamp base. The profile you create should not interfere with the block that sits on top of the lamp base.

- Using angles and arcs, create a sketch similar to that in **Figure 10.27**. It must be a closed, valid sketch, and it must hang over the top and back edge of the base slightly.

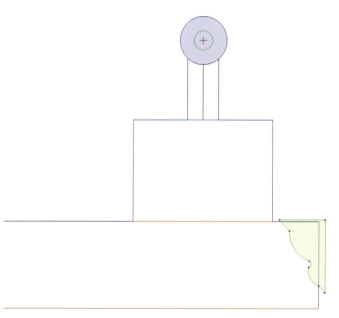

Figure 10.27

- Use the ***Sweep Feature*** to subtract material around the outside of the lamp base. Use the sketch ***sweep profile*** for the profile and sketch ***initial*** for the path (**Figure 10.28**).
- ***Save*** the file.
- Go back to the file ***lamp assembly*** and note how the lamp now looks. You can make adjustments on the sweep profile if it does not look quite right.

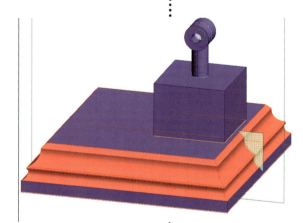

Figure 10.28

- Try the same technique to improve the look of the ***support*** block that sits on the top of the lower base (**Figure 10.29**). Remember to create a new sketch for the block profile. You can use the sketch ***support*** for the path.
- Go back to the lamp assembly file and see if your changes have improved the overall appearance of the lamp (**Figure 10.30**).

Animating the Lamp

In order to create an animation of the lamp you will need ***Variables*** that can be changed. The most logical variables involve the angles of the various parts in relation to the base or each other. If you wanted to move a real lamp similar to the one you have created, you could grab one of the lower arms and move it back and forth. Or, you could push the upper arm and change its angle to the lower arms. Another option is to twist the lamp head and shade.

In **Figure 10.31**, the top of the base and one of the lower arms has been selected with the ***Select Faces*** tool. The ***Orient*** constraint has been applied and

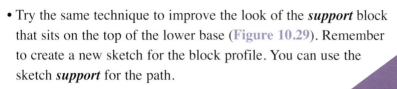

Figure 10.29

Figure 10.30

Figure 10.31

the dialog box shows the present angle between the two selected components.

Entering different values for the Angle and clicking on the **Preview** button will give you an idea of the range of angles that would make sense for the lamp. Write down these angles (Figure 10.32).

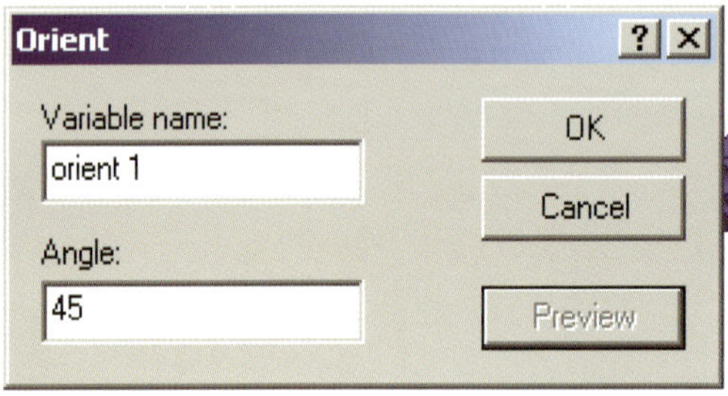

Figure 10.32

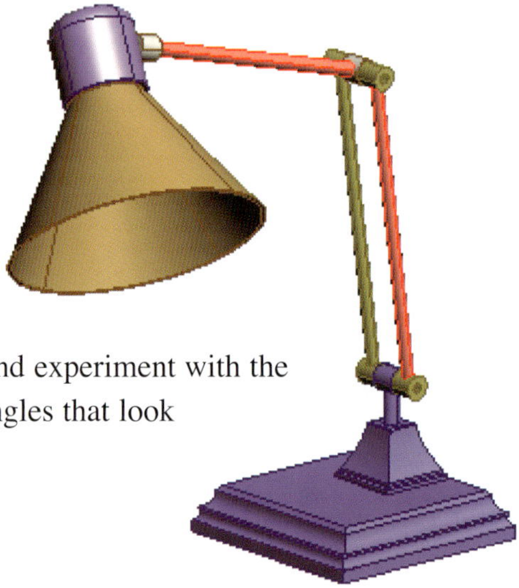

To create a variable of the angle relationship between the lower and upper arms, select them with the **Select Faces** tool (Figure 10.33). Apply an **Orient** constraint and experiment with the angle. Record the range of angles that look appropriate (Figure 10.34).

Figure 10.33

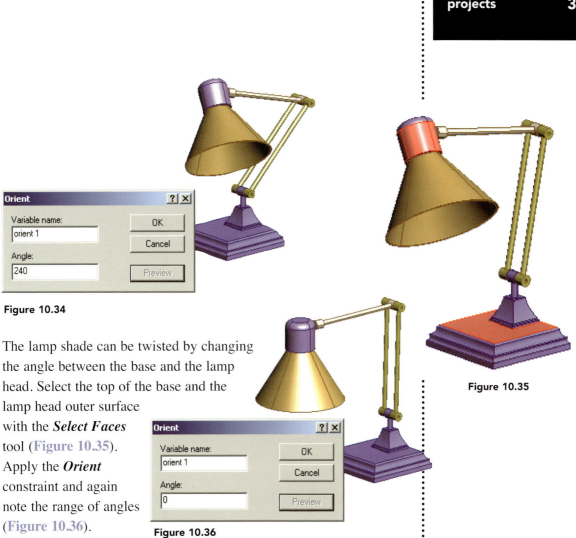

Figure 10.34

Figure 10.35

Figure 10.36

The lamp shade can be twisted by changing the angle between the base and the lamp head. Select the top of the base and the lamp head outer surface with the **Select Faces** tool (Figure 10.35). Apply the **Orient** constraint and again note the range of angles (Figure 10.36).

Project 10.1a Animate the Lamp

Using the Orient constraints for the lower arms, upper arm and lamp head. Try to make at least two variables change at the same time. Save the file as *lampanimate.avi*.

Extension Assignments

You can change the size of the upper and lower arms (length, diameter), as well as improve the transition from the rod to the lamp end. Also, you can change the angle of the lampshade, and other characteristics to improve the look of the finished lamp. Here are a few other suggestions:

- Make pins for the pivots (top and bottom) that will tighten and ensure that the lamp will not slip out of position.
- Make the lamp take on a recognizable design style, such as Art Deco, Arts & Crafts, Victorian, or other.
- Create a bulb as a separate file to fit into the lamp head. You will probably have to modify the lamp head to accommodate the bulb.
- Bring the lamp assembly into the Album Interface and render it.
- Find the center of gravity of the lamp assembly in various positions. Go back to each lamp component and change to a realistic material. Confirm that the lamp will be stable and not tip over. Hint: make the lamp base from a dense material.
- Modify the lamp arms so it can be used over a large drawing table. It should be able to be adjusted so it can reach the center of the table.
- Create a new base for the lamp that can attach to a table. This would be especially important if you choose to create the drawing table lamp.

Project 10.2 Design Style Study: Art Deco Clock

The Art Deco Style

In the first chapter of this book the Art Deco style was described as having geometric curves and a "streamlined" form. This style was applied to locomotive engines, automobiles, buses, skyscrapers, toasters and fountain pens. Almost everything in this style was designed for speed, even things that stood still.

The 1925 Paris Exposition highlighted this new design style as well as some of the new materials that made the production of the Art Deco style possible. The most important of these materials was plastic. Although we take plastics for granted today, in the early years of the Twentieth Century this wonderful new material opened up a whole new world of possibilities in design and manufacturing.

The design of the next project reflects the use of one of the new plastic materials of the Art Deco period — Bakelite. Bakelite was a thermosetting plastic, and it was molded under high heat and high temperature. The Bakelite case for the Art Deco clock would have been relatively heavy and quite durable, unless it was dropped.

10. *Design Evolution, Animation & Style Projects*

The Art Deco Clock

This project will use many Pro/DESKTOP® features and commands you have learned, including the Sweep Profile feature. You will also use the Pattern command that will allow you to reproduce a feature a number of times.

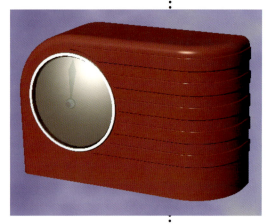

Figure 10.37

Figure 10.37 is a rendering of the Art Deco clock you will be developing.

Clock Body

- *New Design*.
- *Save* the file as *artdecoclock.des*.
- Starting at the *Origin* point on the initial sketch (base workplane) draw a rectangle 7-inches long by 2-inches wide.
- Create an *arc* in the right near corner with a 1.5-inch radius (Figure 10.38).

Figure 10.38

- Extrude the sketch to 4.5-inches high (Figure 10.39).
- *Round* the upper left edge to a 2-inch radius (Figure 10.40).

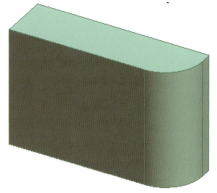

Figure 10.39

348 extension assignments

- Select the base workplane (Select Workplane tool) and create a *New Workplane* named **offset workplane** that is offset 1-inch above the base workplane. Create a *New Sketch* named **sweep path** on this workplane.

- While the **sweep path** sketch is active, select the following sketch lines on the **initial** sketch on the base workplane: right side, arc, and front (*Figure 10.41*).

Figure 10.40

Figure 10.41

- Go to the *Line* pull-down menu and choose *Project*. This will project (duplicate) the selected sketch lines from the **initial** sketch to the **sweep path** sketch (*Figure 10.42*).

One characteristic that is often seen in products in the Art Deco style is parallel lines or grooves. The next few steps will add a series of raised bumps that sweep around the curve of the clock body.

- Looking down on the base workplane, select the frontal workplane and create a *New workplane 1.75-inches behind it (offset)*.

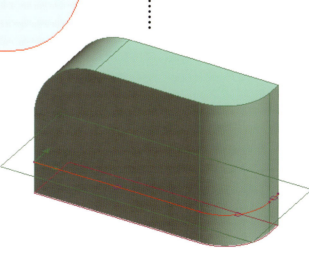

Figure 10.42

- Create a *New Sketch* named *sweep profile* on this workplane (**Figure 10.43**).

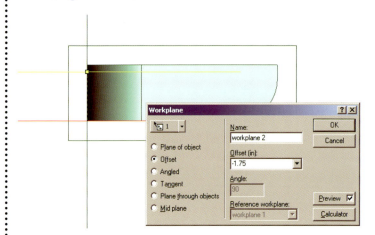

Figure 10.43

- Looking down on the *sweep profile* sketch on the new offset workplane, zoom in to the upper right corner. Draw a small rectangle 0.06-inch x 0.38-inch on the surface of the clock body (**Figure 10.44**). Most of the rectangle should hang over the edge of the clock body.

Figure 10.44

Be sure to keep a visit to KY in your plans. Sharon & U would love to show you some of this part of the US.
   Thanks again. Hello to the girls! Keep in touch & let me know if I can help in any way.

   Kenny.

Tuesday, Mar 20.

Jim,

This is the Pro D book I mentioned. With your background in Pro E, you shouldn't have any problems with Pro D. I think you will find it easy, fun & interesting.

My trip home was easy and uneventful. It is always good to get back, but I was sorry to leave CA so soon.

I appreciated the hospitality & the opportunity to visit with you & your family. From my perspective the workshop went well and I was glad I had the opportunity to help.

- **Constrain** the distance from the top of the rectangle to the top of the clock body to 0.3-inches (**Figure 10.45**).

Use the **Sweep Profile** feature and select the appropriate profile and sketch in the dialog box (**Figure 10.46**).

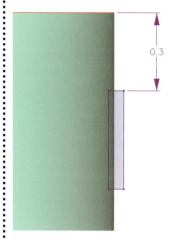

Figure 10.45

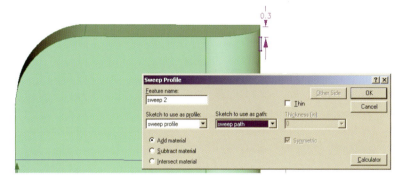

Figure 10.46

- While the *sweep* is still selected (**Figure 10.47**), go to the **Feature** pull-down menu and choose **Pattern** from the list. If the sweep is not selected, choose the **Feature Select tool** from the Design Toolbar and select the sweep first.

Figure 10.47

- Choose the **Select Edges tool** and select the outer edge of the sweep profile sketch rectangle. You will see a green arrow (**Figure 10.48**). The arrow should point down. If it points up, click on the **Reverse** button in the dialog box to change the arrow direction to down.

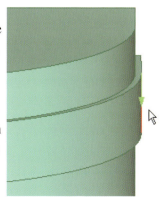

Figure 10.48

- In the Direction 1 tab, change **number of instances to 5**. Enter a value of **0.7 for the Spacing**. The additional sweep lines should preview in yellow. Click OK to close the Pattern dialog box (**Figure 10.49**).

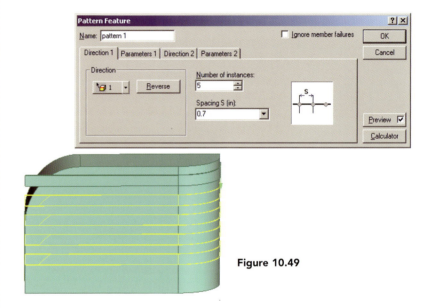

Figure 10.49

Next you are going to change the length of the sweep path line to shorten the sweeps so they line up with the middle of the clock face. This could have been done earlier, but it is important to see that you can go back and make changes as you design, so you will do it now after the sweeps have already been made.

- In the Browser window, double-click on the *sweep path* sketch on the *offset workplane* to select it (**Figure 10.50**).
- Change view by **Shift+W** to look down at the *sweep path* sketch.

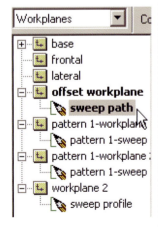

Figure 10.50

- **Draw** a small line 2-inches to the right of the **Origin** point (**Figure 10.51**). This line should line-up with the center line of the radius of the arc used to create the round on the upper left side of the clock body. This line is used to divide the sweep path so a segment of that path can be deleted.

Figure 10.51

- **Delete** the sweep path to the left of the short line (**Figure 10.52**).

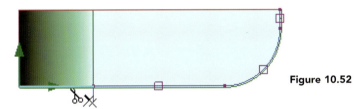

Figure 10.52

- **Delete** the short line you drew to divide the sweep path (**Figure 10.53**).

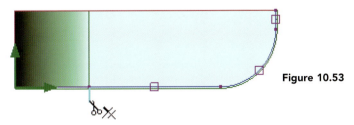

Figure 10.53

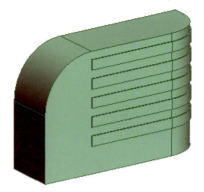

Figure 10.54

- *Update* the file.
- The clock model should now look like the one in **Figure 10.54**.
- *Select* the front face of the model (**Figure 10.55**) and create a *New Sketch* named *sweep trim*. Name the *New Workplane front face*.

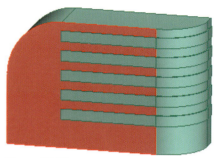

Figure 10.55

- With the *Circle tool* move the cursor to the edge of the upper left arc of the clock body until the small black square appears at the arc center. Draw a 3.2-inch circle (**Figure 10.56**).

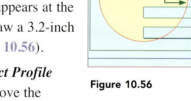

Figure 10.56

- Use the *Project Profile* feature to remove the sweeps inside the circle (**Figure 10.57**).

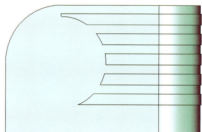

Figure 10.57

- Create a *New Sketch* on the front face workplane named *depression*.
- *Draw* a 3-inch circle concentric with the sweep trim circle (**Figure 10.58**).

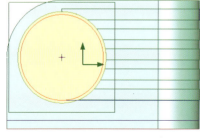

Figure 10.58

10. Design Evolution, Animation & Style Projects

extension assignments   355

- ***Extrude*** the circle 0.125-inches (subtract material, below workplane) to create a one-eighth inch depression in the clock body (**Figure 10.59**).
- Use the ***Round Edges*** feature to round the top and left edges of the clock body with a radius of 0.375-inches (**Figure 10.60**).
- Select the back face of the clock body and Shell it with a wall thickness of 0.125-inch (**Figure 10.61**).
- Create a *New Sketch* named **hole** on the workplane ***front face***.

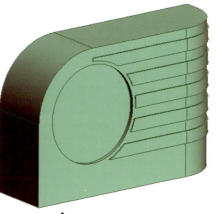
Figure 10.59

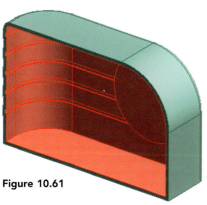
Figure 10.61

Figure 10.60

- ***Draw*** a 0.3-inch diameter circle concentric to the sweep trim/depression circles (**Figure 10.62**).
- Use the ***Project Profile*** feature to create a hole through the clock body for the clock mechanism (**Figure 10.63**).

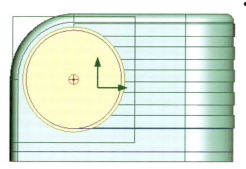
Figure 10.62

Figure 10.63

10. Design Evolution, Animation & Style Projects

- ***Round*** off the edges of the sweep bumps with a 0.02-inch radius (**Figure 10.64**).
- ***Save***.

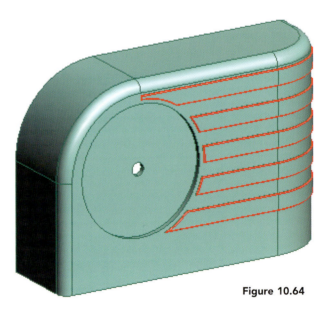

Figure 10.64

Glass lens

The glass lens will protect the clock hands and clock face.

- ***New Design***.
- ***Save*** as ***lens.des***.
- Create a ***New Sketch*** named ***lens profile*** on the ***frontal workplane***.
- ***Draw*** a 3-inch circle with the center at the Origin point.
- ***Extrude*** the circle to 0.0675-inch (1/16th inch).
- Select the front face of the extrusion and go to the ***Features*** pull-down menu. Select ***Modify Solids*** and then ***Deform Face*** from the sub-menu. Enter a value of 0.375 for the height (**Figure 10.65**).

Figure 10.65

- Select the side of the lens with the flat face.
- **Shell** the lens to 0.0675-inch.
- **Save**.

Bezel

The bezel will keep the glass lens in the clock body by friction.

- *New Design*.
- *Save* as *bezel.des*.
- Change the name of the *initial* sketch to *axis* on the *base workplane*.
- *Shift+W* and *Draw* a short vertical *construction line* from the Origin point.
- Add a *New Sketch* called *bezel profile* to the base workplane.
- Move the cursor so that it is 1.5-inches to the right of the Origin point (Snap to Grid) and draw a short vertical construction line. This line will act as the outer limit of the bezel (**Figure 10.66**).

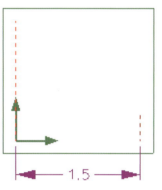

Figure 10.66

- *Draw* an "L" shaped sketch to the left of the second construction line, facing back toward the center axis (**Figure 10.67**).
- *Delete* the extra line segments so you end up with a backward "L" (**Figure 10.68**).

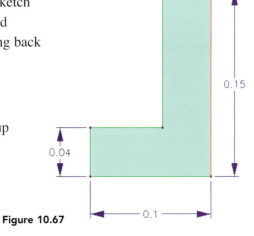

Figure 10.67

Figure 10.68

- *Revolve* the bezel profile sketch around the axis (**Figure 10.69**).
- Select the outside edge of the bezel and apply a radius of 0.04-inch with the *Round Edges* feature.
- *Save*.

Figure 10.69

Clock Mechanism

Although the style of the clock is older, the mechanism is a newer battery-powered model. The clock mechanism will be a model of the outside of a clock mechanism with the three concentric shafts: one for the threaded shaft to fasten the mechanism to the clock body, plus rotating shafts for the minute and hour hands.

- *New Design*.
- *Save* as *mechanism.des*.
- Create a *New Sketch* named *mechanism body* on the *frontal workplane*.

- **Draw** a 2.125-inch square.
- **Extrude** the square sketch to 0.625-inches.
- **Round** the four corner edges to a 0.25-inch radius (**Figure 10.70**).
- Select the front face of the mechanism and create a **New Sketch** named **threaded shaft**. Name the new Workplane **front face**.
- **Draw** a 0.28-inch circle at the Origin point (**Figure 10.71**).
- **Extrude** the circle to 0.185-inches (**Figure 10.72**).
- Select the end face of the threaded shaft extrusion and create a **New Sketch** named **minute**. Name the New Workplane **shaft end**.
- **Draw** a 0.24-inch circle sketch concentric with the threaded shaft sketch (**Figure 10.73**).
- **Extrude** the minute sketch to 0.125-inch (**Figure 10.74**).
- Select the end face of the minute extrusion and create a **New Sketch** named **hour**. Name the new Workplane **minute end**.

Figure 10.70

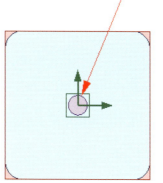

Figure 10.71

Figure 10.72

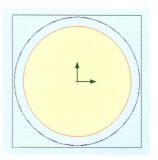

Figure 10.73

Figure 10.74

Figure 10.76

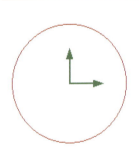

Figure 10.77

- **Draw** a 0.18-inch diameter circle centered on the Origin point (**Figure 10.75**).
- **Extrude** the circle to 0.125 inches (**Figure 10.76**).
- **Save**.

Nut

Make a nut to hold the clock mechanism to the clock body.

- **New Design**.
- **Save** as **nut.des**.
- Create a **New Sketch** named **nut profile** on the **frontal workplane**.
- **Draw** a 0.28-inch circle using the Origin point as the center.
- Using the **Snap to Grid** as a guide, **Draw** a horizontal line 0.2-inches above the Origin point. Make the line about the same length as the diameter of the circle (**Figure 10.77**).
- Use the **Duplicate** command in the **Edit** pull-down menu to make a total of 6 lines around 360 degrees (**Figure 10.78**).
- **Delete** the line segments that hang over the hexagon shape until the sketch fills (**Figure 10.79**).

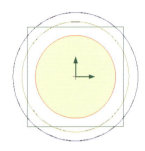

Figure 10.75

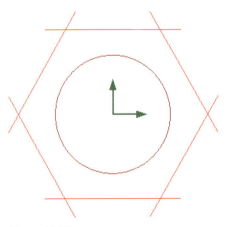

Figure 10.78

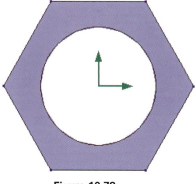

Figure 10.79

- *Extrude* the nut profile to 0.1-inch (**Figure 10.80**).
- *Save*.

Minute Hand

To construct the minute hand you will use a circle construction line that will determine its the length so that it will be the correct size to fit in the depression you created in the clock body.

- *New Design*.
- *Save* as *minutehand.des*.
- Create a *New Sketch* named *minute profile* on the *frontal workplane*.
- Starting at the Origin point, *draw* a circle 2.6-inches in diameter and *toggle construction*.
- *Draw* a small circle 0.24-inches in diameter (**Figure 10.81**).
- *Draw* a 0.32-inch diameter circle concentric with the two previous circles (**Figure 10.82**).

Figure 10.80

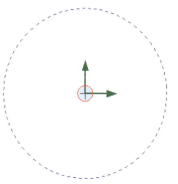

Figure 10.81

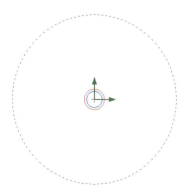

Figure 10.82

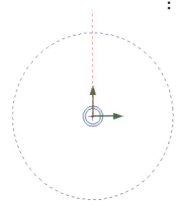

Figure 10.83

Figure 10.85

- ***Draw*** a vertical construction line from the Origin out past the 2.6-inch circle construction line (**Figure 10.83**).

- From the location where the vertical and circle construction lines meet, draw a diagonal line down and to the right (cursor read-out 0.36, -70°), as in **Figure 10.84**.

- ***Draw*** a diagonal line from the previous point to the Origin, passing through the two small circles (**Figure 10.85**).

- Select both of the diagonal lines you have just drawn and, using the vertical construction line as the axis, ***Mirror*** the diagonal lines (**Figure 10.86**).

- ***Delete*** the line segments necessary to make the minute hand shape in **Figure 10.87**.

Figure 10.84

Figure 10.86

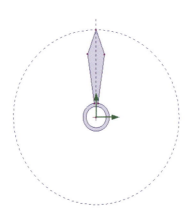

Figure 10.87

- *Extrude* the minute hand sketch to 0.02-inches (*Figure 10.88*).
- *Save*.

Hour Hand

Use the same steps to create the hour hand that you used to make the minute hand. Clock hour hands are usually shorter, so some of the measurements will differ from the minute hand.

- *New Design*.
- *Save* as **hourhand.des**.
- Create a *New Sketch* named **hour profile** on the *frontal workplane*.
- Starting at the Origin point, *draw* a circle 2-inches in diameter and *toggle construction*.
- *Draw* a small circle 0.18-inches in diameter.
- *Draw* a 0.24-inch diameter circle concentric with the two previous circles.
- *Draw* a vertical construction line from the Origin out past the 2.6-inch circle construction line.
- From the location where the vertical and circle construction lines meet, draw a diagonal line down and to the right (cursor read-out 0.3, -70°), as in *Figure 10.89*.
- *Draw* a diagonal line from the previous point to the Origin, passing through the two small circles (*Figure 10.90*).

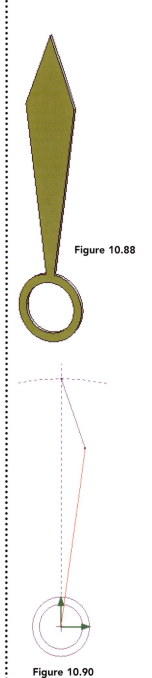

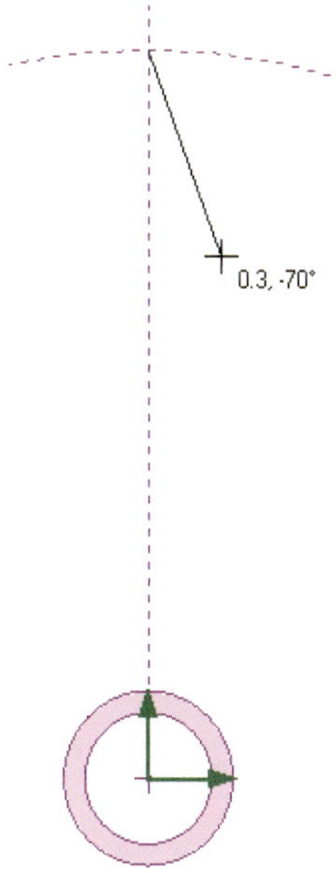

Figure 10.88

Figure 10.89

Figure 10.90

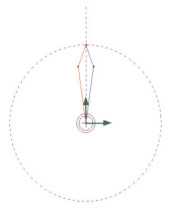

Figure 10.91

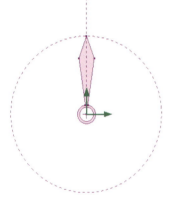

Figure 10.92

- Select both of the diagonal lines you have just drawn and, using the vertical construction line as the axis, *Mirror* the diagonal lines (**Figure 10.91**).
- *Delete* the line segments necessary to make the hour hand shape in **Figure 10.92**.
- *Extrude* the hour hand sketch to 0.02-inches (**Figure 10.93**).
- *Save*.

Figure 10.93

Assemble the Clock

Now that you have modeled all the components, you can assemble the parts to create the Art Deco Clock.

- Start a *New Design*.
- *Save* file as *clockassembly.des*.
- Use the *Add Component* command in the *Assembly* pull-down menu to bring in all the parts of the Art Deco Clock: *artdecoclock.des*, *mechanism.des*, *nut.des*, *hourhand.des*, *minutehand.des*, *lens.des*, *bezel.des*.
- Assemble the mechanism to the clock body with the *Center Axes* and *Mate* constraints (**Figure 10.94**).

Figure 10.94

10. Design Evolution, Animation & Style Projects

extension assignments 365

- Place the nut over the mechanism shaft using the **Center Axes** and the **Mate** constraints (Figure 10.95).

Figure 10.95

- Attach the minute hand to the larger diameter shaft end using the **Center Axes** and the **Mate** constraints (Figure 10.96).

- Attach the hour hand to the smaller diameter shaft end using the **Center Axes** and the **Mate** constraints (Figure 10.97).

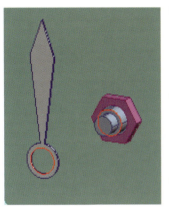

Figure 10.96

- Attach the bezel to the circular recess. The bezel holds the glass lens in place. The lens can be assembled when you are ready to render the clock in the *Album Interface*. In the *Album* you can change the material of the lens to glass so the clock hands can be seen through the lens. If you assemble the lens now you will not be able to see the hands. Use the **Center Axes** constraint (Figure 10.98) and an **Offset Mate** to offset the bezel 0.07-inches away from the bottom of the depression on the clock body.

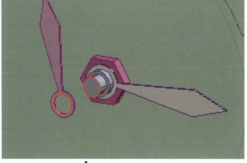

Figure 10.97

Project 10.3 Blusher Case

Background
Most products we use everyday are designed to be inexpensive but durable. If you purchase a product, and it falls apart after only a short time, you probably won't buy the same brand again. Companies know this so they

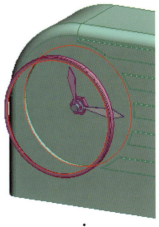

Figure 10.98

must strike a balance between quality and cost. Many products are consumed as they are used, or they contain something that is consumed. Often, the product is thrown away, because it would not be practical to re-fill it.

Such is the case with most so-called "beauty" products. When the chemical compounds contained in the product are used up, the case is discarded. To design and manufacture a case that will last a lifetime is impractical and would cost a great deal. Who would buy such an expensive product, only to throw it away after a short use? But the case must last long enough to provide good service to the customer.

Plastics are most often used for cosmetic cases. Many plastics are durable, they can be colored and textured to create many different "looks," and they are inexpensive to manufacture. **Figure 10.99**

Figure 10.99

shows the "Blusher Case" you will be developing in this project. After completing the development of the blusher case in the next section, you are challenged to design and develop your own blusher case.

Create the bottom case

- Start a *New Design*.
- Change *Units* to *millimeters*.
- Create a *New Sketch* named **bottom shell** on the *base workplane*.
- *Shift+W*.
- *Save* the file as **bottomcase.des** .
- Beginning at the Origin, *draw* a rectangle 64 x 57 up and to the right.
- Constrain the height of the rectangle to 57mm (**Figure 10.100**).
- Using the *Arc or Fillet* tool, drag the right side of the rectangle to a radius of about 110mm.
- *Constrain* the arc to 110mm (**Figure 10.101**).
- Repeat the operation and curve the left end of the rectangle to the same arc.

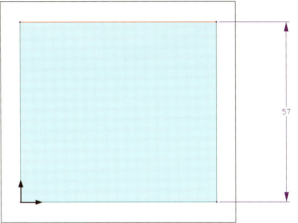

Figure 10.100

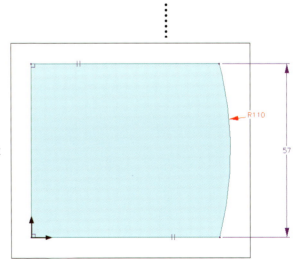

Figure 10.101

- Select both arcs and go to the **Constraints** pull-down menu and select **Equal Radius** from the list.
- **Extrude** the sketch to 6mm thick (**Figure 10.102**).

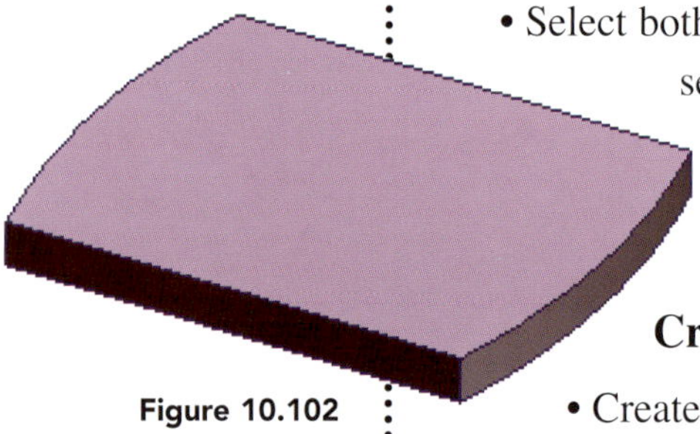

Figure 10.102

Create hinge cutouts

- Create a **New Sketch** named hinge cutouts on the base workplane
- **Draw** a vertical construction line from the mid-point of the bottom line of the bottom shell sketch, past the top edge of the case (**Figure 10.103**).

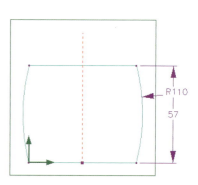

Figure 10.103

- On the same sketch, **draw** a rectangle to the left of the construction line. **Draw** the rectangle so it overlaps the edge of the bottom case (**Figure 10.104**).
- **Constrain** the rectangle so it is 14mm from the centerline, 10mm wide and 5mm from the bottom of the rectangle to the top edge of the case (**Figure 10.105**).

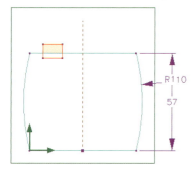

Figure 10.104

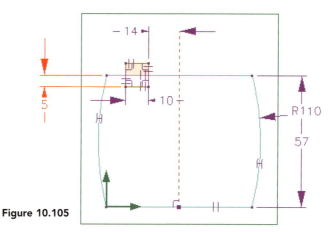

Figure 10.105

- Use the **Select Lines** tool to select all four lines of the rectangle.
- **Mirror** the rectangle using the construction line as the axis (**Figure 10.106**).
- Use the **Project Profile** feature to make the cutout, using the **Subtract material** and **Above workplane** options (**Figure 10.107**).

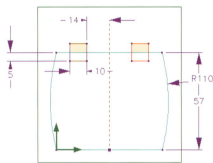

Figure 10.106

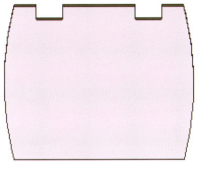

Figure 10.107

Create the hinge pin

- **Rotate** the bottom case so that you can see one of the inside edges of the cutout holes. Use the **Select Faces** tool to select that surface (**Figure 10.108**).

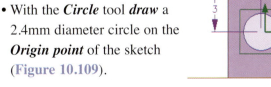

Figure 10.108

- Create a **New Sketch** named **pin profile** on the **New Workplane**.
- Change the viewing mode to **Transparent** so you can see the hidden edges of the bottom case.
- With the **Circle** tool **draw** a 2.4mm diameter circle on the **Origin point** of the sketch (**Figure 10.109**).

Figure 10.109

- **Constrain** the circle 2.75mm from the bottom of the cutout and 3mm from the top (**Figure 10.110**).

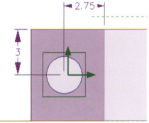

Figure 10.110

10. Design Evolution, Animation & Style Projects

- **Rotate** the bottom case so you can see the cutouts.
- **Extrude** the circle 48mm so it passes through both cutouts (**Figure 10.111**).

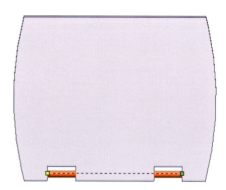

Figure 10.111

Make lip on top surface of bottom case

- Select the top face of the case and create a *New Sketch* named *lip*.
- Use **Shift+T** to change the viewing angle to **Trimetric**.
- Make sure the new sketch you created on the top face of the case is the active sketch (**bold**).
- Select all four lines of the bottom shell sketch (four sides).
- Go to the **Lines** pull-down menu and select **Project** from the list. The **Project** command copies the lines on one sketch and projects them onto another workplane and sketch (**Figure 10.112**).

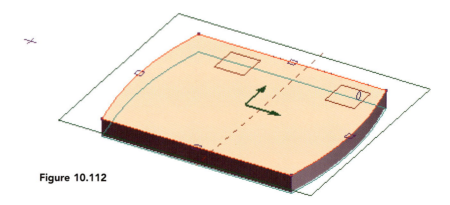

Figure 10.112

- *Shift+W*
- *Draw* a horizontal line across near the top with the *Straight Line* tool.
- *Constrain* the line to 1.5mm from the back edge of the hinge cutout (**Figure 10.113**).
- *Delete* all the lines in this sketch above this horizontal line. Also delete the lines that extend past the right and left edges of the sketch. The sketch should fill (**Figure 10.114**).
- *Save* your work.

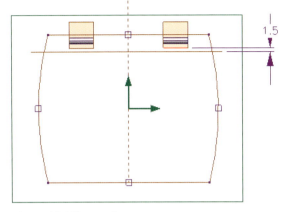

Figure 10.113

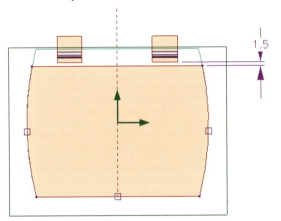

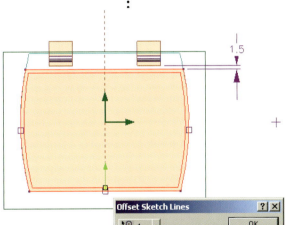

Figure 10.114

The sketch conforms to the outline of the bottom case, but the lip should be set back from the edge so the top half of the case fits snugly.

- *Select* the four line segments of the lip sketch.
- Go to the *Line* pull-down menu and choose *Offset Chain* from the list.
- Enter the negative value –1.5 for the *Offset* (mm) dimension so the offset lines will be inside the selected lines (**Figure 10.115**).

Figure 10.115

- Delete the original lip sketch lines and leave the offset lines. Make sure the offset lines form a valid sketch and fill (**Figure 10.116**).

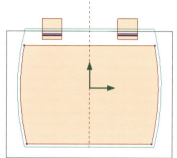

Figure 10.116

- *Extrude* the offset lines to 0.8mm (**Figure 10.117**).
- *Save* your work.

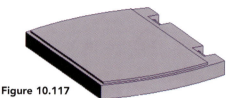

Figure 10.117

Create the cavity for the blusher

- *Select* the top surface of the lip and create a *New Sketch* on this face named **blush cutout**.
- *Shift+W*
- *Draw* a short center vertical construction line from the *Origin* up (**Figure 10.118**).

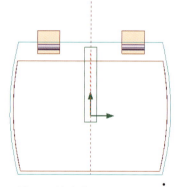

Figure 10.118

- *Draw* a rectangle 58mm x 28mm roughly centered on the construction line (**Figure 10.119**).
- *Constrain* the distance from one side of the rectangle to the center construction line to 29mm.
- *Constrain* the distance from the top of the rectangle to the top edge of the lip to 2mm (**Figure 10.120**).

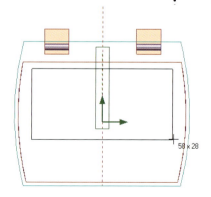

Figure 10.119

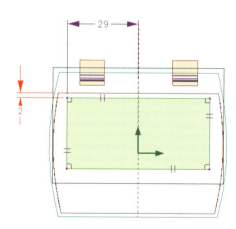

Figure 10.120

- Use the *Arc or Fillet* tool to round one of the corners of the rectangle to 1.75mm radius (**Figure 10.121**).
- *Create arcs* on the remaining three corners.
- *Shift+click* all four arcs and use the *Equal Radius* command in the *Constraints* pull-down menu.
- *Extrude* the sketch, subtracting material, below workplane 5.5mm (**Figure 10.122**).
- *Save* your work.

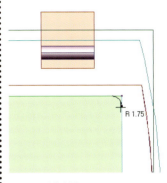

Figure 10.121

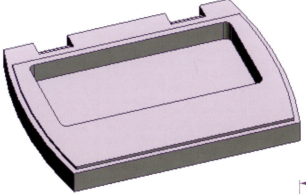

Figure 10.122

Create the cavity for the brush

- On the same workplane as the sketch *blush cutout*, create a *New Sketch* named *brush holder*.
- *Shift+W*.
- *Draw* two horizontal lines (hold down the *Shift* key), the lower one just above the bottom of the lip and the upper one just under the cavity you made for the blush. Start and end the lines off the edge of the case (**Figure 10.123**).

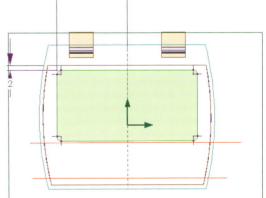

Figure 10.123

- **Constrain** the lines 1mm from each edge (**Figure 10.124**).
- With the **Line Select** tool, select the two lines that form the left and right arcs of the lip sketch.
- Go to the **Lines** pull-down menu and select **Project** from the list. The **Project** command will copy the lines from the lip sketch to the active sketch (**Figure 0.125**).

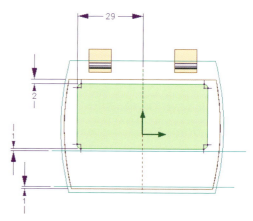

Figure 10.124

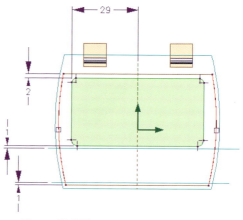

Figure 10.125

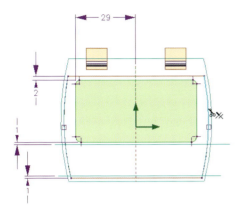

Figure 10.126a

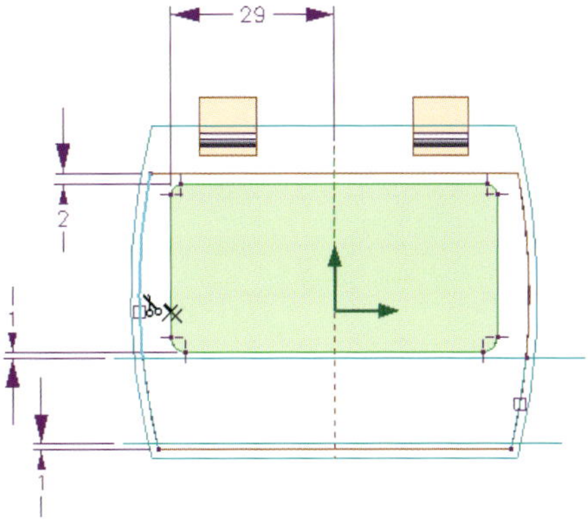

Figure 10.126b

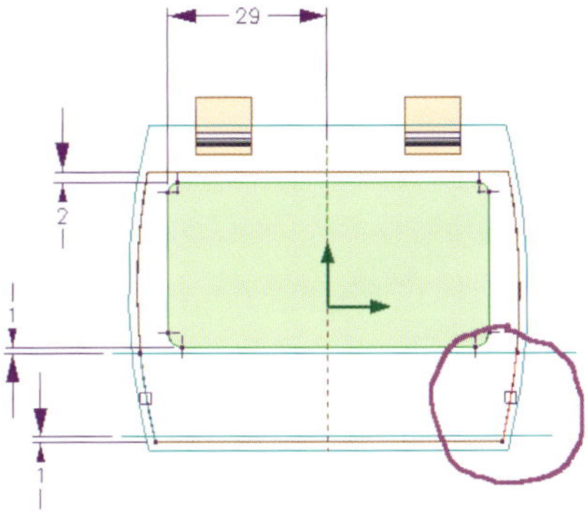

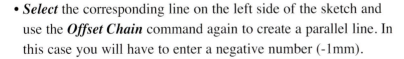

Figure 10.127

- **Delete** the top portion of the projected lines above the two horizontal lines of the active sketch (**Figures 10.126a & b**).
- **Select** the remaining portion of the projected line on the right (**Figure 10.127**).
- Use the **Offset Chain** command to create a parallel line 1mm in from the selected line (**Figure 10.128**).

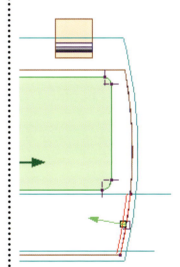

Figure 10.128

- **Select** the corresponding line on the left side of the sketch and use the **Offset Chain** command again to create a parallel line. In this case you will have to enter a negative number (-1mm).

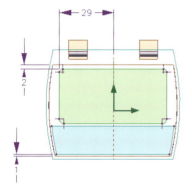

Figure 10.129

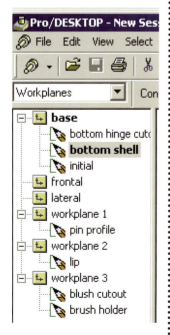

Figure 10.132

- *Delete* all the lines necessary to create a valid profile for the sketch. There will be quite a few lines and you may have to zoom way in on each corner to make certain that all overhanging lines have been deleted. The sketch will fill when you have deleted the last stray line (**Figure 10.129**)
- *Extrude* the sketch, subtracting material, below workplane 5.5mm.
- Round the four outside edges of the case to 0.8mm radius (**Figure 10.130**).
- Round the four bottom edges to a 0.7mm radius (**Figure 10.131**).
- *Save* your work. Do not close the file.

Start the Top case

- Start a *New Design*.
- Create a *New Sketch* named *top shell* on the base workplane.
- *Shift+W*.
- *Save* the file as *topcase.des*.
- Go to the *Windows* pull-down menu and open the file *bottomcase.des*.
- Go to the *Workplanes Browser* window and open the base workplane. Double click on *bottom shell* sketch (**Figure 10.132**). The lines of the sketch should now be selected (red). If not, Shift+click on all the lines on that sketch.

Figure 10.130

Figure 10.131

10. Design Evolution, Animation & Style Projects

extension assignments 377

- *Copy* the selected lines with the keyboard shortcut *Ctrl+C*.
- Go to the *Windows* pull-down menu and open *top case.des*.
- Make sure that the *top shell* is the active sketch, and use the keyboard shortcut *Ctrl+V* to *Paste* the sketch lines you copied from the other file.
- *Extrude* the sketch to 5mm, using the option *Below workplane* (*Figure 10.133*).
- *Save* your work.
- *Rotate* the top case so you can see the underside.
- *Select* the underside and use the *Shell Solids* feature with an *Offset* value of 1.75mm. Make sure *Inside* is checked (*Figure 10.134*).

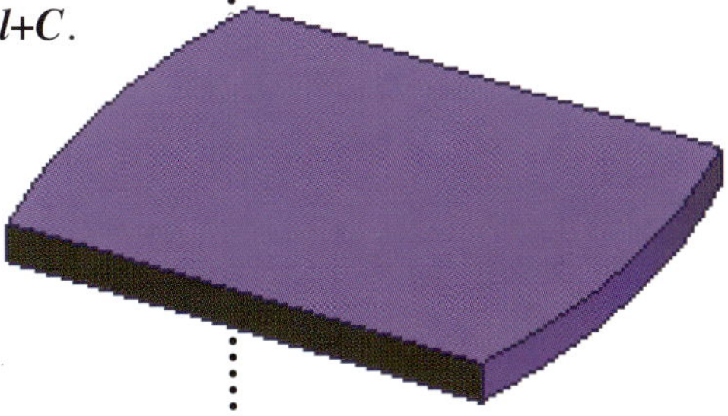

Figure 10.133

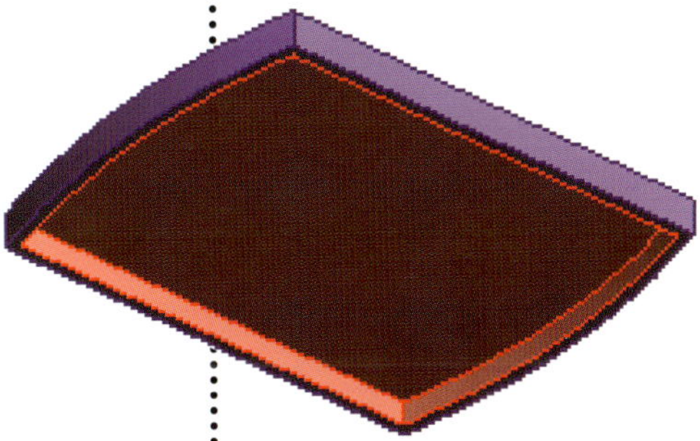

Figure 10.134

Make the hinge pegs on the top case

- *Rotate* the model so you can see the underside.
- Select the bottom surface inside the shell with the *Select Faces* tool (*Figure 10.135*).
- Create a *New Sketch* named *hinge pegs* on the selected face.
- *Shift+W*
- *Draw* a vertical construction line from the *Origin* point. This line will be the axis for a *Mirror* command.
- *Fix* the position of the construction line (*Constraints* pull-down menu and select *Toggle Fixed*).

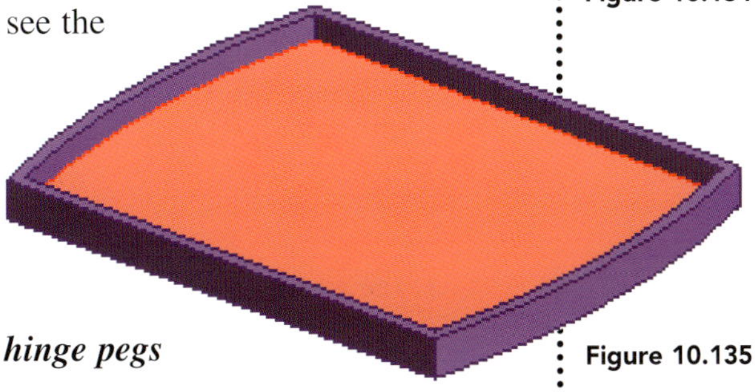

Figure 10.135

- To the left of the construction line, **draw** a small rectangle about 9.5 x 4.5 (**Figure 10.136**).

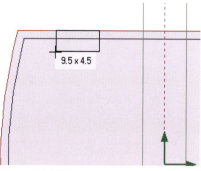

Figure 10.136

- The edge of the rectangle should be even with the edge of the case and it should extend into the shell cavity.

- **Constrain** the distance from the center construction line to the edge of the rectangle to 14mm. (**Figure 10.137**).

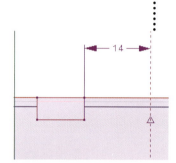

Figure 10.137

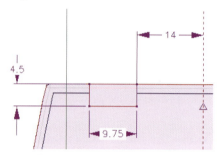

Figure 10.138

- **Constrain** the dimensions of the rectangle to 9.75mm long and 4.5mm wide (**Figure 10.138**).

- **Mirror** the rectangle using the construction line as the axis (**Figure 10.139**).

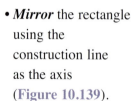

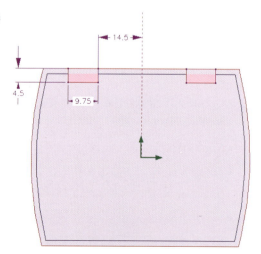

Figure 10.139

extension assignments

- **Extrude** the two rectangles 7.6mm. They are on the same sketch so they will extrude together (Figure 10.140).

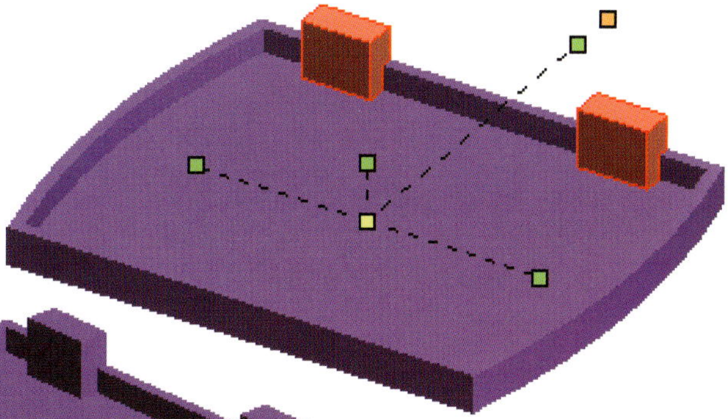

Create snap-in holes for the hinge

- Using the **Select Faces** tool select the outside end of one of the hinge pegs (Figure 10.141).

- Draw a 2.4mm diameter circle located 2.25mm in from the back edge of the hinge peg and 3mm up from the face of the top case (Figure 10.142).

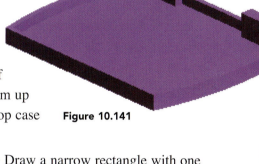

Figure 10.140

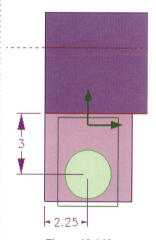

Figure 10.141

Figure 10.142

- Draw a narrow rectangle with one end beyond the edge of the hinge peg and the other end almost to the bottom face of the the lid (Figure 10.143).

- Delete the lines that cross the circle to make the sketch a valid profile. The sketch will fill when you have deleted the last interfering line (Figure 10.144).

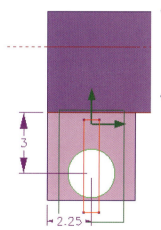

Figure 10.143

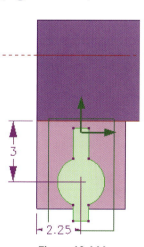

Figure 10.144

- Use the ***Project Profile*** feature on the sketch to ***Subtract material Thru the entire part*** and ***Below workplane*** (**Figure 10.145**). These slots allow the top case hinge pegs to snap onto the hinge pins on the bottom case.
  - ***Round*** the four side edges and the top edges of the model to a 0.8mm radius (**Figure 10.146**).
- ***Save*** your work.

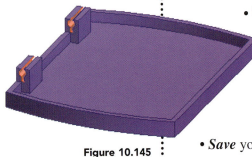

Figure 10.145

  - Select the top face of the case and create a ***New Sketch*** named ***text***.
    - ***Shift+W***
    - Choose the ***Add Text Outline*** command in the ***Line*** pull-down menu.
  - Type in the word ***MAYBELLINE*** in the dialog box. Choose Arial font, a letter height of 4.25mm, and increase the spacing by moving the adjustable pointer two notches. Click ***OK***.

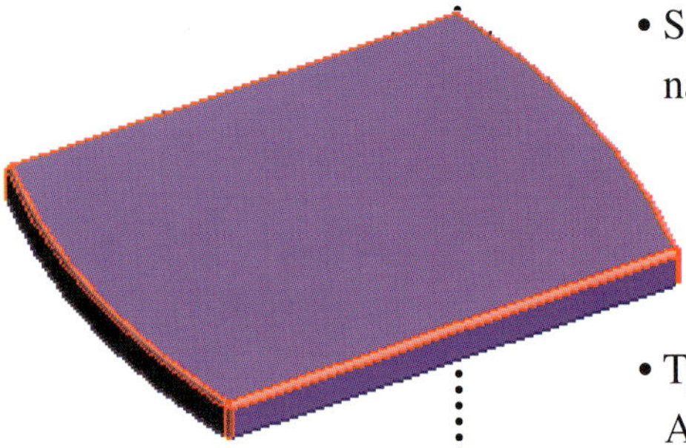

Figure 10.146

- Move the text (while it is still selected) to the lower center part of the lid (**Figure 10.147**).
- ***Extrude*** the text 0.6mm.
- The top of the case should look like **Figure 10.148**.

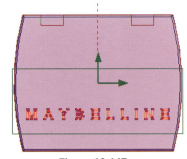

Figure 10.147

Figure 10.148

Assemble the top case and bottom case

- Start a *New Design*.
- *Save* the file as *caseassembly.des*.
- Use the *Assembly* pull-down menu to add the top case and bottom case to the file (**Figure 10.149**).
- *Fix* the bottom case in position.
- Use the *Center Axes constraint* to join the hinge pin on the bottom case and the circular part of one of the hinge slots on the top case (**Figure 10.150**).

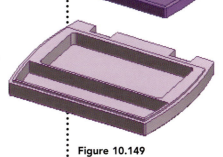

Figure 10.149

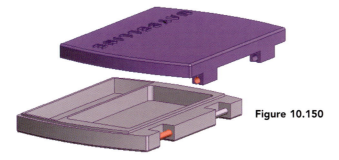

Figure 10.150

- Select the two facing surfaces on the hinge pin and hinge peg and use the *Mate* constraint (**Figure 10.151**).
- *Save* your work.

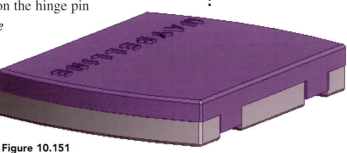

Figure 10.151

Extension Assignments for Blusher Case

- Create a window in the top of the case so a customer can see the color of the blush powder.
- **Round** the inside edges and corners of all depressions for more efficient manufacture.
- Render the case in realistic materials and place in an appropriate setting, similar to a commercial photography shoot.
- Animate the case lid slowly opening and closing as you might see in a commercial.
- Animate the case rendered in the *Album*.

Test Your Knowledge

Design Projects

The following projects are not step-by-step. Each will require you to use the skills you have developed in using Pro/DESKTOP®, along with your creativity and imagination. There is not one right solution to these problems, but this does not mean that all solutions are good.

Each project is presented as a design problem, with background information to help you understand the nature of the problem, a design brief to focus your creative efforts, and specifications that detail the design requirements of your solution.

Project 10.4 Sci-Fi Movie Props

Background
The script for a new science-fiction movie called "Alpha Centauri" has been approved and filming is set to begin this summer. The look and "feel" of the film is supposed to remind audiences of the old 1930s, 40s, and 50s sci-fi movies, like the original black-and-white **Flash Gordon** and **Buck Rogers** movies, although it will be shot in color. The costumes, ships, ray-guns and everything else in the film must have that streamlined look. The film's producers have noticed that the "retro" style, as seen in cars like the PT Cruiser and Chevy's new SSR pickup truck, is popular and hope to capitalize on this trend with their movie. They do not want a "Star Wars" or "Star Trek" modern appearance to the film. Instead, they want audiences to think they are watching an old movie version of the future.

The storyline is about the discovery in 2054 of radio signals from a planet circling the Alpha Centauri triple star system. At about 4.35 light years from earth, it is our closest neighboring star. Explorers from earth will lead a mission to find out who (or what) lives there.

The story begins with the voyage, which takes about a year with the star drive engines (its about 25.5 trillion miles away). When the explorers get to the star

test your knowledge 384

10. Design Evolution, Animation & Style Projects

system, they find a battle going on between inhabitants of the planet, the good "Centaurians" who are quite human-like, and a species of insect-looking warriors. One of the earth ship's crew, Kira, calls them the "Insectoids." The name sticks. The Insectoids are systematically taking over planets and are working their way toward earth. Our explorer crew join the Centaurians to help defeat the Insectoids, thus saving the earth from almost certain attack.

As with any film of this type, props are necessary to carry off the image of the future and provide the actors with devices that don't exist today. Props are generally appearance models that do not have to actually function. Special effects teams will fill-in whatever is necessary to make it appear as if the props are working as they should.

design brief In Pro/DESKTOP, design and model the props that will be used for the film "Alpha Centauri." Each prop needs to be the appropriate size and to scale, and also have that "streamlined" look of the old science-fiction films. A partial list of required props follows, but there are many more that will be needed for a major motion picture like "Alpha Centauri."

Each prop should be designed in 3D and rendered in the Album environment of Pro/DESKTOP. Actual model props should be produced if time and facilities permit.

Partial Prop List
✓ communicator to reach ship in orbit (each crew member will carry one)
✓ hand-held medical diagnostic unit
✓ portable computer
✓ ray-gun pistol-1
✓ ray-gun pistol-2
✓ ray-gun rifle-1
✓ ray-gun rifle-2
✓ personal rocket back-pack for getting around on the planet
✓ wrist-watch/short-range communicator

- ✓ space helmet
- ✓ back-pack oxygen unit for helmet
- ✓ star ship – for crew of 10
- ✓ shuttle craft – for crew of 5

Starting Points

Starting any new project requires inspiration. The goal of this section is to help you find that inspiration by looking at what others have done on related projects.

Review parts of films and search the internet to become acquainted with the "streamlined" Art Deco style of the 1930's, '40's and '50's, and what people of that time thought the future would look like. Draw a few sketches and save some photos of good examples for later reference and for your portfolio documentation.

Search the internet for images with the key words "space ship" and "raygun" and sketch features you might be able to use in your designs. Again, save some photos and sketches for your portfolio.

Find photos of cars from the 1930's through the 1950's. These reflect the "futuristic" view of the time, with fins and lots of chrome. Look up "Art Deco style" on the internet.

Specifications

Prop designs may be developed in one file (no assembly necessary); prop designs must be developed full-size. For example, a communicator should be developed in inches or millimeters but a shuttle should be developed in feet or meters; prop designs need to reflect a style of the 1950s version of the future; prop designs must be rendered in the Album interface, with appropriate materials, colors, etc.; final designs should be rendered with lighting and background effects. Your final project should be printed in color or viewed on the computer screen as a jpeg image. If you know how, you might want to post your design to a web page.

Project 10.5 CD Amplifier

Background
Many hand-held MP3 and CD players provide plenty of power to drive a pair of earphones to quite a loud volume. But there are times when it would be nice to be able to listen to MP3s or CDs without the earphones. A small battery-operated product that would plug into the earphone jack of the hand-held player and provide adequate volume through self-contained speakers would be nice for camping trips or picnics.

Design Challenge
Katodyne Power Systems manufactures consumer electronics products. The company has identified a market for a small portable stereo amplifier for people who own hand-held MP3 and CD players and like to use them in locations where there is no access to household electricity.

Katodyne has manufacturing facilities for injection-molding and printed circuit board production. The company seeks design proposals for this new product.

design brief
Design and develop the case for a battery-operated, low power stereo amplifier with two speakers. The product is intended to connect to a hand-held MP3 or CD player. The design must use standard electronic components and batteries. The components must be held securely in place to prevent damage.

Specifications
- Create a printed circuit board component to be used in the assembly, 3-inches wide x 2-inches long x 0.0625-inches thick. Provide mounting holes if necessary.
- Create a speaker component to be used in the assembly, 3-inches wide x 3-inches long x 2-inches high. Provide four mounting holes, one in each corner of the 3 x 3 face.
- Create a 9-volt battery model to be used in the assembly.
- The product must accommodate two amplifiers, two speakers, two 9-volt batteries, an on/off switch and one potentiometer volume control;
- The product must be compact;

10. Design Evolution, Animation & Style Projects

- The product must be designed to travel, so components should be secured in place;
- The product must be contemporary looking and aesthetically pleasing.

Starting Points

The first step in any design work is to become familiar with the "state of the art." In other words, what have others done to solve similar problems? Here are some suggestions to start you on your investigation:

- Look at MP3 and hand-held CD players for style ideas. You might consider designing your product to go with some of the popular models. However, you would not want your design to be too closely tied to one manufacture's MP3 or CD player, because you want to appeal to as large a customer base as possible. After all, companies must make money to stay in business.

Project 10.6 Communication Device of the Future

Background

Just twenty years ago telephones needed to be plugged into a wall jack and computers were bulky things that required heavy monitors. The few people who used computers used them for word processing but little more. The world wide web hadn't been invented yet and fax machines were the size of a kitchen stove. The development of communication technology has brought us things that people twenty years ago didn't even dream of.

Design Challenge

Your challenge is to design the next generation of communication devices. It might do the same things that a number of existing devices do separately (like the new cell phones that store and play MP3 files), or it might do something new that we don't have a product for yet.

Some future thinkers believe that these new devices will be worn on our wrist,

test your knowledge   **388**

10. Design Evolution, Animation & Style Projects

while others think that they will become part of the clothes we wear. What do you think?

In the next few years electronics will become smaller and more efficient, so products may become smaller (like the new notebook computers that used to be called laptop computers, and digital assistants becoming more like notebook computers).

Think about how people might access its functions. For example, using a keyboard computer works on a desktop or notebook computer but it doesn't work very well when trying to send text messages on a cell phone. You will need to devise ways for machine-human interaction.

design brief Design and model in Pro/DESKTOP® a new communications device that will be released in the year 2010.

Specifications
Accompanying your 3D CAD designs must be a one-page report that addresses the following questions:

- What new technologies that do not exist today will be required to make your product workable?
- What purpose will the new product have and what products or devices available today will it likely replace?

10. Design Evolution, Animation & Style Projects

Project 10.7 Headlight for Bicycle

Background
Products for bicycles are very marketable items and sell well to both younger and older adults. Most people would like a modern-looking product to attach to their bike, so the appearance of the light is very important.

Design and model a bicycle light that is made from several individual parts, such as the light body, lens, battery, reflector, cap, etc. It should be "modern-looking" and will be manufactured from plastic.

Specifications
- The light will be powered by two D-cells side-by-side.
- You must model the D-cell.
- It should have a reflector of at least 2-inches in diameter, but it may be larger.
- It must have some way to attach it to handlebars.
- In your final assembly, bring in the handlebars you created in Chapter 8 and attach the light to them.

11

pro/DESKTOP® and engineering drawing

Figure 11.1

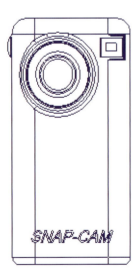

Figure 11.2

In this chapter you will learn how to:

- Create a custom drawing format
- Use the custom drawing format with an engineering drawing
- Import dimensions from a Design file into an engineering drawing
- Create new dimensions in an engineering drawing

Introduction

Design work takes creativity, research, trial and error, and collaboration with other people who have a stake in the final design. Designers often begin the design of parts and products and find that their ideas do not work out. So, they start again, sometimes from the very beginning. Good design must balance many different requirements, and sometimes those requirements conflict. For many designers, this is what makes the work so interesting and challenging.

Engineering drawings are created when the design work is completed. Engineering drawings are sometimes called **technical drawings,** and while they may take a number of forms, the terms are most often used to refer to **orthographic drawings**. Orthographic drawings are drawings made from looking straight down on an object perpendicular to the plane of the object. The camera in Figure 11.1 is represented in an orthographic front view in Figure 11.2.

11. Pro/DESKTOP and Engineering Drawing

introduction

Orthographic drawings are sometimes called three-view drawings because it usually takes three views (the front, the top, and one side) to get all the information necessary to fully describe the object. Many objects, however, require more than three views. There are instances in which an object can be fully described in only two views, but these objects are circular, like the kind of model you would make with the Revolve Profile feature.

Technical drawing is a very important part of engineering and product development. The use of computer-aided design programs and the use of computer-controlled machines in manufacturing have changed the way these drawings are created and used.

It was just a few decades ago that technical drawings were only created by hand drawing. Draftsmen (they were typically men) sat or stood in front of a drawing board and used T-squares, parallel rules, and mechanical devices called drafting machines to carefully draw and letter orthographic drawings. The creation of these drawings took many hours and sometimes days or weeks to complete. When the drawings were done, they were used by machinists and other skilled workers to create the parts illustrated on the drawings.

Today, many companies develop engineering drawings automatically with the CAD programs they use to design the component. With the creation of engineering drawings at the "touch of a button" the job of a draftsman is rapidly disappearing.

Engineering Drawings

Engineering drawings are precise. That is, these drawings provide the reader with the exact specifications to make the part. Typical engineering drawings show the size and shape of parts, the location of holes, slots and other features, the surface finish, and even the way in which parts are welded, if that is an aspect of the design.

When a skilled worker has a good set of engineering drawings, all the information to make the part is included on those pages. Good drawings leave no question unanswered, so the person making the part does not have to go ask questions of the designers.

With more and more companies using automated equipment to manufacture parts and products, the emphasis on engineering drawing is changing from making the part to checking the part after it has been made. Engineering drawings are used in quality control (sometimes called quality assurance) to make certain that the part has been produced to the specifications required by the design. Quality control workers will carefully measure and test components against the engineering drawing specifications.

Engineering drawing is a kind of language. You have to know the language to read it. Entire textbooks are devoted to understanding and reading engineering drawings, but you do not need to have that kind of in-depth knowledge to create them with Pro/DESKTOP. In this chapter you will only be introduced to engineering drawings and how to automatically create and print them.

Third-Angle versus First-Angle Projection

When you start a new Engineering Drawing you are asked to choose a template in the dialog box. Two choices include third-angle and first-angle projection. The angle of projection refers to the placement of views in an orthographic drawing. **In Figure 11.3** you see cameras

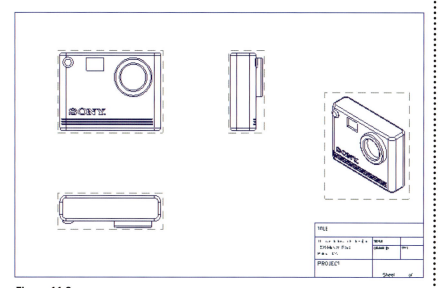

Figure 11.3

formatted in first-angle projection. Note the placement of the front view (the view with the most detail) and the view below it. If you were to rotate the top of the camera toward you, you would see the view below the front view. If you were to rotate the left side camera toward you, you would see the view to the right of the front view. First-angle projection is used in Europe and many Asian countries.

The same camera is formatted in third-angle projection in **Figure 11.4**. Note the placement of the front and other views in third-angle projection. If you were to rotate the top of the camera toward you, you would see the view above the front view. This is the top view. If you were to

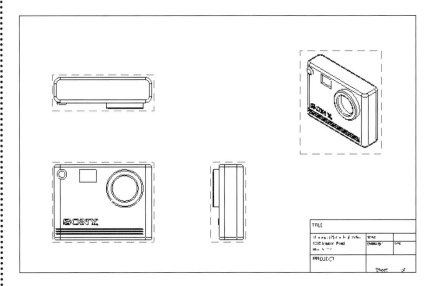

Figure 11.4

rotate the right side of the camera toward you, you would see the view on the right of the front view. This is called the right-side view. Third-angle projection is used in the United States.

Technical Drawing Standards

The American National Standards Institute (ANSI) creates the rules for technical drawings for the United States. Standards have been developed for both English units (inches, etc.) and metric units.

The International Organization for Standards (ISO) has its headquarters in Geneva, Switzerland, and has developed standards for the almost 100 nations that form its membership. The ISO uses metric units as its standard.

11. Pro/DESKTOP and Engineering Drawing

Paper Sheet Size	Inches (WxH)	Millimeters (WxH)
A0	43.8 x 33.1	1189 x 841
A1	33.1 x 24.4	841 x 595
A2	24.4 x 16.5	595 x 420
A3	16.5 x 11.7	420 x 297
A4	11.7 x 8.3	297 x 219
A5	8.3 x 5.9	210 x 149
ANSI A	11 x 8.5	279.4 x 215.9
ANSI B	17 x 11	431.8 x 279.4
ANSI C	22 x 17	558.8 x 431.8
ANSI D	34 x 22	863.6 x 550.8
ANSI E	44 x 34	1117.6 x 863.6

Figure 11.5

Figure 11.5 shows the specifications for each of these formats. For example, the standard ANSI B is the one you would choose if you want to use 11-inches by 17-inches paper size, sometimes called tabloid size. ANSI A is the choice for US standard 8.5-inches x 11-inches letter size paper.

The ISO standard uses "A" sizes. The A4 size is the letter size where metric units are the standard. While the United States still uses the ANSI standard, most of the rest of the world uses the ISO standard.

These organizations have developed standards for much more than drawing paper sizes. Rules for views and dimensioning, including where the dimensions should be located, how the numbers are presented, and how dimension tolerances are represented are part of the standards. In addition, the standards suggest the size, shape and elements of drawing title blocks. Pro/DESKTOP provides a title block for drawings that meet these guidelines. The lines and title block of a drawing are saved as a ***Drawing Format*** in Pro/DESKTOP.

Drawing Formats in Pro/DESKTOP

Formats are sketches that lay under an engineering drawing. If you want a special border, title block, name, or any other text or lines included on the drawings you make, then the way to do it is with a custom drawing format. Figure 11.6 shows a custom drawing format that has a full border and a title block with the name of a school.

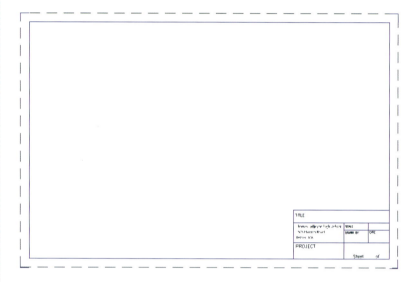

Figure 11.6

The Drawing Format files are located in the Pro/DESKTOP Program folder and are titled A0 to A5 and ANSI A to ANSI E. Figure 11.7

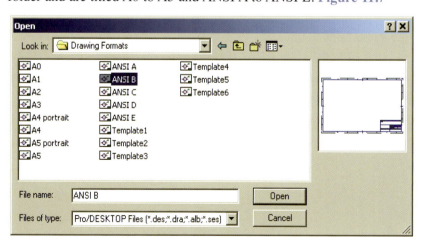

Figure 11.7

11. Pro/DESKTOP and Engineering Drawing

shows the files that are included with the Pro/DESKTOP program. Note that there are two files that are called "portrait." ***Portrait*** and ***Landscape*** are terms used to describe the orientation of a drawing. **Figure 11.8** shows both of these orientations. The portrait orientation on the left is higher than it is wide. The landscape orientation on the right is wider than it is high. The A4 and A5 format files labeled portrait give you the option for a pre-defined drawing format in the portrait orientation.

Figure 11.8 Portrait orientation (red) and landscape orientation (blue).

Creating a Custom Drawing Format

Creating a custom format requires several steps. You must modify an existing format file and save it as a new file.

Exercise 11.1 Custom Drawing Format

In the Engineering Drawing Interface, ***Open*** an existing drawing format and ***Save*** it as a new file. This protects the original file.

Open a Drawing Format

- Choose the ***Open File*** icon.

- Navigate a path to the ***C: Drive > Program Files > PTC > Program > Drawing Formats***.

- Choose either ***ANSI A*** or ***ISO A4*** (**Figure 11.9**) and ***Save As*** a new file named ***custom format-1*** on the Desktop or other appropriate location. Save the file to your floppy, zip or USB pen drive. It is unlikely that you will be able to save this in the Drawing Formats directory, as administrative permissions are needed to save files in this location. This is an important step as you do not want to modify the existing format file.

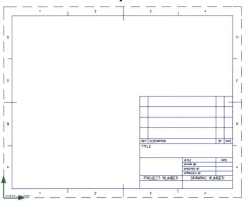

Figure 11.9

- Close the *ANSA A* or *A4 file*. When you use the *Save As* command, Pro/DESKTOP does not open the new file as you might expect. You must close the file you opened and then Open the new file name you saved.
- *Open* the file *custom format-1.dra*.

One of the disadvantages of the existing ANSI A / A4 formats provided by Pro/DESKTOP is that there is not much space for the actual drawing because the title block takes up so much room. Of course these are small formats and more complex drawings will require larger paper sizes. But, we can change the format drawing to provide a bit more room.

Modify the Lines in a Drawing Format

- With the file *customformat-1.dra* open, look at the Browser window on the left side of the screen (**Figure 11.10**). Note the sketches listed under the drawing *sheet 1*. Each sketch describes the lines and text on the format drawing.
- *Double-click* on each pencil icon to the left of a sketch name and note the lines or text that are selected (in red) on the drawing. To delete lines or text (or change text), the appropriate sketch must be the active sketch (bold text in the Browser).
- Select the *Title Block Thin* sketch by double-clicking on the pencil icon. A number of lines within the title block are selected in red.
- Use the *Delete* key to delete these lines (**Figure 11.11**).
- Go back to the Browser window and select the *Title Block Thick* sketch by double-clicking on the pencil icon.
- Click once off to the side of the title block to deselect the lines.
- Use the *Select Lines* tool to select the top horizontal line and the next horizontal line down on the title block.

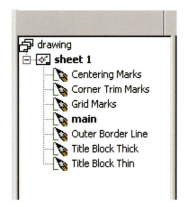

Figure 11.10

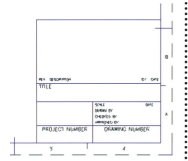

Figure 11.11

- Use the **Delete** key to delete these lines (**Figure 11.12**).
- Readjust the length of the left line by using the **Select Lines** tool. Select it and drag it down until it meets the top horizontal line (**Figure 11.13**).

You can add or delete lines in this fashion. Use the **Drawing tools** you are familiar with from the Design Interface to create borders or lines in a title block. For this project the Grid Marks, Corner Marks and the Centering Marks of the standard title block were deleted (**Figure 11.14**).

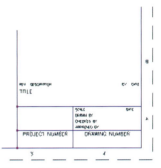

Figure 11.12

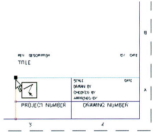

Figure 11.13

Figure 11.14

Next, you will modify the text in the title block. Text is not entered directly on the drawing, but entered into a dialog box instead.

Modify Text in a Drawing Format

- Using the **Text Note** tool, select the text you want to erase and use the Delete key. For this project the numbers on the outside of the drawing border were deleted along with some of the other text that fell outside the new title block. Note that the word "title" was dragged into the bottom section of the title block.

 Text Note tool

- To enter new text, select the **Text Note** tool and while holding down the **Shift** key, drag the cursor with the mouse. The word **Note** is created. If you do not hold down the Shift key while you drag the mouse, a note with a leader line is created.

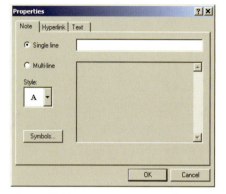

Figure 11.15

- Double-click on the word *Note* that you just created and a dialog box appears (**Figure 11.15**). You can choose to enter only one line of text or multiple lines of text. By selecting the Text tab in the dialog box you will get the options shown in **Figure 11.16**. You can choose the size of text (height) and even rotate the text so you can make title blocks along the edge of the drawing. **Figure 11.17** shows an architectural style title block that was created using these options. This style of title block is useful when you have multi-sheet projects and want to bind the folio on the left edge.

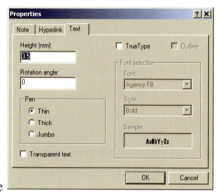

Figure 11.16

- *Save* your work.

Figure 11.17

Exercise 11.2 Create a Design File

First, you will create a file in the *Design Interface* that includes constraints. This file will be used in the *Drawing Interface* in the next several sections.

- Start a *New Design*.
- Create a *New Sketch* named *side profile on the lateral workplane*.
- *Save* the file as *bracket-1.des*.
- *Draw* the sketch you see in **Figure 11.18** on the side profile sketch. Be sure to constrain it with the sketch dimensions shown.
- *Extrude* the sketch 1.5-inches below the workplane.
- Select the face of the bracket (**Figure 11.19**) and create a *New Sketch* named *bearing holes* and a *New Workplane* named *front face*.

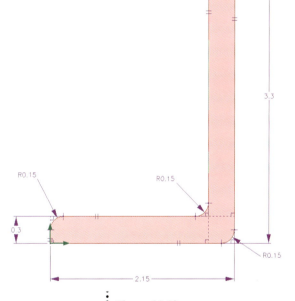

Figure 11.18

Figure 11.19

- **Draw** the three circles in the locations indicated in **Figure 11.20**.
- Use the **Project Profile** feature to create the holes through the bracket.
- Select the top face of the lower part of the bracket (**Figure 11.21**) and create a **New Sketch** named **mounting holes** and a **New Workplane** named **top face**.
- **Draw** the four, 0.25-inch holes on the sketch in the locations indicated in **Figure 11.22**.
- Use the **Project Profile** feature to create the holes through the bracket (**Figure 11.23**).
- Use the keyboard shortcut **Shift+T** to change to a **Trimetric** view.
- **Save** your work.

The bracket you have created in the Design Interface will now be used in the Drawing Interface.

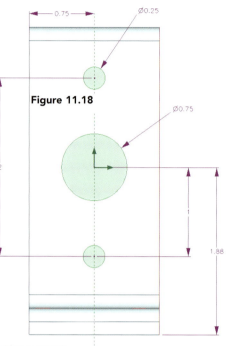

Figure 11.18

Figure 11.21

Figure 11.20

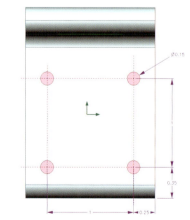

Figure 11.22

Figure 11.23

Exercise 11.3 **Using a Custom Drawing Format**

When you have completed a design and want to put it in an engineering drawing, you can use the custom drawing format to present your work for printing. Use the following steps to create the engineering drawing.

- *Open* the design file *bracket-1.des* if it is not already open.

- With a design file opened in the Design Interface, choose *New Engineering Drawing* from the *File* pull-down menu.

- Select the top center template, which gives you a new A2 size drawing with third-angle projection. Make sure the *Design in session* radio button is selected and the correct file name appears in the Design window on the right side of the dialog box. The A2 size is usually too large to print on a standard printer (24.4" x 16.6"), but the size will be reduced later.

- Click *OK* to close the dialog box.

- *Save* the file as *bracket-draw.dra*.

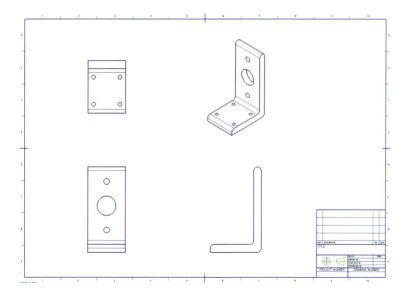

Figure 11.25

The drawing in **Figure 11.25** is the result. It contains the standard three views (front, top or plan view) and right-side, plus a trimetric view.

Note that it is possible to import other views from the Design file if necessary. Go to the **Drawing** pull-down menu and select **Add Modeling View** at the top of the list. You can choose to add a view from any workplane or from the Design Window. Do not add any views at this time.

Next, you will change the drawing format and paper size to **ANSI B** by using a custom drawing format. In the previous section you modified an **ANSI A** sheet. If you want an **ANSI B** sheet you will need to create your own using the same process you used on the **ANSI A**.

- Go to the **Drawing** pull-down menu and select **Sheet Setup** from the list (**Figure 11.26**). The **Drawing Sheet Properties** dialog box appears.

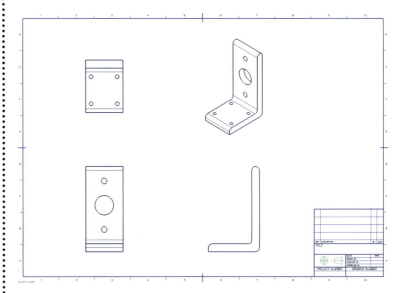

Figure 11.26

- Click on the *Browse* button and locate the custom drawing format file you wish to use. Ours was found in *Drawing formats>Program>Pro/DESKTOP 8.0* folder on the *C: drive* (Figure 11.27).
- Select the drawing format file and click *Open*.
- Click *OK* to close the *Drawing Sheet Properties* dialog box.

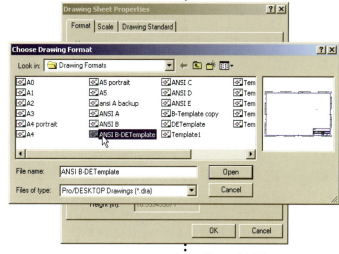

Figure 11.27

Now, the four views do not fit the smaller drawing sheet (Figure 11.28), so you must scale the views to make them fit.

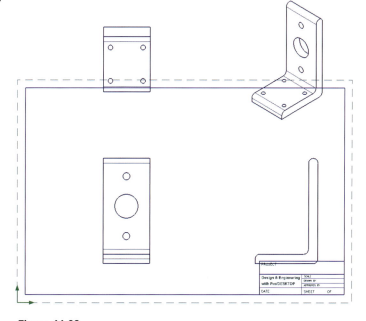

Figure 11.28

Select Views Icon

- Click on the ***Select Views*** icon on the right toolbar and, holding the ***Shift*** key, select the dashed lines around all four views (**Figure 11.29**).

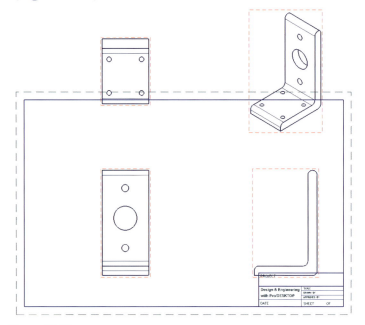

Figure 11.29

- Go to the ***Drawing*** pull-down menu and select ***Sheet Setup*** from the list. Click on the ***Scale*** tab.

- Change the scale for ***Paper*** from 3 to 2 (**Figure 11.30**). The rule is, to make a view smaller, reduce the value of the ***Paper*** in this dialog box. Click ***OK*** to close the ***Drawing Sheet Properties*** dialog box.

Figure 11.30

The size of the four views has been reduced (**Figure 11.31**) but they need to be moved.

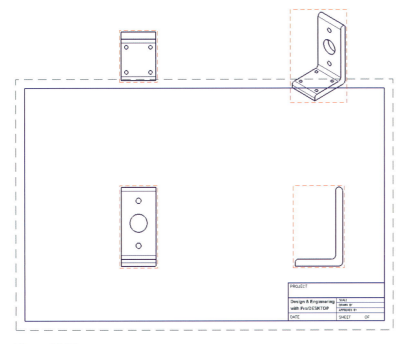

Figure 11.31

Views can be moved around to create the spacing you want.

- Click on the **Select Views** icon on the right side of the Drawing Screen.
- A dashed-line box appears around each view. Select the box by clicking on the line and releasing (it turns red), and then click and drag the view into position (**Figure 11.32**).
- Drag each view to the positions in **Figure 11.33**, where the front view is in the lower left corner, the top view (or plan view) is above it, and the right side view is to the right of the front view.

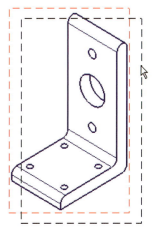

Figure 11.32

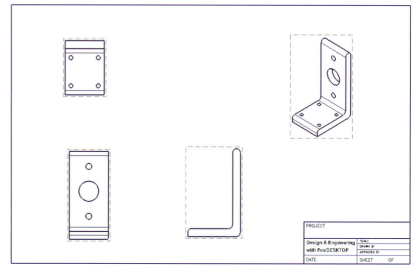

Figure 11.33

- Move the isometric view to the upper right corner. Allow room around each view for dimensions that may be added later.

When you have moved the views into approximate positions, you can use the *Align Other Views* command to make sure that the edges of each view align accurately with other views.

- Select the dashed line around the ***front view*** with the ***Select Views*** tool. Go to the ***Drawing*** pull-down menu and select ***Align Other Views*** (Figure 11.34). The top and right side views now align with the front view as in Figure 11.35.
- ***Save*** your work.

Figure 11.34

11. Pro/DESKTOP and Engineering Drawing

engineering drawings   411

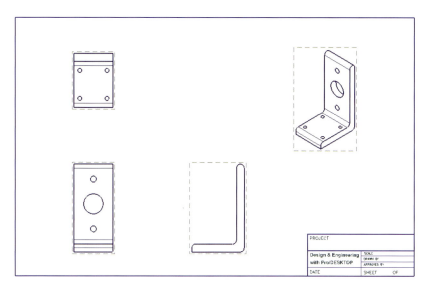

Figure 11.35

Exercise 11.4 Dimensioning Parts in Engineering Drawings

Engineering drawings provide detailed and accurate information about a component. To do this, dimensions that specify size, shape, location of holes and other details are included. In this next section you will learn how to import dimensions you used in your *Design* file into a *Drawing* file.

- Open the drawing file **bracket-draw.dra** if it is not already open.
- *Save as* a new file named **bracket-draw-1.dra**.
- Go to the **Dimension** pull-down menu at the top of the screen and select **Import Sketch Dimensions** from the list (Figure 11.36).

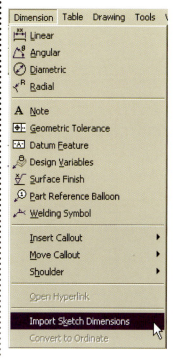

Figure 11.36

The dimensions you used to constrain the sizes and locations of holes and the overall shape of the bracket in the Design file are now visible in the Drawing file (**Figure 11.37**).

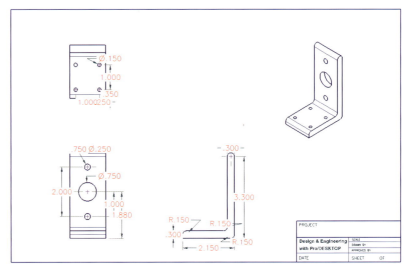

Figure 11.37

- Click once off the drawing sheet to deselect the dimensions.

A problem that immediately becomes evident is the placement of the dimensions on the drawing. It is unclear which detail of the drawing is related to which dimension because they are all crowded together. In the next step you will move the dimensions around to "unscramble" the tangle.

- Click on the ***Drawing*** pull-down menu at the top of the screen and select ***Sheet Setup*** from the list.
- Click on the ***Drawing Standards*** tab and then on the ***Modify*** button (**Figure 11.38**).

Figure 11.38

You now can modify quite a number of drawing standards, but right now we are interested in the size of the numbers on the drawing.

- Click on the *Text* tab and change the *Height* (in): to 0.1-inch (**Figure 11.39**).
- Click *OK* to close the *Standards* dialog box and click *OK* again to close the *Drawing Sheet Properties* dialog box.

The drawing should now look like **Figure 11.40** with smaller size numbers.

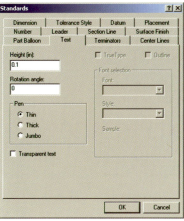

Figure 11.39

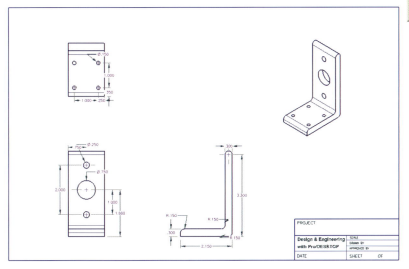

Figure 11.40

Now, the location and position of some of the annotations can be changed to make the drawing even clearer.

- Click on the *Select Annotations* tool on the right side of the screen. An annotation provides additional information that helps clarify details. In this case, the annotations are measurements.

Select Annotations tool

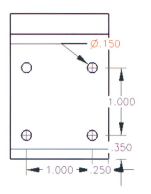

Figure 11.41

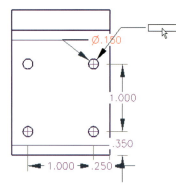

Figure 11.42

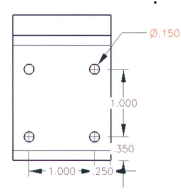

Figure 11.43

Annotations also include notes about materials, surface finishes and other information that would help someone construct the object.

- Move the cursor over the number Ø.150 on the top view. It describes the diameter of the holes in the base of the bracket. It will pre-highlight in bright blue (It may take a second or two for the pre-highlighting to happen.).
- Click once to select the annotation (**Figure 11.41**).
- Drag the annotation up and to the right as shown in **Figure 11.42**. When you release the mouse button, the dimension of the hole should look like **Figure 11.43**.

To move the location of annotations on linear dimensions (such as that in **Figure 11.44**) you must select the *dimension line* instead of the number (annotation) itself.

Figure 11.44

There are many rules and "conventions" (meaning standards) for the placement of dimensions on an engineering drawing. It is beyond the scope of this book to go into them. But here are a few rules of thumb for dimensioning:

- Avoid placing dimensions on the part itself.
- Locate dimensions between views when possible.
- Locate dimensions on a view that shows the shape of the part.
- Make sure you show the overall dimensions of a part.

In **Figure 11.45** the dimensions have been moved around to help make the final drawing more clear.

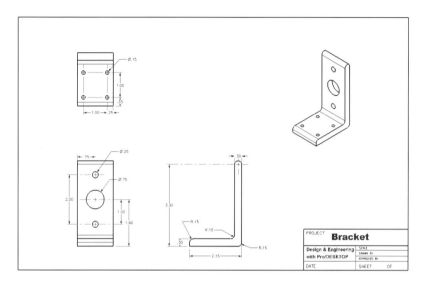

Figure 11.45

View Properties

There are a couple of interesting options available that can be set separately for each view. Making hidden lines visible is one such option. ***Hidden lines*** in engineering drawings are the edges of corners or holes that fall inside of a solid object. For example, **Figure 11.46a** shows views of a solid. In **Figure 11.46b** the hidden lines of the hole and the cut-out corner are shown.

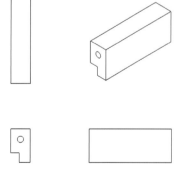

Figure 11.46a

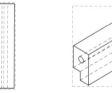

Figure 11.46b

Another option is to **show shading** in a view. While this is generally not done in an orthographic view, shading can help communicate the shape of the object in the isometric or trimetric view (**Figure 11.47**).

Figure 11.47

Exercise 11.5 Change View Properties

- Open the **bracket-draw.dra** drawing file if it is not already open.
- **Save as** a new file named **bracket-draw-2.dra**.
- Click on the **Select Views** tool on the right side of the screen. A dashed box appears around each view.

Select Views tool

- Select the **right side** view by clicking on the dashed box around it.
- **Right mouse-click** and choose **Properties** from the floating menu.
- Check the box **Show hidden lines** in the **Properties** dialog box (**Figure 11.48**).
- Close the box by clicking **OK**. The hidden lines now appear as dashed lines in that view (**Figure 11.49**).

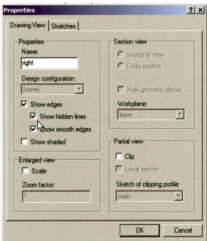

Figure 11.48

- Select the *trimetric view* with the *Select Views* tool by clicking on the dashed box around it.
- *Right mouse-click* and choose *Properties* from the floating menu.
- Check the box *Show shaded* and close the dialog box by clicking *OK*. The trimetric view is now shaded (**Figure 11.50**).

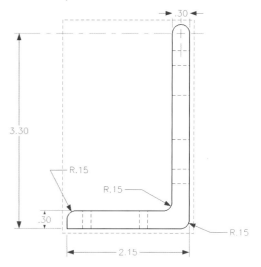

Figure 11.49

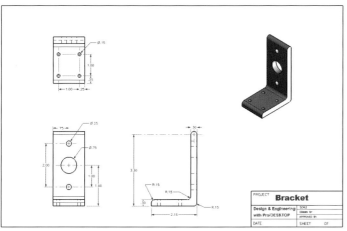

Figure 11.50

- Choose another tool to get rid of the dashed lines around each view.

Notice that you can change the size of a selected view, so if you want the trimetric view to be larger than the other views you can do so.

Adding New Dimensions to Engineering Drawings

Often, you will need to add a dimension that you did not create in the Design file to an engineering drawing. Pro/DESKTOP gives you several dimensioning tools for drawings.

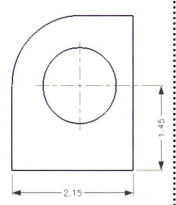

Figure 11.51

- **Linear Dimension tool** – Used for dimensioning a linear distance, such as the length of a side or the distance between the center of a hole and an edge such as found in **Figure 11.51**.
- **Angular Dimension tool** – Used for dimensioning the angle between two planes or other objects (**Figure 11.52**).
- **Diametric Dimension tool** – Used for dimensioning a diameter, such as the various diameter parts of the object in **Figure 11.53**.

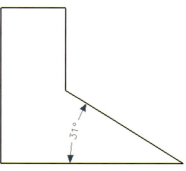

Figure 11.52

Linear Dimension Tool

Angular Dimension Tool

Diametric Dimension Tool

Radial Diametric Tool

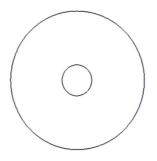

Figure 11.53

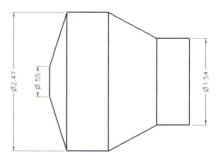

- **Radial Diametric tool** – Used for dimensioning a radius, such as the inside radius on the left and the outside radius (round) on the right on the object in **Figure 11.54**.

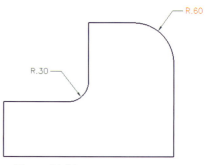

Figure 11.54

11. Pro/DESKTOP and Engineering Drawing

engineering drawings 419

When you are applying dimensions on complex objects, Pro/DESKTOP may slow down a bit so be patient and wait until a line or annotation is selected (turns red) before dragging into position.

Exercise 11.6 Creating Dimensions on an Engineering Drawing

Create the *Design File*

- Start a *New Design* file.
- *Save* the file as *supportblock.des*.
- On the base workplane, initial sketch draw a 2-inch by 4.5-inch rectangle (**Figure 11.55**).
- *Extrude* the rectangle to 1.5-inches high.
- Place a *New Sketch* named *extension* on top of the solid.
- *Draw* a 2-inch by 2-inch square on the new sketch.
- *Extrude* it to 1.5-inches (**Figure 11.56**).
- Use the *Round feature* to create a 0.75-inch fillet where the bottom and top extrusions meet.
- Use the *Round* feature to create a 0.5-inch round on the top right edge (**Figure 11.57**).
- Place a *New Sketch* named *hole* on the front of the object.

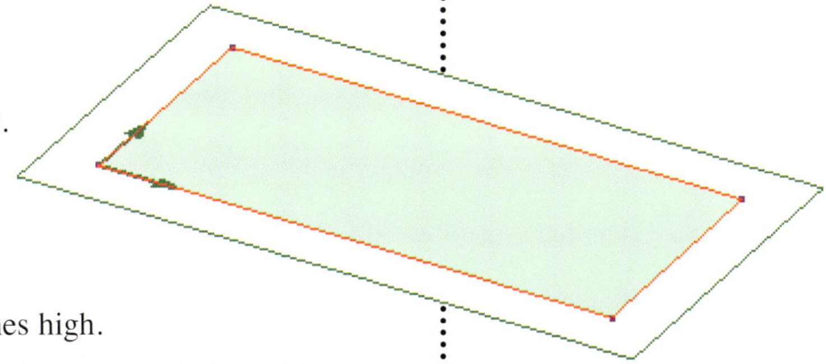

Figure 11.55

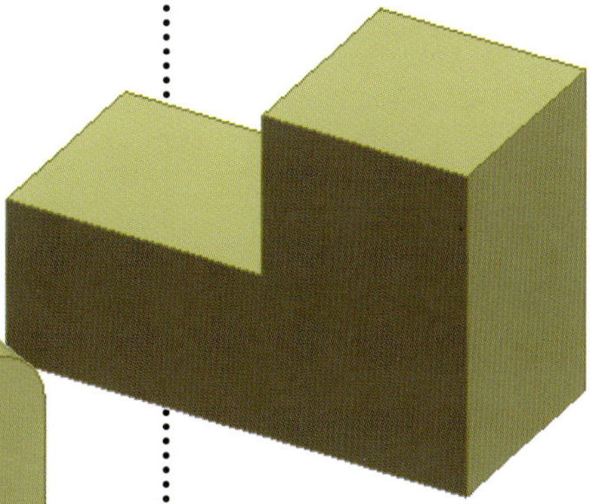

Figure 11.56

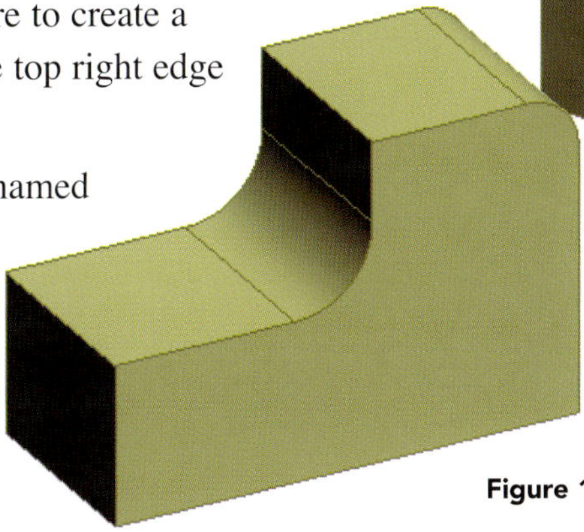

Figure 11.57

- **Draw** a small circle on the hole sketch and **Project** it through the object to make the hole (**Figure 11.58**).

Create the Engineering Drawing

The file **supportblock.des** must be open.

Figure 11.58

- Start a **New Engineering Drawing**.
- Select the **New 3rd Angle Projection** option on the **New Engineering Drawing** dialog box. Click **OK** to close the box. The engineering drawing appears with four views (**Figure 11.59**).
- **Save** drawing file as **supportblock.dra**.

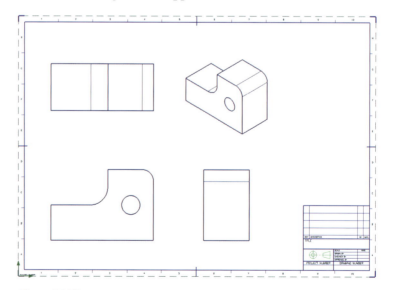

Figure 11.59

- Click on the **Linear Dimension** tool and select the bottom object line of the front view (**Figure 11.60**).

11. Pro/DESKTOP and Engineering Drawing

engineering drawings 421

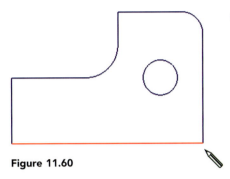

Figure 11.60

- Using the same technique you have been using when in the **Design Interface**, click on the top horizontal line on the **right side** view and drag to the right (**Figure 11.61**). The height of the object is dimensioned.

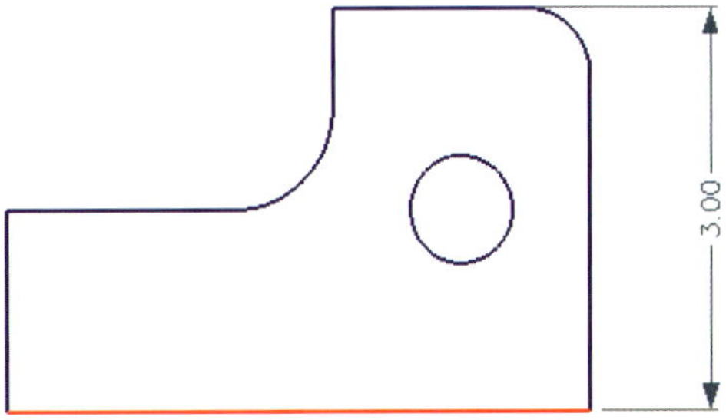

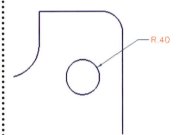

Figure 11.61

- Using the **Radial Dimension** tool select the hole circle on the front view and drag up and to the right. Note that the hole is dimensioned as a radius (**Figure 11.62**), which is not commonly done. Next you will change the radius dimension to a diameter dimension.

- While the radius dimension is still selected, *right mouse-click* and select **Properties** from the floating menu.

- Click on the **Measurement** tab and select *diameter* for the size (**Figure 11.63**).

- Click **OK** to close the dialog box.

Figure 11.63

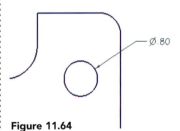

Figure 11.62

Figure 11.64

The hole measurement is now a diameter, as seen in **Figure 11.64**.

Add Hidden Lines

- Use the *Select Views* tool to select the dashed box around the top view.
- Right mouse-click while the box is selected and choose *Properties* from the menu.
- Check *Show hidden lines* to make hidden lines visible in the top view.
- Repeat the same process on the right side view.
- Select the *trimetric view*, right mouse-click and choose *Properties* from the menu.
- Check *Show shaded* to make the trimetric view appear shaded.

Your engineering drawing should now look like **Figure 11.65**.

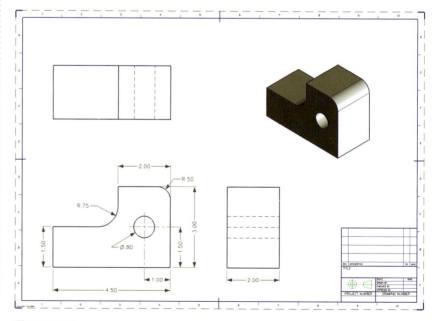

Figure 11.65

Create Center Lines

- Choose the **Select Features** tool on the right side of the screen.
- Select the circle (hole) on the front view. It may take a moment before it turns red.

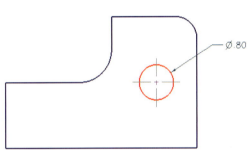

- Go to the **Center Line** pull-down menu at the top of the screen and choose **Center Points** from the list (**Figure 11.66**). The front view should now look like **Figure 11.67**.

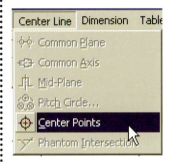

Figure 11.66

Figure 11.67

The hidden lines in the top and right side views may seem confusing, so you will extend the center lines to the other views.

- Using the **Select Features** tool, hold the cursor over the hidden lines that show the hole in the top view. Click once to select these hidden lines (**Figure 11.68**).

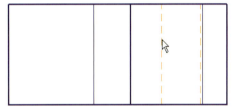

Figure 11.68

- Go to the **Center Line** pull-down menu and choose **Common Axis** from the list (**Figure 11.69**). The top view should now look like **Figure 11.70**.

Figure 11.69

Figure 11.70

If you would like to join the center line on the top view to the center line on the front view, here is the procedure:

- Using the **Select Features** tool, select the center line in the top view and the vertical center line in the front view (holding down the **Shift** key). Both lines should be red (**Figure 11.71**).

- Go to the **Center Line** pull-down menu and choose **Common Plane** from the list (**Figure 11.72**). The drawing should now look like **Figure 11.73**.

- Dimension the rest of the support block, making sure you properly locate the hole. Your finished engineering drawing should look something like **Figure 11.74**.

Figure 11.72

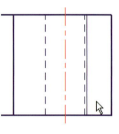

Figure 11.71

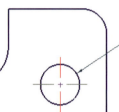

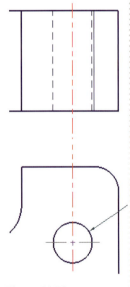

Figure 11.73

Figure 11.74

Summary

Engineering drawings are created when the design work is completed and further changes to the design are not currently planned. These drawings are used for quality control applications and when parts are to be hand-made.

Two standards for engineering drawings have been developed. One set, called ANSI, is used within the United States and another called ISO, covers most of the rest of the world. ANSI standards are generally in inches (although there are ANSI metric standards) and ISO standards are in metric measurements. While ANSI uses third-angle projection, ISO generally uses first-angle projection as a standard.

Pro/DESKTOP allows the use of custom drawing formats so that engineering drawings can be printed on personalized sheets with custom title blocks and borders. Most companies create custom formats to include the company name and other information that will be printed on every drawing created.

Pro/DESKTOP automatically creates engineering drawings from Design files. These drawings can be custom dimensioned or dimensions created in the Design Interface can be imported directly into the drawing. It is often necessary to adjust the position of imported dimensions for drawing clarity.

Engineering drawings can be created from any of the previous projects in this book, so there is ample material from which to work.

Test Your Knowledge

Create Engineering Drawings from the following projects in this book. Include all dimensions.

Exercise 2.5 Digital Camera Model
File: *camera-1.des*

Exercise 5.2 Wheel
File: *wheel-2.des*

Exercise 6.1 Ballpoint Pen
File: *ballpoint-1.des*

Exercise 6.2 Energy Drink Bottle
File: *bottle-1.des*

Exercise 6.4 Triumph Valve
File: *intakevalve.des*

Exercise 8.5 Propane Nut
File: *propanenut.des*

Make Multiple-Sheet Engineering Drawings from previous book exercises and projects.

Exercise 7.1 Ballpoint Pen Assembly
Files: *pentop.des, penbarrel.des, inkcartridge.des, penassembly.des*

Project 10.1 Desk Lamp
Files: *lampbase.des, lowerarm.des, upperarm.des, lamphead.des, lampshade.des, lampassembly.des*

Project 10.2 Art Deco Clock
Files: *artdecoclock.des, lens.des, bezel.des, mechanism.des, nut.des, minutehand.des, hourhand.des, clockassembly.des*

Project 10.1 Blusher Case
Files: *bottomcase.des, topcase.des, caseassembly.des*

keyboard shortcuts

Arc Drawing Tool	T	Onto Face	Shift + F
Autoscale	Shift + A	Onto Workplane	Shift + W
Autoscale Selection	Shift + S	Open	CTRL + O
Circle Drawing tool	C	Parts, Select	P
Components Browser	Shift + C	Plan View	Shift + P
Configurations	Alt + 3	Previous View	ALT + Left Cursor
Constraints	N	Print	CTRL + P
Delete Line Segments	D	Rectangle Drawing Tool	R
Design Rules	Alt + 2	Right Elevation	CTRL + R
Dimension Constraint	Z	Save	CTRL + S
Duplicate	CTRL + D	Select All	CTRL + A
Edges, Select	E	Shaded View	F10
Ellipse Drawing Tool	I	Spline Drawing Tool	B
Enhanced View	F12	Straight Line	S
Faces, Select	F	Toggle Construction	CTRL + G
Feature Browser	Shift + E	Toggle Fix	CTRL + F
Features, Select	A	Toggle Reference	CTRL + R
Front Elevation	Shift + N	Toggle Sketch Filled	CTRL + Shift + F
Half Scale	Shift + H	Toggle Sketch Rigid	CTRL + Shift + R
Hide Other Sketches	CTRL + H	Transparent View	F11
Isometric View	Shift + I	Trimetric View	Shift + T
Line, Select	L	Tumble	Shift + W
Manipulate View	Space Bar	Undo	CTRL + Z
New File	CTRL + N	Update Design	F5
New Sketch	CTRL + K	Wireframe View	F9
New Workplane	CTRL + L	Workplanes Browser	Shift + Z
Next View	ALT + Right Cursor	Workplanes, Select	W
		Zoom In	Shift + Z

Pro/DESKTOP File Types
Pro/DESKTOP uses its own file types to store design, drawing and album files. The file extensions for these files are **.des**, **.dra**, and **.alb** respectively. Computers using Windows 98, 2000, NT and XP will not see the file extensions when viewing file names, but an icon associated with the file will reflect the file type.

Graphic File Types
Here are a few useful descriptions of graphic file types used in Pro/DESKTOP. If you are printing or uploading pictures on the web, it is helpful to be able to make an educated choice between file types.

File Type	File Extension
Bitmap	**.bmp** (Images in bitmap format are represented as small dots in a grid. This image type is not very high resolution.)
JPEG	.jpg
TIFF	.tif
VRML	.vrl

Import File Types
Files can be imported into the Design Interface and the Drawing Interface of Pro/DESKTOP. In the Design Interface, most imported files can only be used as sketch lines in the development of 3D objects. With the new eighth version of Pro/DESKTOP, importing Pro/ENGINEER® files has become much more seamless because both programs share the new PTC Granite engine.

In the **Drawing** Interface, only **DXF** or **DWG** files can be imported.

Export File Types
Pro/DESKTOP can export a number of different file types to be used for printing, output for use in CNC machining and rapid prototyping, export to other CAD software programs, VRML (web virtual reality files), and Windows Media Player video files.

The Design Interface allows export of several 3D geometry files, including Stereo Lithography (**STL**), **IGES, STEP, VDA, SAT** and **Medusa**, as well as image files, including **JPEG**, **Bitmap** and **VRML**.

The **Drawing Interface** allows export of **DWG** files as well as the graphics file types **JPEG** and **Bitmap**.

The **Album Interface**, because it is primarily a graphics medium, offers a number of different graphic file types as export options. Files can be saved as **JPEGs**, **TIFFs** and **Bitmaps**. In addition, Pro/DESKTOP version 8 allows animations files in the Album to be exported as Windows **.avi** movie files.

vocabulary & glossary of terms

Asymmetrical
When the features on one side of a line or point are different than those on the other, the shape or form is asymmetrical.

Axis
The point or straight line running through the center of an object around which the object is symmetrical. The center around which something rotates. *Axes* is plural of axis.

Chamfer
When an edge has been cut on an angle, such as when an edge has been filed, it has been chamfered.

Circumference
The linear distance around the outer edge of a circle. Sometimes it is called the perimeter.

Colinear
In Pro/DESKTOP, two lines or edges of a solid are colinear when they share the same axis. If you draw a straight line and delete a short part of the line in the middle, the two parts of the line that remain are colinear.

Concentric
When two or more circles or arcs (parts of a circle) share the same center axis, they are concentric.

Constraint
In Pro/DESKTOP, a command applied to restrict the size or shape of a sketch, such as dimensions, rigid or fixed commands, or geometric limitations such as tangent or perpendicular. In Pro/DESKTOP assemblies, constraints are restrictions on the freedom of movement of one component in relation to another, such as center axes, mate, align, offset and orient.

Diameter
The distance from one side of a circle to the other that passes through the center point.

Dimension
A distance constraint used to specify the length, diameter, or radius, of a line or object. Dimensions used in the Design Interface are constraints and become Pro/DESKTOP variables. Dimensions can also be created in the Engineering Drawing Interface.

Draft
The taper angle of the sides of a mold so that a cast part can be easily removed.

Form
A three-dimensional figure that includes length, width, and depth. A cube is a form and it is based on the two dimensional shape of a square. When a two-dimensional figure (shape) is extruded, projected, revolved or lofted in Pro/DESKTOP, the result is a form.

Helix
A three-dimensional spiral form, such as found in a spring or spiral staircase.

Industrial Design
A career that involves the development of products for industry. Industrial designers often work with engineers, production managers and others to create successful products.

vocabulary & glossary of terms

Intersect/Intersection
Where two or more things meet, such as the intersection of two lines.

Line
When a point is moved through space a line is created. Lines can be straight or curved.

Parallel
Two lines that maintain an equal distance from each other are parallel. When two lines next to each other are extended to infinity but do not intersect they are said to be parallel.

Perpendicular
At a 90 degree angle. Two lines are perpendicular when they intersect at a right angle.

Point
A location in space, defined by its position. In Pro/DESKTOP, the Origin point is located by x,y coordinates (0,0).

Radius
The distance from a center point to a point on the circumference of a circle or arc.

Shape
A two-dimensional figure that has length and width. Shapes can be geometric (square, rectangle, circle, ellipse, etc.) or they can be organic (containing shapes that might appear in nature, such as a leaf or insect wing).

Solid 0
A term used in CAD to describe a file for a 3D object that contains all the geometry to make it.

Symmetrical
When the features on either side of a line or point are identical, mirror images, the shape or form is symmetrical.

Tangent
When a line touches a curve (or arc) at only one point.

index

Add Text Outline, 53-56, 185-187
Album Interface, 20, 115, 123
Arcs, 113-114, 151-152, 157
Assembly Constraints, 243
　Align, 247
　Fix Component, 245
　Center Axes, 245, 259
　Mate, 247
　Orient, 249
　Offset, 248
Browser Window, 25, 30m 63m 111-112, 117, 139, 148, 243, 257
Center Lines in Engineering Drawings, 423-424
Change views, 31-33, 97
Configurations, 311
Constraints, Sketch, 89-91

Construction Lines, 100, 162-165
Design Toolbar, 26
Dimensioning Engineering Drawings, 411-414
Drawing Tools 150-156
Duplicate Command, 167, 172
Engineering Drawing Formats, 397-402
Equal Radius, 152-153
Image Properties, 118
Intersect Material, 70
Manipulate, 93
Mass Properties Variables, 299
Mirror, 175, 209
New Sketches, 31, 53, 97-98, 111, 130

New Workplane, 53, 133, 137, 140, 144
Pattern, 351, 292
Persepective, 116
Prehighlighting, 47, 88
Properties Dialog Box, 89-90
Round Edges Command, 60, 64-65, 94, 108
Show Workplanes as Glass, 30
Sketch Dimension Tool, 87-89
Symmetric About Workplane, 68
Toggle Fixed, 100
Toggle Sketch Filled, 44
Update Button, 64, 116
Valid Sketch Profile, 44, 159-161
Variables, 298-304